Bread of Dreams

To my students

Bread of Dreams

Food and Fantasy
in Early Modern Europe

Piero Camporesi

Translated by David Gentilcore

Polity Press

First published as *Il Pane Selvaggio* copyright © Il Mulino 1980

English translation © Polity Press 1989

This translation first published 1989 by Polity Press
in association with Blackwell Publishers Ltd.
First published in paperback 1996.

Reprinted 2005

Polity Press
65 Bridge Street
Cambridge, CB2 1UR, UK

Polity Press
350 Main Street
Malden, MA 02148, USA

A CIP catalogue record for this book is available from the British Library.

ISBN 0–7456–0349–1
ISBN 0–7456–1836–7 (pbk)

Typeset in 10½ on 12 pt Baskerville
by Colset Pte Ltd
Printed and bound in Great Britain by
Marston Book Services Limited, Oxford

For further information on Polity, visit our website: www.polity.co.uk

Contents

Preface by Roy Porter		1
Introduction		17
1	The 'Disease of Wretchedness'	26
2	Elusive Bread	35
3	Sacred and Profane Cannibalism	40
4	'They Set Out into the World of the Vagabond'	56
5	'They Rotted in Their Own Dung'	63
6	The World Turned Upside Down	78
7	'Famine of Living' and 'Times of Suspicion'	86
8	Night-time	92
9	Ritual Battles and Popular Frenzies	103
10	*Medicina Pauperum*	108
11	'Tightness of Purse'	115
12	Collective Vertigo	120
13	Hyperbolic Dreams	131
14	Artificial Paradises	137
15	Poppyseed Bread	146
16	The 'Fickle and Verminous Colony'	151
17	Putrid Worms and Vile Snails	163
18	A City of Mummies	172
19	The Triumph of Poverty	178
Notes		185
Index		205

Preface

by Roy Porter

Though extraordinarily prolific as a historian, Piero Camporesi remains relatively little known to more general British readers, because his works have, till now, hardly been translated from Italian. Confronting them may, at first sight, present the Anglo-American reader with certain problems, because they deal with strange subjects in unusual ways (this is what makes them so arrestingly important). It may be useful, therefore, first of all in this Preface, to say a few words about the special nature of Camporesi's historical studies, explaining why they can seem so exotic.

Over the last generation, one of the most urgent and insistent calls amongst historians has been the demand for history to become more holistic, more 'total'. Traditional scholarship, it has been complained over and over again, was preoccupied with the doings of far too narrow a section of society – those who governed, those who fought, those who employed. Indeed, even with respect to members of the governing elite, old-style history was interested in only a fragment of their activities – their public lives as rulers, politicians, diplomats, soldiers, captains of industry, priests and thinkers. Orthodox history gave us little of even these people's lives as a whole, and told us nothing at all about the great majority.

In reaction, the study of peoples, societies and cultures has blossomed over the last generation, most notably thanks to the stimulus given by the *Annales* school. There is neither room nor need here to illustrate how systematic research into parish registers, ecclesiastical records, legal depositions, court reports, tax assessments and masses of comparable documents has utterly transformed our knowledge of the lives of the ordinary people of the past. We now have infinitely more reliable accounts, from the grass roots, of the peasant family and the artisan household, of the economy of the cottage and the smallholding, of the

1

traditional community in village or small town in pre-modern society ('the world we have lost'), and then of the dynamics of the encroachment of industrial–capitalist relations over the last two or three centuries. Demographers have revealed patterns of marriage and childbearing; historical epidemiologists have studied morbidity, mortality and life expectations.

And alongside such accounts of population movements, economic realities, and material culture – the elementary structures of production and reproduction – the popular *mind* has been seriously researched, often for the first time. Replacing old vacuous generalizations, we now possess fine analyses of popular religion (orthodox or heretical), moral and sexual attitudes, traditional views on gender, social order and disorder, living and dying, and so forth.

All this is pure gain. Yet there are, arguably, dangers latent within some of the interpretative approaches used to reconstruct the histories of societies. For one thing, it is easy – especially thanks to the ready availability of sophisticated computer software – for quantitative history to become separated from qualitative history and thereby to claim totemic status as more 'scientific' and thus hegemonic. In the study of population patterns or geo-social mobility, the risk is that we will end up with a proliferation of histogram blocks or lines on graphs, without understanding what these mean in terms of myriad decisions taken by millions of individual people – to marry or not, to breed or not, to move or not. Data mean nothing unless they can be related to the attitudes and actions which make these marks upon history.

But study of the *mentalité* of times past has its problems too. How far, and in what ways, must historians 'make sense' of beliefs and practices – magic perhaps – which do not, *prima facie*, conform to our standards of logic and normal behaviour? One widely followed approach lies in the 'functionalist' assumption that the most bizarre-looking creeds and customs have underlying rational purposes (e.g. creating a common identity, maintaining social solidarity, upholding incest taboos, etc.). Other schools of historians, by contrast, see the 'rationality' of former belief-systems more in terms of the workings of hegemony. It may not be rational for *believers* to believe what they do, but such ('mystifying') belief-systems prove profoundly useful to the ruling groups who encourage and maintain them. The history of Christian millennialism, with its typical injunction to the faithful obediently to await the coming of Christ's Kingdom, may be viewed in this light, as indeed may Christianity as a whole.

Interpretations such as these are useful and indeed necessary, if the popular world-views of the past are not simply to resemble museums of

2

strange beasts to be gawped at – and if they are to escape the condescension of the old folklorist mentality which saw in oral culture vestiges of the 'primitive mind'. Surely it is healthier to treat other people's beliefs as rational than as 'pre-rational' – a danger the French school of historical anthropology, in the tradition of Marcel Mauss, arguably did not avoid.

Yet we may easily run a different risk, that of trimming and tailoring popular consciousness too regularly. It is very easy to gather up disparate beliefs and pour them into scholarly moulds, interpreting them as primitive class-consciousness, as popular protest and resistance to elite values, as economically and demographically functional, or as expressions of imposed ideological social control. It is in resisting such temptations to top and tail popular consciousness according to modern categories that Camporesi has made his most important contribution to the study of the popular cultures of the past.

For the temptations to provide selective, evaluative, pre-packaged accounts of the consciousness of the past are indeed extremely strong. One of the severest challenges facing scholars and readers alike is, therefore, first to enter into, and then to offer convincing accounts of, such collective outlooks, viewed on their own terms. We must deal in an even-handed way with what to us seems sensible and what seems bizarre, what seems progressive and archaic, or sophisticated and naive. And we must grasp how such varied elements typically fitted together into what was for earlier societies – though not necessarily for us – a coherent world view.

The danger, of course, is that we privilege items which seem admirable or 'advanced' to us. As readers, we easily approve of Menoccio, the Friulian miller, who (as Carlo Ginzburg has shown in his *The Cheese and the Worms* (London, 1980)) fell foul of the Counter-Reformation Church for articulating an alternative cosmology; and we do so for precisely the same reasons that historians have traditionally been on the side of his double, Galileo. We cheer both heretics for their rejection of the world-system as dictated by Medieval Scholasticism, and indeed their resistance to intellectual authoritarianism. Likewise, when we read Keith Thomas's *Religion and the Decline of Magic* (London, 1971), it is hard for us not to sympathize with those largely Protestant intellectuals who regarded magic as a system for the understanding and manipulation of nature, lacking truly scientific standards of evidence, observation, experiment and proof; and it is equally difficult not to feel that the emancipation from magic was, as the *philosophes* of the Enlightenment saw it, a true leap forward into a more critical and hopeful frame of mind.

But such preferences lead towards the slippery slope of Whiggishness, which prefers those elements of the mentalities of the past bearing most affinities to the belief-structures of the present, and judges them anachronistically on that basis. Historians need to transcend this selectivity, in favour of what has been called the 'Baptist theory' of history – 'total immersion', or genuinely getting under the skin of the past. We must cultivate a socio-cultural history, warts and all – one in which all elements of earlier belief-systems are accorded explanatory symmetry and 'equal time'. Above all, we must be eager to ask profound questions, which transcend run-of-the-mill issues of family functionalism, political strategies, and economic rationality. What were the dreams and nightmares of earlier cultures? What aspirations jostled alongside the unbearable harshness of reality? What fears and fantasies did they embrace? What were the often only obliquely articulated beliefs organizing the experiences of individual lives? How did the people at large make sense of the world if they did not fully accept at face value the universe of meanings stipulated by authority – by Church or state?

These challenges to read the minds of people at large at all levels are ones from which Anglo-American historians have often shied away, for fear of vagueness. One major reason is that, within English-language scholarship, 'folklore' studies have fallen into disrepute. They have been discredited as trivial and patronizing. As hinted above, the energetic folklore collectors of the Victorian era were excessively eager to pigeon-hole popular beliefs as the vestiges of a primitive mentality, becoming extinguished in the great struggle for intellectual survival in the age of Darwin. Such folklorists reflected a real truth about English society. The extinction of the English 'peasantry', and the great extension of commercial, urban culture, meant the erosion of traditional oral culture rooted in the soil, which gave expression to ancestral beliefs about nature and the cosmos. The result, however, was that the decline of 'folklore' itself was paralleled by the decline of the investigation of 'folklore'. Study of the folk tradition became largely restricted to amateur intellectuals and Sunday collectors.

By contrast, the study of folk and oral cultures has never been thus marginalized – indeed, discredited – within the academic traditions of Continental Europe. And it is thus no surprise that the best research into the minds of the peasant societies of medieval and early modern Europe has come from France, from Italy, and even from Russia (for instance, M. Bakhtin's exemplary *Rabelais and his World* (Cambridge, Mass., 1968)). Historians from countries which have supported to this day a sturdy peasant life have been triumphantly successful in reconstituting the 'little cultures' of the past. In recent years, works by Emmanuel Le Roy Ladurie such as *Montaillou* (London, 1978) and *Carnival* (London,

1980) have achieved notable success amongst Anglo-American readers, particularly because they decipher so expertly the structures of thought and action of rural society.

But Le Roy Ladurie is just one of a host of French scholars who have mined the archives – ecclesiastical records are particularly compendious upon what the Church saw as the outrageous errors of popular beliefs – for evidence of what was a largely pre-literate *mentalité*. The works of most remain largely untranslated. For example, Françoise Loux, coming from the traditions of French ethnography, has surveyed peasant lore largely through analysis of proverbs. Fascinated in particular by the history of the body, she had drawn attention to beliefs which to us, at first sight, seem paradoxical or perverse, but which in fact encode a substantial logic of their own. Much peasant lore, for instance, seems to glory in mud, filth and excrement. We might conclude that the traditional peasantry were dirty – and indeed 'uncivilized'. But these conclusions would be radically false; for within their value-system, dirt (itself, of course, a notably relative phenomenon) was commonly regarded as a form of protective armour for the skin. Whereas we associate cleanliness with health, in traditional peasant culture, health, hygiene, and warmth required a sort of dirty living.

Many of the best French studies remain untranslated. Readers confined to the English tongue, however, may find some of its more fruitful insights incorporated in studies by Robert Darnton, particularly his volume of essays entitled *The Great Cat Massacre* (Cambridge, Mass., 1984). What Loux has done to understand the inner codes of proverbial wisdom, Darnton has done for fairy stories. The bizarre, mysterious and often perverse aspects of such stories (their transformations of identity, their savage cruelty) can be made, through close reading and examination of common structures, to yield insights into how peasants made sense of their world. Magic, the supernatural, disguise, surprise events, coincidences – all these loomed large in the hopes and fears of those who made poor and precarious livings off the land, overshadowed by the powers of nature, darkness, and the unknown, the arbitrary and unpredictable fortunes of birth, life and death, the social exactions and exploitations of the strong and the malign. In a broadly comparable way, Peter Burke's *Historical Anthropology of Early Modern Italy* (Cambridge, 1987) decodes some of the, at first glance, more peculiar features of the popular street culture of the Renaissance – its theatricalities of social power, the symbolic significance of food and drink, clothes and gesture. Burke demonstrates how they should be read as meeting the needs of people living in a face-to-face, pre-bureaucratic society in which personal presence was supremely important.

We might place the works of Camporesi roughly in the same camp with studies of this kind. It is, in fact, hard to label them: they defy being exclusively identified as either social history, intellectual history, historical anthropology or any other sub-specialism. Professor at the University of Bologna, Camporesi's writings – which are copious indeed! – are undoubtedly impregnated with the Marxist viewpoint of that institution and city. But Camporesi certainly does not proclaim his works as toeing the line of Marxist orthodoxy, and he is extremely careful to avoid the reductionist trap of assuming that past idea-complexes are merely the reflections of certain class interests. Rather, the Marxist influence in Camporesi is visible in a pervasive concern to explore the dialectics of consciousness with the realities of material existence.

Camporesi's *oeuvre* possesses great shock value. All his works address themselves to features of past cultures which seem quite alien to us nowadays. He has explored the potent myths of pre-industrial society – in particular, of the Mediterranean and Catholic worlds – examining their ideas about the sacred and the profane, the mortal and the eternal, the worldly and the other-worldly, the relations between man and nature, man and the animal kingdom. In ways sometimes suggestive of the English anthropologists, Victor Turner and Mary Douglas, he has explored how, why, and where people draw boundary lines in their cosmologies, and the special significance attached to their violation. He has always been fascinated by what people found fascinating – often in the world of demons and marvels and witches and miracles. He has explored where power was thought to lie – so important in the consciousnesses of people often impotent and vulnerable to the oppressions of others. And he has probed these topics not in the abstract but through delving in detail into people's day-to-day dealings, their immediate surroundings, the common objects of their work, and showing how these constituted inflections of their notions of the strange and magic powers in the cosmos, the invisible forces of good and evil, of malice and luck. The familiar and local – the supposed attributes of common substances such as salt and blood, the popular associations of places and names, the accretion of stories and legends that have grown up around heroes, patrons, historical figures, saints and martyrs – provide keys to the larger mysteries of the universe.

For instance, in his latest work, *La Casa dell'Eternità* (Milan, 1987), Camporesi explores that most Baroque of all the fantasies of medieval and early modern Europe: Hell. Its geography, its own upside-down social anti-order, its punishments, its roll-calls of sins and sinners – all of these are shown to have proliferated from the barest texts in the Bible, and from projections out of the familiar scenarios of crime and punishment in the home, and in the ecclesiastical and secular courts. Reality and fantasy interlock, and Camporesi indirectly suggests that the more 'limited' societies of earlier Europe were prone to generate more 'luxuriant' fantasies than the abundant societies of today, with their super-saturation of goods, images and communications.

In exploring such matters, Camporesi was tilling soil touched upon in his earlier writings. In one of the most seminal of these, *La Carne Impassibile*, recently translated as *The Incorruptible Flesh* (Cambridge, 1988), he focused upon a topic which fascinated early modern attention and which seems to defy, not just our *outlooks* nowadays, but above all, our *expectations* as historians about the thought-worlds of the past. Nowadays, exposure to the flesh, in its dead and rotting forms, is disgusting to us. We loathe contact with blood that has been spilt, with corpses and cadavers. But not so in the past. The culture of early modern Europe positively basked in the flesh, believing it had all kinds of wonderful powers, beyond normal human capacity. Dead bodies, if touched, had healing properties; human blood, bathed in, or drunken, could cure or rejuvenate. 'Mummy' – the powder from embalmed corpses – was likewise a potent medicine. The culture teemed with tales of apparently dead bodies coming alive, of suspended animation, of the power of mortified limbs to grow again, and so forth.

These stories of the flesh came from all kinds of different sources: from the stories of the Saints and Martyrs, officially *imprimatur*'d by the Church; from antiquity, whose credulous natural historians such as Pliny had faithfully magnified all manner of wonders; from popular science and medicine, from quacks, from *raconteurs* within both oral and literate culture. For one of the cardinal assumptions pervading Camporesi's historical vision is that the tales of the unusual and the cosmology of the weird and wonderful with which he deals were not simply the mind-fodder of the mere peasantry, the opium of the illiterate, the daydreams of the dregs. Rather these beliefs were current throughout the society, accepted – though not necessarily in the same ways, or to the same degrees, or with the same inflexions – by representatives of all social classes, rich and poor, powerful and downtrodden, *literati* and illiterate. Indeed, what to our eyes is *prima facie* the most troublesome aspect of history as presented by Camporesi is indeed the fact that these 'irrational' ideas were supported and generated so powerfully, and for so long, precisely by the most educated and authoritative members of the society. A parallel is offered in the history of witchcraft, where traditional popular belief in the malign powers possessed by certain people became transformed, in the early modern centuries, into a full-scale, water-tight, punitive demonology by the clergy, professors, magistrates and nation state.

Here Camporesi confounds our expectations in a double way. Not only were popular and 'vulgar' views – about the normality-defying powers of the flesh – supported by the intelligentsia, but the beliefs of Medieval and early modern Christian culture turn out to have been different from, or at least far more complex than, what historians have traditionally suggested. We have always been told that Christianity inculcated a contempt for the flesh, seeing it as mere worm-food, a mass of corruption, a prison house of the soul. That is indeed true, and Camporesi cites abundant instances of ascetics and flagellants. But his point is that the contempt of the flesh, taken to such levels, becomes and endorses its opposite. It expresses a profound fascination for the flesh, as an emblem of life in a world of the inanimate, of change and becoming. It suggests almost a reverence for it, not least because the flesh of those self-scourgers, the great ascetics, became no less an object of veneration, almost adoration, than the bodies beautiful of pin-ups and movie stars nowadays.

Bread of Dreams further explores many of the themes implicit in the above. *The Incorruptible Flesh* focused upon the miracle and mystery of life in a world in which all things grew and then decayed, and in which the threat of putrefaction seemed omnipresent and all-dangerous. The sustainer of life, indeed the very staff of life, was food. Itself organic, itself therefore subject to the laws of growth and decay – itself, indeed, all too often nearing a state of putrefaction – food was a life-source more aboriginal even than flesh and blood. Yet food itself was dead, the once-living cut off for human consumption. So food utterly symbolized the ambiguous cycles of existence, and the interdependence of all things sublunary. It was an organic cosmos in which all changed and was changed. Man fed on animals which had themselves fed on lower forms of life; in turn man would die, and himself be eaten by the worms. Thus all was transformation, all was interconnected in a cosmic alchemy – compare cheese and worms as the basis for a cosmology in Ginzburg's book. The most elementary and direct realities of a material, countryside culture fermented into the most vivid imaginative cosmology.

What moved the masses most in the societies of five or three hundred years ago? It was not, *au fond*, politics or religion, or art or ideas, or even sexuality, argues Camporesi. It was, above all, hunger, and the urgent need to relieve it through food. The axis of famine and food, and the fears and fantasies linked with them, form the core of his inquiry. Using sources as varied as ecclesiastical records and official reports, proverbs, scurrilous verse and popular drama, Camporesi explores the diverse features of a way of life in which, for the vast majority of a society of small-scale peasants, labourers, wanderers, paupers and vagabonds, Lenten living was a cruel and perpetual necessity as much as an act of Christian holiness, and in which a public feast could be the apogee of a lifetime's aspirations.

Camporesi shows how hunger and satiation, eating and drinking, digesting and defecating, in all their aspects, dominated both private and public, official and unofficial cultures. There is no need to summarize here in any detail all the themes covered in the book. It is, however, worth mentioning a few. Camporesi shows the enormous symbolic significance attached to having enough to eat. Eating well was more important than being rich, famous, or of high status – conspicuous food consumption in fact stood as the very proof of all these attributes. The man able to eat handsomely, with a groaning board, with ovens, fires, and cooks, the man able to stand feasts or run soup kitchens for the poor, was recognized to be the grand man. The fat man was – as in so many third world cultures these days – the visible embodiment of the successful man, the man who had literally incorporated his success, become his own corporation (the obsolescent Victorian colloquial connotation of 'corporation' is apt). This prevalent symbolism of body size and shape is, of course, utterly alien in the light of the fashionable connotations of today's Western societies of superabundance, where fat is corrupt – diseased even – and lean is fit.

Of course, as Camporesi never forgets to emphasize, such symbols are never univocal: they are resources which can be used in a variety of different ways in the culture. As a figure from the past, the fat man is enviable. Yet often enough that enviability becomes the target of criticism, when he keeps all his fat to himself as an alimentary miser – or indeed when he has no business being fat at all, as with the gross monks and friars of popular satire. Through their gluttony, such people are thus condemned out of their own mouths.

Camporesi further expatiates upon the meanings of different sorts of food – which were thought healthy and which unhealthy? which patrician and which plebeian? what precise associations were carried by flesh and vegetables? by red and white meat? by fowl and fish? which foods were considered especially clean and unclean? wholesome or indigestible? which were appropriate for those who worked with their hands, or their brains? Foodstuffs, raw and cooked, bespoke a symbol system which identified the social order no less than did the clothes people wore or the idiom they uttered.

He is also deeply concerned with popular physiologies. How did

9

people envisage what actually happened to the food they ate? How did digestion work? How did potential nourishment get transformed into actual nutrition through the action of the stomach, turning into the fluids which in turn created new, fresh, warm, red blood, which, as demonstrated in *The Incorruptible Flesh*, was standardly viewed as the very life-force itself? Camporesi thus explores how the acts of eating, digestion, and defecation formed the core of a popular cosmology concerned with explaining living and dying, change and process, the tendency to decay and the capacity to resist it.

It was a culture in which all dreamed of eating flesh (meat was nourishment, taste and status) but in which eating the flesh of certain animals was taboo, and above all, the notion of eating *human* flesh was utterly charged with feelings of abomination, yet fascination. Tales of anthropophages, and of tribes which practised cannibalism, proliferated. How could it have been different within a religion whose most sacred ritual was the ceremonial repetition of an act of cannibalism? Popular culture, in its orgiastic drunken feasts, mocked the sacred cannibalism of the eucharist. In the world-turned-upside-down respite of Carnival, eating and drinking necessarily assumed the parodic overtones of the blood and body of Jesus Christ.

Above all, Camporesi focuses upon the reality and the metaphor of *bread*, that staff of life which is the symbol of survival but which, taken on its own, was equally the marker of object poverty. We live today in a society in which the eating of bread has become a dietary irrelevance – no-one now recommends it as indispensable for the needs of life or health – and simultaneously therefore a cultural fossil. Bread nowadays carries few connotations, except archaically (as in 'Give us this day our daily bread'). Precisely the reverse was true in pre-modern times. Bread marked the divide between life and death. Bread stood for the body within Christian symbolism. Making, breaking, and distributing bread carried profound connotations of friendship, communion, giving, sharing, justice – indeed, literally, *companionship*. Different sorts and qualities of bread marked status, and were connected with 'ingrained' notions of nutritional value, good and bad taste and tastes, distinct occasions, seasons, times of the year, rituals and ceremonials. When Marie Antoinette politely suggested to the French mob that they should go and eat cake, she indirectly acknowledged that the want of bread was the severest blow which the people could sustain.

Various of these themes have been dealt with in their specialized ways by historians of nutrition and diet, economic historians, historians of religious ritual, secular etiquette and manners, and so forth. The great triumph of Camporesi is to interlink them all. His powerful imagination enables him to recreate the central importance of hunger as a moving force in history – both as what we might call a real 'gut' drive, and as the stimulus to fantasy, to rebellion, to utopias – the idea of a land of Cockayne, where none will any longer be hungry. The promise of food moved peasants to revolt more than the abstractions of justice, and the ritual world of Carnival depended upon its guarantee of release through bingeing. Not least, he suggests, the fact that so much food was mouldy and rotting, coupled with peasant use of herbs and vegetables with narcotic qualities, constituted a physiological cause for intoxicating fantasies: the 'delusions' of the past were toxicologically produced by hunger, or by the food people ate.

In Camporesi's breathtaking vision, covering several centuries of early modern peasant society, and focusing chiefly but not exclusively on Italy, real social history and *l'histoire des mentalités* fuse; not with the exemplary rigour that *Annales* history has often demanded, but with a tremendous flair and imaginative insight which is apt to disguise the fact that Camporesi is also immensely erudite in the byways of research.

Camporesi is not, however, an easy writer. Partly this is a problem of the relative unfamiliarity of his source materials and range of cultural reference for English readers. His central topics – Carnival, the Counter-Reformation Church, the popular stories of saints and heroes – do not have their blazingly obvious equivalents in the actual lived-world of early modern England. This may, in part, be an optical illusion due to the orientation of English history-writing. Socio-cultural historians have concentrated on the religious politics of popular culture in early modern England – the roots of the Levellers and the Diggers, as it were – but, despite pioneering work by E. P. Thompson, popular customs and beliefs remain under-researched. Simon Schama's recent *Embarrassment of Riches* (London, 1987) – a study of the fabric of urban living in the golden century of the Dutch republic – shows how a 'bourgeois' and 'Protestant' culture manifested surprisingly many of the features of the world depicted by Camporesi, not least the semiotics of food, drink and consumption as a whole.

Nevertheless, real difficulties are presented by Camporesi's work. He covers a vast amount of ground in a grand sweep. He encompasses many centuries, emphasizing the *longue durée* from the high middle ages through to the building of the modern, mass state in the nineteenth century. He habitually juxtaposes popular songs and tales, learned theology, the lives of the saints, graffiti, official sumptuary laws, the vernacular lore, books of etiquette and the like. His aim in such juxtapositions is partly to provoke. It is, more importantly, to make points about the very absence of sharp cultural boundaries in earlier centuries. Yet there may

11

remain a residual uncertainty about the quality of his sources or the weight of inferences from them. Does a reference in a sermon necessarily indicate that a practice was common on the street? It is often impossible to tell, and Camporesi does not stop to discuss such interpretative issues down to the last iota. To those readers who may feel unsure as to exactly how to locate Camporesi's exploration of the alimentary imagination of earlier centuries within wider key scholarly concerns, it may be worth addressing certain issues individually.

Food and the Body

Much of Camporesi's work presupposes the powerful presence of a popular discourse concerning the operation of the body, its physiological functions, the conditions under which health could be maintained or sickness would set in. One might think that such questions were reserved for discussion by doctors, and that it was but rarely that people at large addressed themselves to these matters. But that would be a mistake. Recent research into the history of conceptions of the body, into the metaphorical meaning of the organs and into the histories of health and disease, amply bear out Camporesi's perception that lay culture had deeply entrenched and often prominent visions as to the functioning of the body. Above all, right across the cultural spectrum, from the highest medical authorities down to common opinion, life was seen as a continual process of consumption, in which the energy and strength of the individual constitution depended upon constant supplies of adequate nourishment and stimulus from outside, and upon the equally efficient disposal of bodily wastes (without which, poisoning would set in).

The healthy body was thus the body with an efficient through-put system. Its effective working was easily endangered. Many sorts of food would upset the system. Too much meat was potentially dangerous. For meat itself was corrupting flesh. If it remained too long in the stomach, it could itself engender corruption, for example breeding intestinal worms. But too much vegetable food was likewise seen as a potential health threat, for it was thought to be acidic, hard to digest, and often leading to wind, cholic, fluxes and dysentery. That is why bread was widely believed so desirable a food: solid and substantial, yet not subject to decay, and only hard to digest if its quality were poor. In her *Geschichte unter der Haut* (Stuttgart, 1987), Barbara Duden has recently studied the concepts of the healthy body held by a sample of eighteenth-century German country women, as revealed by their medical records. She finds that they believed that health largely depended upon proper diet, and that bread was widely seen as the safest nutritive staple, especially to be recommended when pregnant women began to suffer from *pica*, having longings for exotic foodstuffs. Likewise, in his *The Body and Society* (Oxford, 1984), the historical sociologist of food and health, Bryan Turner, has emphasized the associations in eighteenth-century English writings of a high bread-content diet with certain ideas of earnestness and responsibility. George Cheyne, a fashionable physician, argued that a diet rich in seeds would avert nervousness, hypochondria, stomach diseases and many of the other prevalent disorders of the day.

Consumption and the Consumer Society

The consumption of bread was thus essential for sustaining the constitution. But historians also acknowledge, in line with Camporesi's perception, that food was a crucial item of social exchange. The better our understanding of the medieval economy, the more we grasp how sophisticated were the systems of exchange in operation, sometimes involving money, sometimes simply involving the bartering of goods in kind. Even amongst relatively self-sufficient peasant economies, items of diet such as salt would have to be purchased, and carried great exchange value, and thereby symbolic value. The miller's services were needed. Often the baker was the only person in the village owning an oven: he would bake people's bread and other dishes, as well as selling bread ready-made. Trading and marketing focused upon grain and bread.

Nothing secured or threatened socio-political stability so frequently three or four centuries ago as the operations of market arrangements for the buying and selling of grainstuffs and the sale of bread. Everywhere market regulations laid down in enormous detail the legal price for grain and bread (the ingredients, size and quality of a loaf). Typically grain could legally be sold only in the full market, between certain hours, under public view. Magistrates not normally sympathetic to popular aspirations would nevertheless ensure that market regulations upholding the price and quality of bread were sustained. Improper dealers in grain and traders in bread – those who hoarded or adulterated – were the bogeys of folklore, and were often attacked or prosecuted. Perhaps the most prominent form of social protest in early modern Europe was the grain riot or the bread riot – popular disturbances which often won some sympathy from the authorities.

Thus bread was at the heart of a complex transition from relatively autarkic economic conditions to market relations. Trading in grain and bread was central to the development of market relationships; yet trade in these commodities was too sensitive to be left to market forces. Thus bread was central to that struggle which E. P. Thompson has identified between the 'moral economy' and 'political economy', because maintenance of a fair price for bread was tantamount to saying that labouring people had the right to live. When the authorities were no longer willing or able to sustain adequate grain supplies, what typically resulted was either revolution – as in France – or famine.

Bread and Famine

As Camporesi emphasizes, the folklore and mythologies of early modern Europe were indeed haunted by the fear and threat of famine – of being what we colloquially call 'starving hungry', as a result of dearth and deprivation, or, worse still, literally starving to death. Obviously many poor people individually starved to death, but so did large proportions of the entire population of many regions in Europe in bad years right through the eighteenth century. Famines were the product of the concatenation of multiple circumstances. Obviously they could result from absolute failures of food production – from crises brought on by disastrous weather conditions. They typically also involved breakdowns in the market mechanism for getting food supplies to areas of gravest need. Sometimes war was to blame for this.

Yet in many ways the eighteenth century proved a turning-point. Those precise capitalist pressures which had traditionally been so greatly feared as the causes of shortfalls were in fact lubricating the market. In eighteenth-century England, famines killing off sizeable numbers of people had ceased to happen. Indeed, for a while, thanks to advances in capitalist agriculture, England became a grain exporting nation. In the nineteenth century, imperialism resulted in a mass importation of primary foodstuffs to Europe which ended the threat of mass starvation. The nineteenth century, the century of industrialization, was a century of poverty, but it was not a century of mass famine. The spectre of mass starvation began to retreat, and, with it, the centrality of food, and bread, to popular consciousness began to wane.

Hunger, Hallucination and Fantasy

One of the most startling claims in this book is Camporesi's view that much of the population of earlier Europe was living in some sort of drugged condition. This, he suggests, was sometimes the effect of mere

14

hunger, producing dazed or stupefied states. Sometimes it was the result of eating tainted bread, made from mouldy, verminous flour, or stale food whose condition had deteriorated. Sometimes it was through accidental or deliberate adulteration – mixing flour with mash, bran, potatoes, vegetable leaves or chemicals to make it go further or to transform the taste. It was also thanks to consuming all manner of fermented drinks, mushrooms, distillations and the like, and applying or sniffing lotions, oils, essences, etc.. Such intoxication – the equivalent perhaps of betel-chewing in Asia or the use of coca leaves in South America – perhaps inured populations to lives of toil, tedium and general hopelessness; perhaps also provided hallucinatory experiences which stimulated that vision of the tangibility of the supernatural which is so central to early modern religious experiences; and perhaps accounts for bizarre phenomena such as witchcraft possession and religious convulsionism.

Camporesi's is a rather startling claim, difficult to assess. Should we treat this as a flight of fancy, an ingenious suggestion, or does it contain a deeper truth? It should at least be clear that Camporesi is not here offering a crude reductionist resolution – he is not suggesting for a moment that we can simply explain away the religious and occultist consciousness of earlier times by referring to mere chemical hallucinogens. Nor is he necessarily saying that our forebears were leading their lives any more under the influence of artificial stimulants than we do nowadays with our diets of tea and coffee, cigarettes and alcohol. Camporesi's point, as I take it, is that historians need to address themselves to the myths by which people live, and the totality of the conditions which support these collective fantasies. Many factors must inevitably be involved in creating and reproducing the most ingrained beliefs – the brainwashing power of education, of all the media continually active in the transmission of images – songs, incantations, paintings. Many of these are drummed into the mind in infancy, almost subliminally; many sink deep into consciousness through repetition, through association (the dark, rich, incense-laden air of the church with its ritual – the equivalent for earlier ages of television or the rock video nowadays), through habituation. Consciousness-affecting drugs and food may be a further element amongst many others. Just as 'junk food' is today claimed to produce subtle alterations to the mind, so the junk bread of the past may have disturbed body and mind, while producing subtly altered mental states which enabled the poverty and deprivation the better to be borne.

It would be easy for the stolid Anglo-Saxon reader to feel suspicion of, and resistance towards, Camporesi's alluring theses: they join together what are commonly kept asunder in academic scholarship; they are undoubtedly speculative; Camporesi's vision moves too fast to dot every 'i' and cross every 't' with a scholarly footnote (though the visible apparatus of learning is impressive indeed). Above all, he invites us to confront the strange. And instead of scaling down the strange into the familiar, he invites us to see *everything* as strange – not least, by implication, the set of values within which we ourselves are operating, our own culinary fantasies, our obsessions about size and weight and dieting, which lead to the diseases of our own age – anorexia, bulimia – which are every bit as weird as the flagellomania of the past. Camporesi's history defamiliarizes, but it does not wallow in the exotic for its own sake. Rather it insists that we make the heroic act of understanding which is necessary if we are to understand our own past – and our own present.

Roy Porter
Wellcome Institute for the History of Medicine, London

Introduction

The flight of the ragged and starving masses of the modern era into artificial paradises, worlds turned upside down and impossible dreams of compensation originates from the unbearability of the real world, the low level of sustenance, dietary deficiency and (for contrast) excesses; these inspired an unbalanced, incoherent and spasmodic interpretation of reality. This resulted in the construction of a model of existence different from the one elaborated in the same period by rationalist intellectuals like Galileo, Bacon and Descartes, who laid down a firm foundation in the construction of a world machine: a mental and physical 'works' regulated by a coherent mechanical and logical apparatus, a perfectly and inexorably self-adapting system of fittings and attachments.

Meanwhile, at the lower level of 'civil' society – in the subordinate world of instrumental and 'mechanical' beings, tyrannized by their daily use of 'vulgar breads', in which the mixture of inferior grains, often contaminated and spoiled by poor storage, or, as happened not infrequently, mixed (sometimes deliberately) with toxic and narcotic vegetables and cereals – the troubled rhythm of an existence verging on the bestial contributed to the formation of deviant models and delirious visions. The dichotomy between the 'bread of princes and great masters' and the 'bread for dogs'[1] (effectively described by Giovanni Michele Savonarola, 'most excellent physician' at the University of Padua in the second half of the fifteenth century) is transformed into a dietary metaphor of the two different cultural systems that find their focal point in bread. Bread – a polyvalent object on which life, death and dreams depend – becomes a cultural object in impoverished societies, the culminating point and instrument, real and symbolic, of existence itself: a dense, polyvalent paste of manifold virtue in which the nutritive function intermingles with the therapeutic (herbs, seeds and curative pastes

17

were mixed into the bread), magico-ritual suggestion with the ludico-fantastical, narcotic and hypnotic.

Among the most common and popular foodstuffs that permitted the transition from a human condition on the verge of the unliveable to a drugged and paranoid dimension was poppyseed bread (the poppy was cultivated in vast areas of Europe with what today would be called industrial methods). It was a bread disguised and flavoured, and in addition spiced with coriander seeds, anise, cumin, sesame-seed oil, and all the possible delectable additives available in the 'vegetable kingdom', with which man dwelled in a close intimacy, today unthinkable. In areas where it was cultivated, even the flour of hemp-seeds was used in the kitchen to prepare doughs and breads which 'cause the loss of reason' and 'generate domestic drunkenness and a certain stupidity'.[2] One could doubtless regard this as having been directed not so much from above (as is sometimes supposed), as desired and sought by the masses themselves, consumed as they were by disease, hunger, nocturnal fears and daytime obsessions.

The collective journey into illusion, followed by 'domestic drunkenness' – with the help of hallucinogenic seeds and herbs, arising from the background of chronic malnourishment and often hunger (which is the simplest and most natural producer of mental alterations and dream-like states) – helps to explain the manifestation of collective mental delirium, of mass trances, of entire communities and villages exploding into choreal dancing. But it could also be the path which allows us to catch a glimpse of a two-sided mental model of the world, born under the ambiguous and equivocal sign of dualism, conditioned by a hallucinated and altered awareness of reality, where the layers are overturned, the universals reversed, the world ending up head-over-heels, with head on the ground and feet in the air. The result of an altered measuring of space and time, based on a non-Euclidic geometry and a magical, dreamlike perspective where the relations and proportions are regulated by different instruments of verification and measure from those employed in the cultural areas where classical logic predominates, which are none the less not able to separate themselves totally from contamination introduced by the 'culture of hunger'.

At this point it appears evident that poverty and low subsistence levels 'influenced the categories of logic once again shown to be non-universal and, instead, generated by cultural conditions' (A. M. Di Nola). Poverty also attacked the sense of time which in a world of destitution never leads into the future (inheritance of the rich), unless ironically, but is consumed in the present, or in the obsessive repetition of an ever-identical past, recurring immutably, on a fixed date, like a constant nightmare.

As with the curse and nightmare of decayed flesh and destroyed spirit, so with the worms that consume the bowels even before death can overtake the body. These were the almost permanent guests of an infected social body, and this ineradicable obsessive belief in mass infestation, having become a repulsive metaphor, was projected on to the 'verminous populace' of tramps and beggars, the voracious worms of the granaries of the rich. But the global projection of a widespread demonism, an evil contamination (in the guise of repulsive insects, and using the mask of the foul *animalcula*), also took possession, invading and bewitching the pauper's body and soul in the name of Satan.

The spectre of this vampirish society of people possessed becomes visible, fleeing the painful recognition of the *brevitas vitae* and the fear of death, while trying desperately and cruelly to prolong life by sucking yound blood, opening and closing the veins of its own and others' bodies. This society is possessed by a corporeal culture neurotically sensitive to the internal circulation of the humours and convinced of the absolute primacy of good human blood, its 'marvellous properties', which – if distilled in an alembic to become the 'elixir of life, that is, life-giving fire' (as written in *Secreti diversi et miracolosi* by an anonymous author who passed himself off as the great Gabriele Fallopio)[3] – not only cures every infirmity, but retards death and restores youth.

The purging of the blood and the ridding of impurity ('the evil tempers,' recalled Levino Lennio, 'mix with the humours'[4]) were the decisive moments of every therapeutic activity based on the expulsion of corruption and evil, since 'the dismal and black humour in the blood generated horrible spirits and, if the blood is not purged, it causes lycanthropy and fears and ugly thoughts, such that one sees men rave and become spellbound in foul and filthy places, among graves and corpses, because the infected spirit desires things similar to itself'.[5]

Seen from this perspective, the image of a febrile and sleepless society comes into view, attempting to resist the nocturnal visitations, the presence of the night-dwellers (incubi, goblins, vampires, witches and werewolves), and to protect itself from the painful aggression of the dreadful and horrible dreams by means of a whole magical pharmacology that induced forgetfulness and serenity, bestowed *giovialità* and *cordialità*, enlivening the heart and cleansing the blood, bewildering and stupefying. It also prevented the medical neurosis from approaching to get its hands on some astounding secret prescription which would finally offer the key to entering into a protected existence, neither tiresome nor eaten away by disease. Having fallen into this necromantic and alchemistic dimension of affinity, attractions, senses and agreements between things and elements, of proportions, analogical relationships, and of revealing *signaturae*, the popular and learned pharmacopoeias, without distinction, also included in their magical realm culinary recipes where the enchanted plants entered with all their 'devilish' vegetable powers. Wormwood, for example – a plant of 'feminine, lunar and nocturnal meaning', used 'particularly for the treatment of dysmenorrhoea and for difficult births' by the tribes of North America (Lévi-Strauss),[6] and regarded as providential for the womb by the herbalist of the Old World as well – was considered the mother of all herbs, *herbarum mater*, from which all others descended as offspring. 'A medicinal herb', of entirely feminine virtue, 'many call it the *matricaria*, especially women, for whom it is itself a treasure. They use it with cheese, eggs, etc., to make *tortelli* during the feasts for Holy Mary. For this reason certain women call this the herb of Holy Mary.'[7]

Woman's treasure, regulator of the female cycle (and because of this governed by the moon), protector of the reproductive organs and female fertility, the *matricaria* (mother of herbs) was associated in its benign properties with the supernatural power of the mother of the Omnipotent, and then reconsecrated in the Christian baptism of herbs with the Virgin's name. It was ritually eaten as a food filled with enigmatic powers (in their form, too, these stuffed *tortelli* resembled a half-moon), on the day when it emanated the greatest therapeutic energy.

The culinary recipe, the sorceress's 'compositions', the apothecary's prescription, the herbalist's unguent, and the ointment-seller's remedy all coincided, in practice, in this type of 'magical pharmacology', interpreted as the secret knowledge capable of rendering people healthy, invulnerable and rich. Likewise, they overlapped in the constant, sleepless search for magical herbs and roots bestowing oblivion and ecstasy, in dreams and nocturnal diversions, witches' philtres and necromantic potions.

The cuisine of the imaginary, dream-inducing diet, sacrilegious gastronomy (cannibalistic, vampirical and dung-eating), human ointments and plasters, profane oils and sacred unctions, 'mummy' fragments and cranial dust, medicinal powers *de sanguinibus*, breads filled with seeds and powders bestowing oblivion, expansive and euphoria-producing herbs, narcotic cakes, stimulating roots and aphrodisiacal flours, aromas and effluvia of devil-chasing plants and antidotes for melancholy (*balneum diaboli*), and 'seasoned' and 'fostered' spells created a network of dreams, hallucinations and permanent visions. By altering measures, relations, proportions and backgrounds, they made 'three fingers seem like six, boys armed men, and men giants . . . everything much bigger than usual and the whole world turned upside down'.[8] It was observed how real massacres and imaginary battles, wild warriors and avenging angels were 'depicted in the air', because, as Tommaso Campanella gravely asserted, 'nature is wise and devilish' and 'future things are foreseen in the air'.[9] An aerial theatre that prefigured to men the 'signs' of things to come: a symbolic reading of the future conducted with eyes raised upwards.

Mass witchcraft, especially where customs were 'rustic and wild': this was where 'new and unheard of things appeared to urban on-lookers, not ever witnessed by bewitching Medea perhaps until now, with such frequency and number of people of every sort, *quod vix credibile est*' (Marin Sanuto).[10] In the mountain areas more than in the plains, more sterile than fruitful, inhabited by a 'rancorous people, almost all completely deformed, without any custom of civil living', 'more diabolical than Christian', where the priests themselves 'were the principal sorcerers', where 'wanton old men' and 'bitter women' appeared 'more beautiful than either Paris or Helen'. In this wild and alpine 'earthly paradise full of the joys of the world', reached by means of a witchly ride or *viazo*, the rancorous savages – restored by 'malmsey . . . pine-nuts cinnamon and confections of all sorts . . . all joyful and at ease' – could confuse the image of 'Our Lady' with the simulacrum of the devil.

In reality, not only the crippled mountain-dwellers or those of the forest, but the people of the town and city as well, lived immersed in a world of expectation, in a suspended and bewitched condition, where portent, miracle and the unusual belonged to the realm of the possible and the everyday: the saint and the witch (in her own way, a saint of a different type) reflected the two ambiguous faces, the face side and reverse of the same neurotic tendency towards the separation from reality, the voyage into the imaginary and the leap into the fantastic.

The saint – eccentric wizard of ecstasy in a body consumed by penance and privation, his mind altered by fasts, like certain hermits kept alive by roots and herbs (but which ones?) – was equipped with shamanistic powers (trance, levitation, knowledge of the language of animals . . .). The 'immeasureable treasure of most holy poverty' possessed by the father of the *Fraticelli* produced the same effects of an upsetting withdrawal from reality, and in the process stimulated the same sense of the real and the impossible, as experienced by those who, suffering and subdued by an involuntary poverty, victims of an alienating indolence, fell into shocking hallucinations and stupefied contemplations of unreal worlds.

The diminutive St Francis who, transfigured and strengthened, ardent and fiery, raises the giant Brother Masseo (the dwarf who became a giant and vice versa) into the air and throws him far away, or the mad *uomo di Dio* of Assisi who stripped and placed himself like a fakir upon the red-hot coals of a fireplace in order to convert (that is, change to another logic) a 'woman of beautiful body', both belong to the same culture of reversal in which the other face of the sacred was hidden: the culture of the profane, which confused creation with destruction, everything with nothing, the possible with the impossible.

The conjuring exploits of St Francis, his 'fakiresque' tricks with fire, belong to the same sort of discourse as the exhibitions practised by the pedlars of the sacred, the sellers of prayers and *brevi*.[11]

In Florence during November 1509, a wandering charlatan known as 'the Spaniard' – who often climbed up on to a bench to sell his prayers, following his text with an example, like a good preacher – began his market-performance of the supernatural in this way:

> 'In order that you will believe that this comes from a saint who performs miracles, and that what I tell you is true, come and lead me to a hot baker's oven, which I will enter with this prayer.' And so he was led to this oven, at the Holy Trinity, with the people behind and many of the leading citizens . . . On arrival at the baker's he said: 'Give me some uncooked bread' and threw it in the oven to show that it was hot, and then he stripped down to his shirt and dropped his trousers to his knees, and in this way he entered till high up, and stayed there awhile, and picked up the bread and turned around inside. And note, the oven was hot, he brought out the bread, and he didn't harm himself at all. When he had got out of the oven, he was given a torch and he lit it, and lighted as it was he put it in his mouth and kept it there until it was extinguished. And many other times on the bench, over the course of several days, he took a handful of lighted tapers, and held up his hand for a length of time, and then he put them burning into his mouth, so that they went out. And he was seen to do many other things with fire: raising his hands into a pot of oil that was boiling on the fire, was seen many times by all the people. And thus he sold as many of the prayers as he could make; and I say that among all the things I have ever seen [the observer is Luca Landucci, a Florentine spice merchant] I have not seen a greater miracle than this, if it is a miracle.[12]

The boundaries between the real and unreal, possible and impossible, sacred and profane, abstract and concrete, holy and cursed, purity and filth, and indecency and sublimity are extremely fleeting and uncertain. It could almost be said that the structural ambiguity of folk culture – with its two-dimensional view and its double-edged mental machinery – invaded, with its demonic animism, the spaces where the 'superior' culture was attempting to devise different systems of knowledge.

In reality, western Europe, at least until the seventeenth century, has the appearance of an enormous house of dreams where the diurnal regime becomes confused with the nocturnal, and which is master of surrealistic mythologies whose shadows project themselves even on to the gloomy nosology of the humours tinted with ink and soot, perfecting the ancient figure of the werewolf. This melancholy offspring of nocturnal corruption, with tainted and putrefied blood, is reborn (having freed itself from its cadaverous mask, tormented by black bile, and having become the literary model of Medieval French) in the *Bisclavret* of Marie de France,[13] having emerged from the early medieval medical apologues, thirsting for blood and meat: 'Those who are afflicted with lycanthropy, leaving their houses at night, imitate wolves in every way and, until the arrival of daylight, wander mostly about the gravestones. They are noted to be characterized by the following: pale face, eyesight weak and dry, tongue very arid, saliva lacking in the mouth and an excessive thirst'.[14]

The Europe of dreams and nocturnal hallucinations, repelled by mind-boggling cannibalism while at the same time yielding to the spell binding appeal of blood ('there is neither thing nor food', observed Girolamo Manfredi, a Bolognese doctor–astrologer of the late fifteenth century, 'that is more agreeable to man's nourishment than human flesh'[15]). The Europe that, as Jacques Le Goff has splendidly perceived, turned repeatedly to 'agents of oblivion' more than to the professional witch, *domina herbarum et ferarum,* and that had the first innovators of the artificial delights and narcotic sweetness accompanying a concocted and directed diet of dreams in the women of the home: the mothers, grand-mothers, aunts, godmothers, the wet-nurses who nursed the infants, and the domestic casters of charms.

At least until the end of the eighteenth century the habit of adminis-tering an infusion of poppies steeped in water to slightly restless children survived in the Italian countryside. This custom was widespread in France as well, since Josèphe Raulin, towards the middle of the eight-eenth century, described as 'always suspect the narcotics which . . . all too commonly are given to children to calm them'[16], and the celebrated author of the *Avis au peuple sur sa santé* (1760), the Lausanne doctor Samuel André Tissot, recognized that 'les remèdes tirés de l'opium . . . leur [aux enfants] sont d'une absolue nécessité.'[17] (It is unnecessary to recall here the *Medicina pauperum,* 1641, by Jean Prevost, superintendent of the botanical garden in Padua, and doctor to the students of the University, and *Le médecin des pauvres,* 1669, by Paul Dubé, since they belonged to two partially different cultural areas and periods.)

In the seventeenth century the botanist to the Grand Duke of Tuscany, Paolo Boccone, a tireless traveller, noted that the women of Moravia,

> in order to induce sleep in babies who cry in the cradle or in bed, place beside the baby a bunch of *solanum hortense*, upon which the baby quickly quiets down and falls asleep. The cause of this effect must be attributed to the narcotic effluvia, and also because the pores of the babies are susceptible and they are more capable of receiving the effect of these plant effluvia than adults.[18]

The belief that the emanations and effluvia of the volatile aromas and essences passed rapidly through the pores of the skin and were absorbed almost instantaneously was one of the commonplaces where learned knowledge and peasant doctrine coincided perfectly. From Albertus Magnus, who believed that the effluvia of opium, thorn-apple and crocus could be absorbed even at a distance, it passed to Ambroise Paré, who none the less took a critical position on this matter in *De vulneribus sclopetorum*, and to Fallopio, Fioravanti, Cardano (of the *De subtilitate*), and Robert Boyle, author of a singular *Tentamen porologicum*, who (as in another of his works, the *Specificorum remediorum concordia cum corpuscolari philosophia*) not only upheld the therapeutic benefit of wearing medical substances hung from the neck, but solemnly declared to have been cured of a haemorrhage simply by holding in his hand moss taken from a human skull.

In this general faith in the simultaneous absorption through the skin's pores, the greases, oils, ointments, plasters and poultices occupied a privileged position in the transmission of pharmacological messages, both harmful and beneficial. (Also valued were the 'umbilical' laxatives – the *epomphalia* that were applied on the skin of the abdomen – while self-styled doctors, charlatans, experimenters and wandering herbalists successfully peddled 'miraculous secrets which are taken in by the body as ointments, without having to take anything through the mouth'.) Society of old was made up of a swarm of people, oiled, smeared, anointed and spiced, violently odorous and unbearably smelly, where everyone was in turn anointed and anointer, and where the sense of smell dominated heavily, as Lucien Febvre has emphasized. In this regard at least, Campanella's *City of the Sun* is not at all utopian, resembling rather a normal report on the customs of an ordinary European city:

> They eat what is most beneficial and suitable according to season . . . The Solarians make great use of fragrances . . . [they] chew some marjoram, parsley, or mint and rub it on their hands. The

older folk use incense . . . they often wash their bodies with wine and aromatic oils . . . they observe the stars, inspect herbs . . . they use prayers, fragrances, head comforters, sour things, gaiety, and fatty broths sprinkled with flour. In preparing tasty dishes that are a delight they have no equals. They make great use of mace, honey, butter, and many aromatic herbs . . . they know a secret, marvellous art by which they can renew their bodies painlessly every seven years.[19]

In this aromatic world of sensitive skin and magnetic pores, in order to prevent nursing infants from falling victim to 'terrifying dreams', 'hideous dreams', and 'fantasies' that 'by inciting dreams disturb the sleep', the wet-nurse, for her part, had to maintain a strict diet, eating 'lettuce in broth or in boiled salad and poppyseeds': sedative substances that were transmitted to the infant along with the milk. And furthermore, every night the anointing ritual took place beside the cradle: the infant was 'smeared from one temple to the other with a poplar ointment [in which poplar buds were mixed with black poppy, mandrake and henbane], rancid oil and a little opium, and a bit of vinegar, spreading this on the nostrils as well. A more effective remedy', advised the Roman doctor Scipione Mercuri, who died in 1615, 'is to boil lettuce seed and white poppyseed, with a little saffron and vinegar, in the rancid oil, spreading this over the temples with a cloth. A small amount of white poppy syrup taken through the mouth will also help.'[20]

Thus prepared and 'seasoned', the infant was entrusted to the dark arms of the night. The initiation into controlled dreaming and the artificial ease of opium-induced sleep began with swaddling clothes. From infancy to old age narcosis ruled supreme.

In the 1771 *Antidotario* of the medical college of Bologna – in which *pilulae hystericae opiate* were advised along with *pilulae ad longam vitam* – the medical prescription of Nicholas of Salerno for insomnia still held the place of honour. Cinnamate, seeds of henbane and white poppy, mandrake root, nutmeg, violet and rose oils, juniper and opium (as well as purslane, endive and lettuce seeds) were mixed in enormous doses. *Requies magna* was the name given to this agent of oblivion and sleep, ambiguously and ominously allusive. However, something new was taking place: *parce infantibus*, advised the sober, austere instructions of this funereal treatment. With difficulty the child of Jean-Jacques Rousseau was being born.

1

The 'Disease of Wretchedness'

'One was really tired of being in the world,' noted a French rural curate in his diary during the seventeenth century,[1] interpreting the desperation of the most wretched parishioners who died of hunger in his village.

At the beginning of the same century a Bolognese canon, Giovan Battista Segni, recalled that 'in Padua in 1528, every morning throughout the city twenty-five or thirty dead from hunger were found on dung heaps in the streets. These paupers did not even resemble men.'[2]

A terrible passage, coming from one of the most learned cities in Europe, that ominously illuminates the last stage in a troubled metamorphosis: the long miserable voyage towards the destruction of what is human and the passing birth of the man/animal in daily contact with dung, attracted by the mirage of its soothing, fermenting heat. A nauseating refuge for whoever was forced to sleep naked on excrement, like a second Job.

During times of famine, even those less devastating, the starving were transformed into grotesque likenesses of human beings: into dried up mummies exhausted by the toil of staying alive and the unbearable effort of keeping on their feet. 'One sees almost everyone reduced to the formless thinness of a mummy, so much that . . . the skin hides nothing, supported by the skeleton with very little flesh. And go where you like, in the streets one meets up with nothing but sadness, melancholy, weakness, sorrow, misery and death.'[3]

In the villages and in the afflicted and calamitous cities, lurid rags wearily stirred, inhabited by fleeting emaciated shadows, wasted by hardship: the metaphysical forms of Sorrow, Misery and Consumption. The urban scene then came to resemble terrifying concourse – to use an image dear to a classical writer on hunger, St Basil – traversed by spider-men, skin dried out and ashen, eyes sunken in hollowed-out bony

26

sockets, like the kernels of dried nuts. St Basil's *Homilia dicta tempore famis et siccitatis* painted a masterly portrait of these starving men which would remain an inimitable model until the time when famine stopped tormenting the West. It is a dramatic stereotype, whose memory also re-emerges, enduringly, in a famous passage of the *Divine Comedy*.

> The disease of the starving, I mean hunger, is a pitiable affliction. Of human calamities hunger is certainly supreme. It brings about the cruellest end of all deaths. Hunger is a disease that torments with slowness, a pain that endures, a sickness that lasts, and is hidden in the bowels, a death that is always present and ever-lingering. Since it consumes the natural humour, the heat becomes cold, the bodily form is consumed, and strength is weakened little by little. The flesh becomes thin, and remains attached to the bones like a spider-web; the colour is lost entirely, since the vermilion disappears from the blood, which becomes thin: nor for this does it turn white. While a sad emaciation overcomes the person; while the body becomes livid, to whoever looks it seems miserably covered in a colour between pallid and black. The knees no longer support, but shuffle because of the weight. The voice is weak and feeble; the eyes weakened and without their natural support in the cavities, sunken in the sockets like dried nuts in their skins. The stomach is empty, sagging and deformed, because it has neither fullness nor any distension of the bowel projecting out, but is supported and maintained by the bone behind . . . The torment of hunger forces many to cross the limits of nature, that is, to feed on the bodies of people related by blood or friendship, and the mothers who give birth to children only to put them back into the womb with horror.[4]

The same bruised flesh and black facial colour, the same deathly-pale form is described in French evidence of 1683: 'some thousands of poor people, with blackened and bruised faces, subdued like skeletons, the majority leaning on crutches and dragging themselves along as best they could to ask for a piece of bread'.[5]

A great gloomy and dazzling literature has etched the chilling *topos* of famine into a malicious and cruel portrait. Procopius of Caesarea, in the suite of Belisarius, was able to observe at close range the horrors of the Gothic–Byzantine war, in the sixth century. Echoing St Basil, he outlined this chilling scene in a memorable page:

> All of them first became lean and pale; for the flesh, being ill-supplied with nourishment, according to the old saying 'laid hold upon itself', and the bile, having now the mastery of their bodies by

reason of its excess, lent them almost its own appearance. And as
the malady developed, all moisture left them, and the skin became
very dry so that it resembled leather more than anything else,
giving the appearance of having been fastened upon the bones. And
as they changed from a livid to a black colour, they came to resemble torches thoroughly burned. And their faces wore an expression
of amazement, while they always had a dreadful sort of insane
stare. And they died, some because of the lack of food, and others
too by sating themselves too much with it. For since all warmth
which nature kindled within them had died away, whenever anyone fed them to satiety, and not little by little, just like infants newly
born, the result was that, since they were as yet unable to digest the
food, they died much more quickly. Some too, overcome by hunger, fed upon their comrades. And it is said that two women in a
certain place in the country above the city of Ariminum ate seven-
teen men; for these women, as it happened, were the only inhabitants of the place who survived, and consequently it came about
that strangers travelling that way lodged in the little house where
these women lived; so they would kill these strangers while they
slept and eat them. Now the story goes that the eighteenth stranger
was roused from sleep, just when these women were about to lay
hands upon him and, leaping up and learning from them the whole
story, killed both of them. Such, then, is the story which they tell.
And most of the people were so overcome by their hunger that if
they happened upon a bit of grass anywhere, they would rush to it
with a great eagerness and, kneeling down, would try to pull it from
the ground. Then, finding themselves unable to do so because all
strength had left them, they would fall upon the grass and their
outstretched hand and die. And no one ever laid them in the earth,
for there was in fact not a man to concern himself about burying
them; and yet they remained untouched by any of those numerous
birds which have the habit of feeding upon dead bodies, for they
offered nothing which the birds craved. For all the flesh, as I have
previously stated, had already been consumed by starvation.[6]

Many centuries later, in the same territory of Rimini which had witnessed the Gothic–Byzantine horrors, in a village located in the
immediate vicinity of the 'Gothic Line', episodes of clandestine butchery
and the consumption of dead soldiers took place during the terrible
winter of 1944. Their flesh, in part fresh and in part preserved, helped to
resolve the crisis of survival within the small indigenous community,
supplying a providential ration of food high in protein. These were

sporadic excesses, foreign to a non-cannibalistic culture, but into which society could always slide when the general picture was altered.

The generations preceding ours, used to fighting against practically endemic famines, had tried to elaborate a series of precepts against famine which went from toasted bread to the roasted liver of every animal. In cases of absolute emergency, urine was recommended for hunger and thirst: 'We read . . . such a thing, of buildings fallen into ruin, with no hope for life remaining, for seven days and nights only urine was drunk, so that hunger and thirst were endured.'[7]

There were those who believed in the pills of Avicenna (*globuli contra famem*), as large as common walnuts, made with ground almonds, lique-fied beef fat, the oil of violets and the juice of marshmallow roots.[8]

Among all the perils that conspired to bring about the decay and destruction of the human body, hunger was the cruellest; but, like other calamities, it escaped every mechanism of control. Man's sense of impo-tence in the governing of his own destiny became dismally more acute towards the end of the sixteenth century.

The soul itself could not 'hold out against the world, the flesh and the devil.'[9] Like Job, condemned to bear not only the miseries and troubles of the human condition, but also the punishments sent by God, and to eat daily the 'bread of sorrows', man – upon whom weighed the dark preoccupation of old age and death, and the irreversible journey into nothingness – also had to protect himself from the 'enemy intestines' and the

> discord of the elements in the four humours which fight among themselves: the choler with the phlegm, and the blood with the melancholy. If one of them wins, which is an easy thing, the bal-ance of all the human temperament is upset, leading to a thousand infirmities, so that our own humours, on which life is based, become our enemies which fight among themselves for our destruction.[10]

The continuous and mortal offence that man had to inflict upon plants and animals in order to survive corresponded to this never-ending inte-rior battle of the four humours. This implied a universe of violence and permanent conflicts, fought in order to preserve an uncertain and pre-carious existence, along with the death of things and the murder of nature:

> We live by force, as we eat for force the food which the earth gives us as a result of sweating and ploughing. We dress as a result of the force we use in stripping the animals of their wool and skins, almost

29

stealing from them their own clothing. We find shelter from the cold and protect ourselves from storms with the force we use against plants and rocks . . . nor can we live except by the death of other things . . .[11]

Rape, violence and theft constituted the dark and sorrowful destiny of man, forced to destroy and ravish all the other forms of creation: 'The things that nature made (birds, fish, trees, herbs and flowers) perish in order to maintain our miserable life, so violent and difficult is it to be able to sustain it.'[12]

Life was fatally destined to ruin and death because of the first parents, Adam and Eve, according to popular belief: 'The body is destined to death because of sin.' To original sin was added the regular action of the devil and the divine scorn for the enormities perpetrated by men. This first and fundamental cause of disease and death was compounded by the malign influence of the stars and the restless cohabitation of the humours.

> Given that in effect death is the extreme of all diseases that can afflict us in this life, so under the name of death we also include all the illness and misery of human life. To that is also added our errors, which day by day are committed and accumulated by us, until our blind will precipitates into all wickedness by the devil's impulse, by which God, provoked to just anger and indignation, allows every kind of illness and calamity to be let loose in us.
>
> The second cause of illness, destruction and deprivation in our bodies is the sinister and malevolent influence of the celestial bodies and the wretchedness of the temperaments.[13]

In order to escape this ghastly dew that fell on mortal faces, the rich drew on a costly but ineffective pharmacopoeia, requiring gold dust and precious stones ground into their distillations or mixed into their most noble electuaries, such as that made from hyacinth, a recipe into which the virtues of the rarest stones were combined.[14] Many people, 'in order to prolong youth and retard old age, make use of viper-tinged wine and prepared viper flesh mixed with other foods.'[15] For the 'poor . . . bereft of riches',[16] empirical and charlatanical medicine recommended the use of *aqua vitae*:

> You must realize that the nature of the world has not produced anything of more marvellous virtue than wine, from which, if we extract the soul – that is, the quintessence, called *aqua vitae* – it is obvious how much more useful this wine will be and what stupendous virtues it will possess; I believe the cards are already stacked

and with its scent it will penetrate the universe as well as the human body.[17]

For the poor, therefore, it was 'drinkable gold . . . marvellous liquid to restore those who are close to death, and to give strength to the aged and convalescent.'[18]

To restore strength and fortify the consumed body, nothing was better than the 'quintessence of capons',[19] obtained by the putrefaction of its flesh in a glass vase which was then immersed in horse manure. Others 'feed and nourish chickens with hellebore, and then these chickens are given as food to those who wish to be rejuvenated.'[20]

Then there were those who believed that the 'prolongation of life is possible',[21] that an elixir of life or quintessence could be concocted: a drinkable gold for extending life for a longer time, 'as one reads about deer, eagles and serpents, who with the herbs they eat renew their lives'.[22]

The earth could hide marvellous secrets, and fables were told of a lucky peasant, a *rusticus*, who 'while digging the ground with his plough, came across a golden vessel full of liquid. Considering it rainwater, he washed his face and drank; his body and goodness, his spirit and wisdom were strengthened, and from ploughman he became the king's porter'.[23]

It was said that a German, having drunk an obscure potion in Saracen lands, 'was prolonged in life to five hundred years'. The honeycomb was singled out as the celestial medicine ideal for producing life.

Many wondered if the spirits (demons and elves) could 'prolong men's lives, rejuvenate the aged, bring back the dead': whether it was possible 'to restore nature, aged and broken down by time',[24] to renew the 'moist root', to draw out the old blood, 'replacing it with fresh blood . . . so that a rotted and emaciated man never goes to ruin and does not allow death to prey on his mortal remains'.[25]

> It is very difficult to discover whether demons can prolong men's lives and cause the aged, weakened by their many years, to be revived and to return to flowering youth . . . And the reason is that up to now no stone, herb, medicine, or other thing has been found in the world which can create this marvellous natural effect of rejuvenating man and prolonging his life . . . None the less, I cannot find any reason for not believing that God created in the world either bird or fish or animal or stone or juice or herb or drop or mineral or jewel or other thing that stores in itself similar virtues capable of renewing man, increasing the strength, restoring the moist root, invigorating the fiery heat, fortifying the constitution and, in short, prolonging life.[26]

31

Authoritative doctors like Cardano were of the opinion that in the New World there had been found 'a fountain of water much more precious than wine, by drinking from which anyone who is aged becomes young'.[27]

Reliable witnesses, informants on the subject who could not be doubted, swore falsely that here and there near-centenarians had seen their hair turn dark, their wrinkles disappear, their teeth grow back: and wrinkled and decrepit old women were all of a sudden relieved of their long hanging breasts, the entire body becoming reinvigorated.

Like the birds of Hibernia ('They die freezing in Ireland for five months, / the birds, yet now they even take to high flight'[28]), certain peoples of the most impervious parts of Muscovy, frozen every year by the north wind, died on 27 November, only to return to life on 24 April – it was not clear whether from 'diabolical trickery' or natural sleep – like dormice.

Everyone knew that to maintain health one could generally rely on 'the things which generate good humour and praiseworthy blood':

So those who wish to maintain their health and retard old age must use those things which generate good and thick blood, and so also with the other humours. As Avicenna said when speaking of old age, saying that old age is retarded when the blood is thick, rich, warm and viscous: then the hair is black. Whereas, when the blood is watery or tends to the watery, then the hair begins to turn white. But the things which generate good blood are fragrant and subtle wines, the meat of young goats, lamb, partridge, pheasant, cockerel and peacock.

Of the herbs: borage and lettuce; and it is better if these are cooked in pies or roasts without broth. And likewise, use those medicaments which have the virtue of modifying the blood, such as absinthe, 'Saracen truffle', wonderful seasonings, fumitory extract, gold and pearls; while the doctor must study those things which cause good digestion, for it is fundamental, since bad digestion corrupts the blood, generating bad and foul humours . . .

Therefore, in digestion lies the entire foundation.[30]

Even if known to everyone, very few people were capable of putting into practice these elementary precepts that fell into the sphere of non-natural things, which had great influence on the problem of staying healthy: 'food and drink, motion and rest, sleep and wakefulness, emptyness and fullness, and so, in short, the passions' (Gregorius Pictorius).

On the other hand, penury and hunger belonged to the category of natural things, which became chronic and endemic in the West during the sixteenth to eighteenth centuries in particular. Like the non-natural phenomena, they had their origin in the economy, the means of production and the political will of the rulers. The precarious relationship between production and demography, and between man and dietary resources was never so compromised as in the period when peasants made up the overwhelming majority of the population.

The fall of man into bestiality constitutes a recurrent *topos* in the great dramatic frescos of provisioning emergencies. It is a motif which, climbing over the corporeal to land at the banks of the incorporeal, is expanded and transformed into the theme of hunger, becoming an essential element in the meditation on death and the art of dying (*ars moriendi*), and passing from hunger to Hunger. It is the conclusive moment in the battle, terrible and without respite, between Life and Death: the conflict between the instinct for life and *thanatos*, between the fatal pull of the sterile world of the shades, bereft of laughter and hunger, and the swarming termites' nest of existence, a voracious feeding mechanism.

Hunger, the prime mover of biology, but also society's 'disease of wretchedness' – antechamber of death which in the judgement of doctors 'is the primary disease',[31] was the closest ally of the epidemic diseases, typical of those societies which had arrived at the nation-state phase of organization, but which nevertheless irresponsibly allowed vast poor and over-crowded human heaps to fall into degradation.

The pace of history has been articulated by the succession of diseases and epidemics, and civic life has moved in harmony with the rhythm of epidemiological laws, which for a long period of time constituted one of the most effective regulators of the demographic game.[32]

In representing the hell of the poor one constant motif is used: the physical degradation of the starving pauper and his bestial metamorphosis. The pages written by doctors and priests often give us passages describing the collective reality with strong and biting dramatic force. Those who daily moved among the hungry and the dying were – more efficaciously than the men of letters (involved in totally different excercises) – the best interpreters and witnesses of the dismal marasmus of wretched individuals and crowds. Their voices agree in underlining the intolerable filth of the beggars, the nauseous and disagreeable stink of poverty, inescapable companion of the 'canine' condition: They did not have the appearance of humans, writes a south Italian doctor during the eighteenth century, 'so haggard and thin were they, and, furthermore, they stank so badly that when approaching citizens or wandering through the streets or churches or public spaces, they caused instantaneous giddiness and dizziness'.[33]

In the pre-industrial age pauperism was eventually contained at a constant level as a result of a whole system of urban assistance and hospitalization (charitable institutions, mendicants' institutes, homes for the aged, hospices, hospitals, etc.), that maintained the number of beggars almost constant, affected to a considerable degree by the epidemic mortality and the morbidity of the old endemic pathologies. The situation, more or less static, began to change when epidemics like the plague mysteriously faded to the point of disappearing after the first decades of the eighteenth century (not much trust can be placed in the theory of auto-immunization). The growth in the population became progressive: while in the north of Italy population seems to have remained stationary, in the south the demographic expansion increased much more rapidly. The tendency towards demographic growth, the causes of which remain unclear even to those expert in the field, brought about profound social unrest when the pauperism of the *ancien régime* could no longer be controlled by the traditional mechanisms of power, and was transformed – under the influence of the large numbers of poor, underemployed and unemployed – into an explosive revolutionary combination.

2
Elusive Bread

Baroque intellectuals and scholars, slightly removed from the threatening crowds of breadless beggars and mountain-dwellers, and the unseemly and mournful processions of the hungry, defended themselves, according to their traditional inclination, by launching cynical and malicious broadsides against the tide of beggars and *formiconi scioperati* ('idle workers').[1] This was the case with Baldassare Bonifacio, who at Treviso in 1629 witnessed tumultuous agitation among the very poor, which he transposed shortly afterwards into the pitiless and hot-tempered sonnets of *Il paltoniere*.

The distress of the few in the face of the crazed surging in the streets, of the innumerable devourers of refuse – the 'grub-men' and 'insect-men' – and the anxiety of the groups in power regarding the great, threatening numbers, the uncontrolled proliferation of the wretched and the spectre of a negative society that, reluctant to be integrated, waves the banner of a society in opposition, all stimulate the obsessive image in Bonifacio's sonnets of the rising tide; water that rises irresistibly in order to bring about the final suffocation. The tension between the castes is transformed into this metaphorical series of verses from which seeps the fearful contempt of the eaters of white bread towards the eaters of dark bread or those who went without bread altogether: the *picchia-porte* ('door-knockers') or *matta-panes* ('bread-crazy')[2] who expanded the 'great cloud of scoundrels and rogues',[3] as threatening as a raging storm of locusts.

In reality, beyond the literary effect and ritual dramatization of tumult and fear, the turbulence of the very poor, while capable of causing anxiety and dread, never went beyond a bit of unorganized looting, incapable of being transformed into anything more than a furious but short-lived rebellion. The linguistic stereotypes of violence and revolt were transmitted from century to century according to litanies of despair that share the same tense and impassioned stamp: as in the fourteenth-century *Libro del biadaiolo*, where famine (similar, in fact, to the sonnets of Bonifacio) speaks with the voices of Dantesque pandemonium. But they remain linguistic stereotypes, while the protagonists of the uprisings themselves 'did not show themselves interested in changing the structures of the society in which they lived'.[4]

In a society fragmented and compartmentalized into very large numbers of guilds, the notion of 'class' could not have any sense. The medieval *status* formed the structure of a world in very slow evolution, where collective life was modified with extreme difficulty and, it could be said, almost with reluctance. Caste and corporation prevented the birth of the idea – an entirely eighteenth-century one – of 'class'. Liberation from the *male di vivere* ('sickness of living') was not pursued politically, but by means of direct-release techniques, such as the great use of alcoholic beverages, sexual practices ('wild' and unrestrained) and ritual feasts (the private or group transgression of the civil or religious norm). Dreams stimulated not revolutionary ferments but voyages into fantastic evasions. The utopias, even the most radical, dissolve into doctrinal and sapiential story-telling. Even the great myth of the Land of Cockaigne – whether in its general desire for fair community ownership of material goods and property, or in the dream of eternal youth and love, not socially controlled, of non-institutionalized *eros* – never remotely entails authentic political and social renewal.

In years of unfortunate conjunctures, the small landowners, forced to sell their fields to the large landowners at usurious prices, ended up begging in the streets. Even the mighty Alvise Cornaro enormously expanded his already ample holdings by utilizing Angelo Beolco, *il Ruzante*, as a trusted agent, mediator and broker.

The bread of the poor, of those dressed in rags, the unemployed, and especially of those who produced it, the peasants, victims of a paradoxical social and economic logic, was a bread forever fleeting, as elusive as a slow-motion nightmare of interminable length. In lean years, the time of the next harvest was dreamed of, in longing expectation, beginning in late autumn: of summer and its fruits, the season in which one could re-experience the taste of the *pan novelo* ('new bread').[5]

The character of Menego in Ruzante's *Dialogo facetissimo*, performed during the famine of 1528, counts on his fingers the months that separate him from 'the fleeting bread': 'January, February, March, April, May and half of June as well, until wheat. (Sigh!) Oh, we shall never make it! Blast, but it's a good long year, this one. I know the bread flees from us, indeed it does, more than sparrows from the falcon'.[6]

The comic stamp of the dialogue (*facetissimo*, 'most facetious', used ironically) also serves to dispel the terrible adversary, hunger, by exorcizing it with laughter. Humoristic whims are indulged by means of the vast inventive repertory of bitter-sweet peasant contrivances and their thought-out artifice in trying to satisfy alimentary requirements: tragic buffoonery invented by those whose flesh is tortured by the wedges of hunger. This cruel image, borrowed from the torture chambers, was then quickly transferred and rendered innocuous by the absurdity of the expedients devised to try to avoid, or at least mitigate, the hard laws of necessary consumption and physiological fate, proposing the use of astringents like the sorb-apple, or the surreal strategem of plugging *la busa de soto* ('the hole underneath'). In that way the excrement, not being able to leave the body, would keep the bowel full, thus neutralizing hunger.

In a strange paradox, illness was desired in order to allay hunger, as Menego explains to Duozo: 'I try hard to get sick because, I tell you, friend, it seems that when I am sick hunger does not come to me; and as long as hunger doesn't bother me, I wouldn't want anything more'.[7]

Uselessly the beggars of the fields recited falsely comforting proverbs: litanies stemming from the resigned and disconsolate millenary cohabitation with hunger. The season of herbs was longed for too, not only that of cereals and pulses: 'with it one can pass all of January, and then the wild plants come out and men feed themselves'. The 'wild plants' would help them to survive, and the buds would be eaten before the flower and the fruit: iris and corncockle buds, ruminated along with grapevine leaves. Burs, traveller's joy, and perhaps even ivy would have met the same end. Almost three centuries later, the farmers of Friuli described by Caterina Percato, the 'peasant baroness', in the *Anno della fame*, mowed the grain in spring while still green in order to survive. Alternating the over-realistic register with a dream-like one, Ruzante composes an extraordinary surrealistic image in order to give a ghostly sense to men near death, having by then arrived at inconsistency on the edge of nothingness. 'I know that we will become so thin as to resemble dead men who have been hung in the smoke, so weak and worn out shall we be'.[9]

The dance of the consumed bodies, so thin and wasted away that they could be hung in the smoke – a rapid, 'smoky' ending of relief to all this hallucinated and grievous dietary humour – marks one of the most sophisticated moments of that literature which borrowed themes, motifs and patterns from hunger.

The dietary boundary between men and animals became fine to the point of disappearing. Sorghum, for example – the dialogue between the two day-labourers corresponds accurately to brutal reality – passed from pig to man, and if there was none, it was bran that became 'good fodder for men', soaked in hot water and formed into a bran mash for the 'pig-men' (*porci et rustici*, or 'pigs and peasants'), so reduced to wallowing as to resemble snuffling animals.

Ruzante reaches the most powerful effects of macabre humour when Menego, outraged in heart and flesh by his rival in love, imagines his own destruction, by self-devourment: 'But nevertheless I shall kill myself . . . And it will be even better, because I myself shall eat me, and so I shall die well-nourished, in defiance of the famine'.[10] The grotesque effect is surprisingly successful and of an irresistible humour (at least for us); except that the weighing and the interpretation could be modified, keeping in mind that episodes of this sort – here only imagined for the amusement of the noble listeners – were actually taking place outside the theatre. The accounts by the missionaries of St Vincent bear witness to the tragic reality of autophagy in France during the seventeenth century.

The shortage in the food supply from which Ruzante departs in order to construct his *Dialogo facetissimo et ridiculosissimo*, 'performed at Fosson in the year of the famine, 1528', corresponds dramatically to the notarial acts of the time (fortunately and deservedly brought to light thanks to Paolo Sambin, and examined with mournful sensibility by Ludovico Zorzi), which furnish a vivid counterpoint to the theatrical game created in order to delight the powerful patron and master, intent on expanding this vast landed patrimony, taking advantage of the misery which forced small landholders and lease holders already afflicted by heavy debts, to sell him their lands at a low price.

It remains an enigma how an audience could enjoy this theatrical action which caused the starving poor (even in the fiction of the stage) to become the means of entertainment and amusement for those who, if not actually the causers of hunger, took generous advantage of the calamities which fell heavily on the people. Leaving aside useless socio-moralistic deprecations and popularistic complaints, the moral insensitivity of Alvise Cornaro which Ruzante voiced in his play serves to indicate, above all, how social sensibility was profoundly different during a 'hard age of conscience and reason that was the Renaissance at its height, when the celebrated liberation of man was replaced by the notion of responsibility over his historical and earthly destiny'.[11] While taking for granted the cruelties of the times and the toughness of life for those whom we can no longer understand, enveloped in the security and protection of civil as well as societal tutelage, we should certainly not interpret Cornaro's laughter in terms of self-flagellation of a masochistic sort, but more like the satisfying, exhilarating response to the oppressive condition of anguish of a 'benefactor' who, although actually performing acts of usury, was conscious of his contribution to the saving of human lives.

The miserable and dramatic reality emerges from the notarial deeds, as in the one documenting the case of the married couple of Rosara who, 'wanting to help and relieve themselves in so much necessity and extremity of living, in such penury that there was never anything worse, indeed they perish from hunger with their very poor family', 'sold to Cornaro the usable property of two fields at the price of ten ducats', receiving, however, only fourteen lire of the price, having already been paid the rest 'before the promise of the contract'.[12] There is also the deed which sadly tells the miserable story of Master Michele Polato of Codevigo: 'Wanting to help himself in such penury of sustenance, indeed he perishes from hunger, he has been begging publicly for two months to be confined, not having any other way of keeping and sustaining his poor life, other than by sale'.[13] (He receives three ducats for his field, having already received seven beforehand.)

Take-overs of the less ample estates, the elimination of the smaller landowners and the merging together of these new lands of which Cornaro came into possession by means of a cunning and disguised appropriation, not a violent one as occurred elsewhere, is a confirmation of the theory of Maurice Dobb. According to this, 'large property grew to adult stature by digesting the small; and a capitalist class arose as the creation, not of thrift and abstinence as economists have traditionally depicted it, but of the dispossession of others by dint of economic or political advantage'.[14]

One might wonder whether the theorist of frugality and restraint, 'sober-life Cornaro', made use of his own over-preached ideology of dietary temperance to cover up a Pantagruelesque appetite for lands and fields.

3

Sacred and Profane Cannibalism

During the period of the Thirty Years War and the Fronde, when the bark of trees and even dirt was utilized in the desperate hope of prolonging the misery of human existence by a few days or hours, the carcasses of animals killed by the plague, even if in a state of advanced decomposition, were roasted to supply miserable hallucinating meals.

Several inhabitants of Picardy, '. . . which we would not dare to say if we had not seen it, and which caused horror, ate their own arms and hands and died in despair'.[1]

However, self-devourment was certainly not unknown in Italy either, since – clothed in a reassuring comic attire – it filtered its way into the theatre of Ruzante.

Undoubtedly these desperate forms of cannibalism were not infrequent in western Europe of the seventeenth century. In 1637, according to other evidence from France which was too densely populated in relation to the availability of protein resources, people looked for the carcasses of dead animals; the roads were packed with people, most of whom were prostrated from weakness or were dying . . . Finally, it even came to eating human flesh'.[2]

However, beyond horror – not historically justified and perhaps not dietetically either – there was whispered praise of cannibalism, not so much for love of paradox as in recognition of its effective contribution in the saving of human lives. The accursed ghost of the *Raft of the Medusa* does not permit moralistic detours. The *quaestio de vita producenda* (the search for nourishment necessary to prolong or save life) has from ancient times been a tricky problem for philosophical meditation and medical science, and not merely an abstraction for theoreticians concerned with the politics of provisioning and social organization.

The uncertainty of sixteenth- and seventeenth-century theologians and casuists over 'whether it is ever lawful to eat human flesh', analysed in the two topical cases of consumption *extra necessitatem* or *in extrema necessitate*, constitutes the sign of a practice, more or less clandestine, and the need to 'violate nature and defeat aversion . . . to like disgusting foods and abominable carcasses'.[3] Not 'ordinary' but 'extreme' hunger, according to the definition of the Jesuit Giovan Stefano Menocchio, who in a chapter of his *Stuore* discusses 'those who, stimulated by hunger, or by barbarous custom, eat human flesh; and whether in any circumstances it can be eaten without sinning'.[4] The hunger which leads to this excess is that which Virgil termed *obscena*; cruellest variant of what Quintilian impeccably defined as 'the ruin of the body . . . most disgusting of evils'; profane variant (born of the condition of necessity) of the sacred banquet practised by many peoples of antiquity, like the Messagetae among whom, according to the account of Herodotus, 'when someone becomes old, all the relatives meet and sacrifice him, and with him other animals; once the meats are boiled they feast. This they regard as most blessed; and those who die from sickness they do not eat, but they bury, holding it a disgrace that the sacrifice did not take place'.[5] This was mass slaughter, by which the group satisfied the magico-propitiatory precept and, furthermore, rid itself of the extra mouths. By balancing the deficit of provisions, it succeeded in helping the youngest to survive, and they, in their turn, would be used in the same way, in a singular path of exchange between the living and the dead.[6]

Pursuing the elimination of the aged with method and rigour, the Khoi overcame old age and exalted youth, according to the speculation on ancient sources conducted, with a certain hidden pleasure, by another Jesuit, François Pomey, a learned delver into thanatological disciplines, in his work on the rituals of death, *Libitina seu de funeribus*.

> The Khoi abstained from mourning . . . since among them it was established by law that sixty-year-olds should procure their deaths with poison; that is to say, so that as lazy and idle people they would not consume the food necessary to keep the adolescents alive. For this reason almost everyone among them enjoyed youthfulness, and so much was old age held in low esteem, that they preferred death.[7]

These poisonous herbs, funeral drugs in a rite of mass suicide, formed part of the cultural baggage of the ancient civilizations: the 'sardonic herb' is also recalled by Virgil and Solinus.

In *De gubernatione Dei*, at the beginning of that seventh book which opens with the splendid scenario of the punishment of the Romans' vices, and the dramatic portrait of the Roman patriciate dancing and laughing

41

on the edge of the abyss ('moritur et ridet') while everything, amidst massacres, butchery and horrors, is tumbling down around them, Salvianus highlights the image of stupefaction and collective vertigo resulting from the effects of the 'sardonic herbs': 'We enjoy ourselves, despite the fears we have in captivity; though we are put in terror of death, we laugh after a fashion through the action of the sardonic herbs which all the Roman people are full of'.

In the ritual sacrifice of the aged, 'laughter is an act of piety which transforms death into a new birth'.[8] By nullifying the homicide, the birth of new lives was propitiated, weeping and mourning abolished, and slaughter and death turned into a collective laugh, even if the elimination of 'idle and mature beings' was motivated in part by the hard laws of food availability, given that the alimentary reserves had to be used to preserve the young and productive nucleus (and so ensure the reproduction of the group), which had to be protected and nourished at all costs.

Laughter and tears, death and life - indissolubly intertwined in the history of men faced with the eternal alternation of creation and corruption, birth and destruction, death and rebirth - have recently been brought to the attention of the West by Slav scholars (Propp, Bakhtin, Jakobson): funeral rites in which the element of play and parody, sneering and laughter, and the offence against death were included, making up a liturgy struggling to enhance life and strengthen its forces against the great cunning and mysterious adversary. In such rites, let us add - lying in the depths of folk culture, which has always made of laughter the most powerful weapon for consolidating life and causing it to triumph over death - comical mime and evil-averting song and laughter constituted the central part of the funereal moment. These rites were 'demonized' by serious clerical learning, and by new ecclesiastical models hostile to laughter and comedy.

The more that ecclesiastical learning strayed from the agrarian sense of life and the seasonal rebirth of nature, the more it forbade in every possible way the obsequies celebrated by the agrarian world. 'The diabolical songs', urged Pope Leo IV in a homily of his during the ninth century, 'which the populace are in the habit of singing over the dead, and loud laughter which they practise, are prohibited by the commandment of the omnipotent God.' None the less, something of this laughter remained in the countryside until the eighteenth century. We would just like to add that the tradition found in the serious/playful epitaph or in laughter at the graveside has its roots in folk rites. Limiting ourselves to a few examples, we could glance through the 'playful epitaphs' of *Il Cimiterio* by Giovanni Francesco Loredano and Pietro Michiele (Venice/Bologna, 1666), or the *Epitaphia ioco-seria* of Franciscus Swertius

(Cologne, 1623), and examine them, bearing in mind the peasant ritual laughter and tricks played on the corpses of widows by 'ceremonial' clowns. A written memorial of this has remained for us in a page of Giovanni Battara's *Pratica agraria* ('near the bier . . . sometimes things are heard which make one die laughing'), and in the late fifteenth-century *Episcopale bononiensis civitatis* ('They let out indecent and unrestrained shouts and yells over the burial ground, telling ridiculous things to those nearby . . . and they do likewise on the day of the requiem').

Death and laughter are tightly bound together in an inseparable dialectic relationship in all cultures of the agrarian type, which have the profound nucleus of their religiosity – a constant relation between earth and sub-soil, fertility and sterility – in vegetable rebirth and reproduction by means of dead seeds. Not by accident the term *homo* is linked to *humus* ('earth'), as Emile Benveniste has recently reminded us.

In the chronicles of the Slav east (not to mention the comic farces on the Resurrection studied by Roman Jakobson, a parallel element of which lies in the very vital and prolific energy inherent in the 'resurrection of the flesh' metaphor, dear to Italian short story writing) one reads that 'On Trinity Saturday, in the villages and hamlets, men and women gather in the cemeteries and weep on the graves with great lamentation. Then the minstrels and buffoons start their show, and having finished their weeping, even they [the men and women] start to jump and dance and clap their hands and sing satanic songs.'[9]

The *carmina diabolica* ('diabolical songs'), anathematized by Leo IV and interdicted by Regino of Prüm in the *De synodalibus causis et disciplinis ecclesiasticis* (*c*.900), reappear in eastern Europe and wherever agrarian culture created as it were an ambivalent sense of life.

A variety of the buttercup, probably mixed with hemlock or other deadly herbs and narcotic infusions, seems to have been the instrument in the group slaughter of the aged of which the voices of the past tell us. According to Pietro Andrea Mattioli:

> That which in Sardinia is called 'rustic celery', some call *Apium risum* ('laughing celery'), since it is believed that those who eat it die laughing; several others who are more to be believed, say that when this Sardinian celery is eaten it causes all the nerves to retract in such a way as to widen and distend the mouth, and whoever has eaten it, as he dies, resembles a person laughing. This herb, which is called 'Sardonia', is really a species of buttercup. When drunk or mixed in foods, it causes insanity, and by making the lips of the mouth retract, it generates a certain spasm so that it really seems as if those who have eaten it are laughing.[10]

To tell the truth, other ancient sources (Helianus, for example) disagree about Sardinian customs and refer to the aged parents being beaten to death, having become useless and unproductive (our civilization knows something of this, the desolation of the elderly outside of the productive machinery). The Meruli succeeded so perfectly in conditioning the no-longer-young that they themselves asked permission of the less aged for the privilege of leaving the living, and climbed of their own will on to the pyre that would consume them (according to the account of Procopius in *The Gothic Wars*). The inhabitants of Marseilles, on the other hand, preferred to distribute free rations of hemlock to whoever asked for it, in order to quicken the end of their suffering and bar the passage to adverse fortune, ever in wait.

A relic of the decimation of old men and the assassination of old women also survived in the mid-Lenten rite that went under the name of *Segavecchia* (literally, 'Saw-hag'). The *vecchia inutile* ('useless old woman') or *vecchiaccia malandrina* ('wicked old hag') was killed by bands of young men, as recounted in the printed pamphlets of eighteenth-century Romagna. The feast was entirely for them: the old woman, rich but miserly, was bled entirely for the benefit of 'young blood'. In Bologna, the 'at least twice-over sexagenarian and arch-decrepit hag' was burnt alive on the rise of the Strada Maggiore (as a 1667 broadsheet of the story-teller Pietro Testi 'the Blind' narrates). But as usual, it is the voice of Giulio Cesare Croce which best preserves the echo of this most remote ritual practice, the controlled shiver of social assassination and ritual elimination:

> A hundred old women found,
> Wrinkled, thin and poorly-fed,
> Disgusting, bitter and ugly,
> Who are no longer good for anything.
> Come on, who wants to come?
> And their names will have a place.
> All into the vase!
> And pull one out by chance,
> Who will take the place?
> Come on, who wants to come? . . .[11]

In times closer to ours, a prestigious intellectual like Marsilio Ficino, son of a doctor, prescribed the drinking of blood drawn from the veins of adolescents as a remedy for the exhaustion of old age, following a universally adopted usage, in his *De sanitate tuenda*:

> Thus the good doctors, using blood distilled and refined by fire, are able to recreate and restore those who are eaten away and

consumed, little by little, by the consumptive fever of old age. Now why can we not also, with the same liquid, occasionally restore and almost bring back to vital strength those people who are half dead simply because of old age?

There is a certain ancient and popular opinion that certain old women, whom we call witches, suck the blood of babies to rejuvenate themselves as much as possible; why should our elderly, who find themselves bereft of any other assistance, not likewise suck the blood of a yound boy, of robust strength I mean, who is healthy, cheerful, even-tempered and who has perfect blood and, by chance, in abundance. Then suck it as would a leach or bloodsucker, from the open vein of the left arm . . . and during the waxing of the moon.[12]

'The mummy expels dead blood', wrote Giovanni Michele Savonarola in the *Practica maior*, while 'the quintessence of human blood' was often utilized 'against hopeless diseases'.[14] According to a Franciscan, Fra Francesco Sirena, druggist at the monastery of Santa Croce in Pavia, the blood most prized for its therapeutic virtues, extracted in the spring, was that of bodies that were 'healthy, of hot and humid temperament . . . because such men have purer blood than any other temperament, and are of the best and most robust complexion of all the other temperaments. I warn, moreover, that as long as it is drawn from those of hot and humid temperament, such as that of people with white and red complexions and somewhat fat bodies, the blood will be perfect, as long as they do not have red hair'.[15] Human cranial powder was also used in the therapy for epilepsy: 'The powder collected from human skulls, coins and water drawn from the vettonica plant serve in the cure for epilepsies'.[16]

It was believed for a long time, at least until the middle of the eighteenth century, that cranial powder was an effective medicine against epilepsy. Superstitious soldiers even believed that 'by just drinking ordinarily from a human skull, the person is rendered immune from the assaults of arms':[17] a 'barbaric' practice (one thinks of Alboin and Rosamund) which has accompanied the battles of 'modern' history.

However, not all skulls were considered of equal value:

Those which are stolen from cemeteries, from people naturally dead, are not valued at all [by druggists and doctors]. But they take singular care to choose those skulls belonging to men who suffered violent deaths, and that, purified and cleansed of all filth, have been in the open air for a few years, like those which justice, for the public infamy of great bandits, exposes in iron cages on the gates of the city to the view of others. The reason why this choice is best, according to them, is that the skull of whoever has passed to the other life by means of a natural death is believed to have none of its innate spirit which has been dissipated in the disease; whereas those which met violent deaths still preserve a part of this spirit and because of such a death this powerful spirit, they say, lies concentrated and nearly hidden inside.

This is confirmed by the *usnea* of the human skull, which (according to Olmonte) is a small plant which, by a seed fallen from the sky, grows in the skull on the nourishing sauce of its alcoholic liquid.[18]

The 'incomparable art' of the doctors, according to the resounding conclusion of Camillo Brunori, had found in the skull an admirable means of inflicting notable injuries on death:

Horrid death, that implacable war,
    Every hour you declare in thousands and thousands of ways,
    And running through the underground caves,
    Proudly you go through many murdered remains:
From these fleshless skulls, in which are locked up
    Great virtue, and that now are your shares,
    Phoebean hand, that your arrogance demolishes,
    Drew great sword and put herself against you;
And with her then come to the defence
    Of man, and he assists in that part
    Where he takes the appearance of a real man;
And defeated, you then flee, and go to one side
    Together with anger and shame incensed,
    You curse our incomparable art.[19]

Aqua divina was the name of a distillation from corpses, and not a few doctors 'proclaimed its supreme magnetic virtue'. It was prepared by following this recipe: 'The whole corpse (killed, of course, by a violent death), with bones, flesh and intestines, is separated into tiny pieces, and this done well, every part of the body is ground up, so that nothing remains unmixed. Then it is distilled with favourable results.[20]

With 'cadaverous' ingredients ('chosen mummy of life') and, in particular, with the blood 'of a flourishing and healthy man', a troche (a type of compress) was prepared, 'notable . . . [and] efficacious in curing abscesses'. To dissolve the tablet a 'secret mixture of human blood was considered perfectly suitable.[21]

The flesh of the mummy mixed with mother's milk was the main ingredient in the preparation of a 'human plaster' manufactured in

Carpi by the Barigazzi family, a clan of barber-surgeons from which
Berengario emerged, a famous anatomist at the University of Bologna
and author of *De fractura calvae sive cranei* (1518):

> Among the medicines for external use, I have never known the
> equal of my head plaster, known also as the human plaster, because
> a notable part of human, or rather mummy, substance enters into
> its composition. I have always heard from the oldest of my family
> that the mummy which enters into this plaster must be part of a
> man's head, and the mummy is dried human flesh. In Venice I saw
> nearly intact bodies of such a mummy. From what I learned from
> my father and also from what I have seen, the old people of our
> family kept one or more such mummified heads in the house, from
> which they took certain parts for the preparation of the plaster.[22]

In the light of such familiarity between living flesh and the desiccated
flesh of the dead, for us almost archaeological, of this cohabitation with
conspicuous bodily fragments (which obviously presupposes a spiritual
co-existence) that have become dry and wrinkled like parchment from
the *morte secca* ('dry death'), the presence of skulls and bones, appears not
alarming, but intimate, almost natural. In the society of old the world of
the living was tied to that of the dead by a thousand threads. The presence of the shades, their voices, signals and mysterious language conditioned the existence of those not yet deceased.

The cemetery – a polyvalent space used for all human activities (very
often it even served as a market) – was at the same time a place of death
and a place of play: an area protected by the bones of some powerful
saint. Inside the 'sacred' enclosure the rites of life and death, weeping
and laughter, body and spirit were celebrated. Dancing accompanied
burial, and the funereal lament accompanied the ritual banquet. Folk
culture (and *ancien régime* society in general) had a healthily ambiguous
relationship with death: naturally 'equivocal' because it believed that the
ambivalent 'death–life' rhythm constituted the obscure but powerful
principle of human life. The 'other world' dwelt within the world of the
living, constituting the other side of human existence.

In this continual and vital presence of death, the categories of the
macabre and the lugubrious did not have the same sense that is attributed to them today. The almost tactile association and intimacy with the
products of death – corpse, bones, the diseased and dying – also meant a
different relationship with the human body. In its carnality and physical
presence, it represented a boundary place where popular wisdom and
'scientific' culture met, in a syncretism where the traditions were distinguished with extreme difficulty. The medical recipes, whether of popular

or official medicine, constitute a treasury of micro-texts in which the therapeutic encyclopedism of traditional society – in the complicated interlacing of 'sympathies', 'repulsions' and 'affinities' – reveals the magical character of every practice pertaining to the maintenance of health.

The recipes of the pre-industrial age can help to restore the ancient face and sense of death, to interpret with greater pertinence the body–disease–death relationship, to feel more tangibly the corporeal depth and physical presence of an existence which, in its two-sided syncretism, made use of tissues and fragments of the dead to cure the living. One fact strikes us with great clarity: the familiarity with human and animal flesh, with the excretions of the human body and the most repulsive physiological by-products, and the natural intimacy with what was funereal, repugnant, impure, rotten, putrid and nauseating.

It is enough to run through a little work printed many times during the course of the seventeenth century, *Le medicine che da tutti gl'animali si pusso cavare a beneficio dell'uomo, altre volte intitolato il Zomista, e Secretario de gl'animali*,[23] by Alessandro Venturini, in order to see how the list of 'medicinal' animals opens with the entry 'man' (followed immediately by 'woman'): the first of all the therapeutic 'beasts', and follows with dog, pig, horse, wolf, dormouse, rabbit, marmot, hare, salamander, tarantula, spider, and so on. 'Man' in this list is *Homo homini salus* ('man, the health of man'). With a preventive prophylactic aim in mind, or else in curative procedures, hair, menstruum and mother's milk and butter were all utilized. Even more numerous were the 'virtues' to be extracted from the body, starting from the 'marrow of dead bone', to 'human fat', blood, the dried flesh of 'mummies', the excrement and urine of men and boys, sweat, the 'filth of the ears', the 'mucus of the nostrils', the 'dirt to be found around the neck of a man's penis' (to be spread on a scorpion sting), and 'testicles given in powder to the woman after menstruation' to make her conceive, according to the recipe attributed to Trotula da Salerno (eleventh century).

From the druggists' and herbalists' workshops came ointments, pomades, elixirs, syrups, pills and electuaries: products not dissimilar, in their 'repugnant' composition, from the philtres and ointments attributed to witches.

The virtues of the 'true compound of human fat' (effective in curing a great number of infirmities, 'spread cold with a swab or rag on every kind of cut and wound, bruises, sores, scrofula, glands; it is applied hot for the humours, with stuffing in the ears . . .') continued to be praised even at the beginning of the last century, as appears from the *Selva medicinale in cui stanno ristretti varj segreti d'erbe, le quali non vengono stimate da alcuni. Sperimentate da me Pietro l'Ignoto e dedicati a beneficio universale* (Bologna).

The more knowledgeable and authoritative pharmacologists like Johann Schroeder (born at Salzuffeln in 1600, active at Frankfurt, where he died, the undisputed authority in pharamacology) distinguished four types of 'mummy' chosen 'from the cadaver of a dead man': (1) 'The mummy of the Arabs, which is fluid or a condensed fluid substance that exudes from the cadavers in the grave, preserved with aloe, myrrh and balsam'; (2) '[that] of the Egyptians, which is a liquid that comes out of the cadavers, preserved with *pissaphaltum* [pitch mixed with bitumen]'; (3) 'those made with *pissaphaltum* . . .'; and, (4) 'the cadaver roasted in the sand by the heat of the sun'.[24] To these four qualities of mummy, another 'fresher' one was added, made up of

> the cadaver of a reddish man (because in such a man the blood is believed lighter and so the flesh is better), whole, fresh without blemish, of around twenty-four years of age, dead of a violent death (not of illness), exposed to the moon's rays for one day and night, but with a clear sky. Cut the muscular flesh of this man and sprinkle it with power of myrrh and at least a little bit of aloe, then soak it, making it tender, finally hanging the pieces in a very dry and shady place until they dry out. Then it comes to resemble smoke-cured meat, without any stench.[25]

The use of human flesh – even the spiced and scented flesh of mummified corpses,[26] smelling of balsams and age ('the mummy . . . is nothing other than the flesh of the human body buried with precious ointments', according to the definition of Leendert Leys[27] a prestigious Jesuit theologian) – was not only supported in medical therapy by the authority of the great Rasis, but also practised until the eighteenth century in the preparation of certain elixirs and in the therapy for paralisis and apoplexy, so that it became quite difficult and inconsistent to demonstrate that it was morally inappropriate to abstain from this type of alimentation 'in the extreme necessity of hunger' or in 'extremely urgent hunger'. In fact, moral theology found itself in notable embarrassment in dealing with this problem, and it was forced to advance arguments of the sophist type, of little weight or authority. Facing this delirious void, it was not much use recalling the totally abstract principle that it was necessary to nourish oneself with foods derived from beings lower than man, inferior to him in the physical hierarchy, following the natural order that sees the plants fed by the juice of the earth, the animals fed in turn by the plants, and the most perfect and strongest of animals fed by the weakest and most imperfect.

Nor could the theological intimation that in anthropophagy 'in general the whole is confused with the part during resurrection'[27] have a stronger influence.[28]

Resisting the cannibalistic taboo was not easy in the case of dire necessity. It is even harder if one reflects on the singular similarity in taste – according to those who had tasted it – between human flesh and pork. A classic figure of Byzantine medicine, Paulus Aegineta, whose authority remained great until after the Renaissance, had observed that 'among the animals which provide meat for those who go on foot, pork, more than other foods, is the one found to be most familiar in smell and taste to the human body, as some people who have inadvertently tasted human flesh have learned'.[29] Giambattista Moreali – a court doctor active in the first part of the eighteenth century – was a lone voice and gained no following; he held that human flesh, and especially that of adolescents, manifested a violent acidic-verminous odour, similar to that accompanying veal. 'If we had a book *De medicina Antropophagorum*', wrote this doctor who had built an unpublished scientific theory on worms and their odours, 'as we have *De medicina Indorum*, perhaps we would know that human flesh, and especially that of boys, sometimes has a similar odour'.[30]

But men dying of hunger, more 'shades of the dead' than living beings, 'emaciated, wounded and pale because of the extreme discomfort . . . shades and not human bodies',[31] could become the necrophagous butchers of other men (as was demonstrated quite recently by the disaster in the Andes).

In the pontificate of Stephen VII, when everything that man needs to survive was lacking – dogs, mice, cats, with all the other animals that are most abominable were dead, there remaining not even horses or other pack animals – in Italy and France many learned to eat human flesh, although they pecked away very secretly.[32]

We shall never know how many tons of human flesh have been consumed in the modern era, even though the existence of this secret 'pecking' is beyond discussion. It is its clandestine quality that renders this consumption non-quantifiable. This consumption, besides being quite widespread, is indirectly corroborated by the very high number of fairy tales full of ogres, eaters of Christian flesh, 'wild men', and frequent similar episodes in the romantic epics of the fifteenth and sixteenth centuries from the giants of the *Ciriffo Calvaneo*, eaters of children, to the ogre of *Orlando Innamorato*, another in the *Pentamerone*, and the 'savage' Magorto of the *Malmantile Racquistato*, who, 'blacker than midnight',

He has the snout of a bear and the neck of a stork
And a stomach like a large barrel:
He climbs up catapults, and has a mouth like a sewer;
He makes light work of a tub of cooked apples,
He has the tusks of a pig and the nose of an owl,
Who pisses in his mouth and makes waste continuously.

The hairs of his brows cover his eyes,
And some of his nails are half a yard long:
He eats men, and when he catches one,
That day becomes his feast day
Complete with every treat and revelry;
The blood he first uses for his black pudding,
The meat he arranges in vast and good mouthfuls,
And of the skin he makes macaroni.
He then makes toothpicks out of the bones . . .

(Seventh canto, octaves 54–6)

The image of the ogre, which weighed for a long time on the culture of
the West like a heavy memory, is exorcized in the attempt to eliminate it
by means of a comico-grotesque representation, according to the mechanism typical of a culture which had reduced the nightmare of the collective conscience to a bogeyman for the children, induced by the Christian
religious taboo, unknown to other cultures, which places cannibalism not
only under a dietary heading. The Europeans, it seems, ate each other
only in times of dire necessity: during tragic sieges, terrible famines, or in
the case of dramatic destruction. Typical is the account of the five
Spanish soldiers who 'finding themselves in the Indies on the coast of
Xamo, experienced such extreme hunger that they ate each other, until
only one remained, since there was no one to eat him'.[33]

A rare example of wisdom in the midst of so much European bestiality,
Montaigne understood

that there is much more barbarism in eating a living man than a
dead one; to tear apart with hellish torments a body still full of
feeling, to chop it up and roast it to have dogs and pigs bite and
bruise it (as we have not only read, but seen within recent memory,
not among enemies, but among neighbours and fellow-citizens,
and what is worse, under the pretext of piety and religion), than to
roast and eat it after it has passed away.[34]

Almost during the same period when Montaigne was making these
observations, the 'libertine' and 'naturalist' (the definition is Marc
Bloch's) Girolamo Cardano advanced instead a materialistic explanation

51

for the anthropophagy of the Caribs, the aboriginal inhabitants of the West Indies whose habit it was to eat the children fresh out of the wombs of servants, and the enemies captured in battle, fed and fattened in special enclosures, like pigs in sties. At the base of this ritualism, according to the doctor of Pavia, there lay not so much hatred among the tribes or the necessities of war, but the paucity and scarcity of animal flesh and the pleasure of eating a 'dish' high in protein content. An ingenious perception that predates by more than four centuries the theory of Marvin Harris, according to which the 'Aztec priests can be defined . . . as the ritual butchers of a state system dedicated to the production and redistribution of substantial qualities of animal proteins in the form of human flesh.'[35]

> Consequently this rite was induced by hatred (as I have said) and war, as well as necessity, but the good quality of (edible) food and misery rendered it more widespread. In fact, there was no four-legged animal that tasted good: neither pig, ox, sheep, goat, deer, horse nor donkey. Therefore because of poverty they had reached this point.[36]

This naturalistic–economic explanation has above all the merit of not falling into condemnation of 'barbaric' customs and, even if weak anthropologically, has been justified by very modern and reliable dietetic logic. In fact, even a late-Renaissance doctor understood that 'necessity [is] the great alms-giver and liberal bestower of spirit and intellect.'[37]

> [N]o human society is fundamentally good: but neither is any of them fundamentally bad; . . . Take the example of cannibalism, which is of all savage practices the one we find the most horrible and disgusting. We must set aside those cases in which people eat one another for lack of any other meat – as was the case in certain parts of Polynesia. No society is proof, morally speaking, against the demands of hunger. In times of starvation men will eat literally anything, as we lately saw in the Nazi extermination-camps.
>
> There remain to be considered what we may call the positive forms of cannibalism – those whose origins are mystical, magical, religious. By eating part of the body of an ancestor, or a fragment of an enemy corpse, the cannibal hoped to acquire the virtues, or perhaps to neutralize the power, of the dead man. Such rites were often observed with great discretion, the vital mouthful being made up of a small quantity of pulverized organic matter mixed, on occasion, with other forms of food. And even when the element of cannibalism was more openly avowed, we must acknowledge that to condemn such customs on moral grounds implies either belief in a bodily resurrection, which would be compromised by the material destruction of the

52

corpse, or the affirmation of a link between body and spirit, and of the resulting dualism. These convictions are of the same nature as those in the name of which ritual cannibalism is practised, and we have no good reason for preferring the one to the other.[38]

These hysterical 'skin-deep reactions', as the author rightly emphasizes in *Tristes tropiques*, 'do not hold up to a correct appreciation of the facts'. The notion of barbarism is so false and corrupt that it can in no way serve as a point of reference. Precisely those ages which have regarded the 'barbarisms' of 'primitive men' with horror have been bloody beyond measure; and it is pertinent to observe that the distaste for foods prepared with blood (black pudding, blood sausage, boiled blood, etc.) exists in times like the present when massacres and cruel crimes have become a daily practice or rite.

In fact, the considerations of Lévi-Strauss do not run counter to the general impressions of pre-scientific and even Enlightenment thinking. In the words of the French anthropologist, we can hear the echoes (perhaps unconscious) of Cardano and theologians like Leys and others concerned with this particular casuistry.

Looking at it objectively, we can state that the horror for anthropophagy and patrophagy becomes ever more consistent the more western European society is spared the pangs of hunger. The *ancien régime* societies that struggled almost continually against deadly famines did not feel that 'instinctive' repugnance (alibi of protection and false conscience) towards human blood and flesh later theorized in the West. At the end of the sixteenth century, Giovanni Botero noted unemotionally that the inhabitants of Hibernia, or, as others preferred to call it, Ireland, who 'still have much of the rustic and savage . . . esteemed as praiseworthy the eating of their dead parents'.[39]

It is necessary to recognize that with regard to the nutrition of man, the cultural fact has at least as much weight as the pure and simple dietary one. And the Abbé Raynal, gifted with the 'precious liberty of philosophical enlightenment',[40] had already noted that there existed two forms of anthropophagy, one ritual and the other based on dietary shortage:

The Brazilians have the greatest ambition to take prisoners. These are led to the village of the victors, where they are then butchered and eaten with great preparations. The feast is apt to be long, and during it the aged are busy exhorting the young to become courageous warriors, in order to spread the glory of their nation further, and often to have for themselves such an honourable repast. This inclination towards human flesh never causes them to devour those of their enemy killed in action: the Brazilians restrict themselves only to those who fall into their hands alive and who are then killed with several particular formalities.[41]

The Jesuits, on the other hand, urged a 'horror of human blood' upon those who had a relationship of great familiarity with it. In these districts 'a man who wants to please must be covered in blood,' wrote the Abbé Raynal.[42] Blood was the prop of religious ritual, and the 'sacrifice of prisoners' met an unavoidable mythico-ritualistic need for the Indians of South and Central America: the perpetuation, uninterrupted in time, of the 'first murder',[43] the active and fertile memory of the death of the primordial being who had founded the cosmic regime which governed them. The ritual inherent in the 'living idols' – which the Peruvians reserved for prisoners, who were slowly fattened before the sacrifice as objects of reverence and worship – did not escape the attention of Giovanni Botero, who repeatedly emphasized the 'performance', 'comedy' and sacred theatrical ritualism which in the last act became 'solemn feast and meal'.[44]

The ancient inhabitants of Nicaragua celebrated the feast of the god Maiz with a fertility ritual based on collective blood-letting:

Their banner is the image of the devil placed on a spear and carried by the oldest and most honoured priest. The priests proceed with order, singing until they reach the place of the idolatry, and when they reach it they spread tapestries on the ground and scatter roses and flowers so that the devil does not touch the ground. When the banner is halted, the singing ceases and the praying begins; the prelate, by clapping his hands, signals that it is time for everyone to bleed themselves, some from the tongue, others from the ears, and others from the male member, each according to his devotion; then they take the blood on paper and on their fingers and they rub it on the face of the devil as an offering.

During the blood-letting, the youths swagger and dance in honour of the feast . . . In some of these processions they bless Maiz and spray him with blood drawn from the male member, and they split him like blessed bread and then eat him.[45]

Such was the documentary aloofness of the sixteenth-century scholar Mambrino Roseo, of Fabriano, fellow-countryman and near contemporary of Francesco Panfilo da Sanseverino, who in the poem *Picenum* described the orgiastic rites in honour of the goddess of life that were performed in the caves near Cupramontana – in the Massaccio region – culminating in the murder and ingestion of an infant. He was born in a city where tradition, authenticated by the authoritative if biased pen of Flavio Biondo, attributed similar bloody and cannibalistic rites to heretical sects. It is symptom of a non-provincial culture, extremely flexible in interpreting the 'morals of all peoples' (as Joannes Boemus would have said), to which the much more recent idea of unlimited progress and development was foreign. As Mambrino Roseo writes, unmoved:

> When they make war among themselves, their arms are arrows, clubs and stones, and they kill each other without any mercy, and the defeated are put by to be eaten, since among all meats that of humans is commonly used, which they salt, as we do pork, and then they keep hanging in their houses. They live a long time and rarely fall ill.[46]

> When they eat the flesh of the sacrificial victims, there are great dances, drunkenness and smoking, and the priests then drink plum wine.
>   When the priest anoints the cheeks and mouth of the idol with the blood of the sacrificial victim, the others sing, and the people pray with much devotion and tears; then they go in procession.[47]

In reality, as we know, the obtuse ferocity of the Iberian peoples (famous since antiquity) constituted the worst possible case of barbarity: 'There are those who claim to have found some people [among the Spaniards] so barbaric that they had trained their dogs to find and devour savages; and others reported to have sworn to slay, in honour of the twelve Apostles, twelve Indians a day.'[48]

Compared with this monstrous apostolic genocide, ritual anthropophagy, or even that practised because of an 'inclination to human flesh', is absolutely comprehensible. Without being an anthropologist, even the Abbé Raynal realized that 'no society is morally protected from hunger' (Lévi-Strauss). As Raynal noted:

> The savage can be seized with a canine hunger in the same way as a civilized man . . . All the moral vices that bring civilized man to theft must also bring the savage man to the same crime. Now, the only theft that a savage can be tempted to do is that of taking another savage's life, whom he believes is good to eat. Laziness is everywhere an anthropophagy; and from this point of view, anthropophagy is more common in society than in the depths of the forest . . . if opulence is the mother of vices, misery is that of crimes; and this principle is not realized less in the forests than in the cities . . . civilized man steals and kills to live, the savage kills to eat.[49]

4

'They Set Out into the World of the Vagabond'

When the crises of existence became more acute, during the tense moments of food shortage (although famine constituted an almost permanent structural feature of the old regime, even in its milder version of 'need' and dearth, and beyond the high peaks of malign and perverse conjuncture, very frequent in the pre-industrial era), the threat of hunger's Grim Reaper, the divine punishment of which ranting preachers warmed, lacerated the most deprived, the least protected and least secure, making their terrified faces turn pale. The 'famine of living' – as it was described at the time – upset the price curve, forcing the price of foodstuffs to a level inaccessible to urban artisans and labourers, while the withered countryside saw its cultivators (generally too numerous in relation to the low yield of the land) fleeing towards the heaven of the cities in order to beg – new mendicants – for bread from public charity.

Day by day, the houses were emptied of household goods, pots and saucepans changed hands, clothes and linen were pawned (in times of famine usurers and speculators made enormous profits) and the hearth became ever darker until it went out completely, the cold penetrating piercingly into the empty and desolate interiors.

> A bad thing is famine
> that causes man to be always in need,
> fasting against his will,
> Lord God, send it away . . .
>
> I sold the bedsheets,
> I pawned the shirts
> such that now my uniform
> is that of a rag-pedlar,
> to my suffering and greater distress

only a piece of sackcloth
covers this flesh of mine.[1]

This painful 'flesh of mine' has been carefully deleted – along with the *lamenti* of many anonymous *poveri homini* (even though reflected, transposed and toned down with scarce reference by popularizing intermediaries) – not only by the popular literary tradition, but also by the historico-critical exposition with no interest in any but purely formal interpretations. This latter type of study has preferred to erect illustrious monuments to its 'shining examples', and similar 'feminine' pretences, preciously imitative, rather than listen to and interpret messages originating in the non-illusory, but purely dramatic realm of 'lower' literature. Now, however, the times seem inclined to a different reception of the messages coming to us from poor, distant 'transmitters', from the cities of rags, the lands of hunger, the dens of scrofula and scabies.

The voices, of the wretched, the miserable and the alienated, weak and plaintive, have never found citizenship in the beautiful palace that is literary history, which has been reproducing itself, from the Risorgimento onwards, on the same élitist model into which the so-called 'lowly' of Manzoni just managed to squeeze (though meeting difficulties and suspicion). Considered in an ambiguous and hypocritical light, fundamentally Jesuitical, they were manoeuvred by a class-oriented culture which used them as ingredients in the most varied ideological 'sauces', only to ignore them as social components even when approaching the ambiguous area of populism.

It is not really surprising then that the 'question of language', reborn with each new generation, should perform a mystifying role in this great national deceit, re-invented periodically in order to alienate – along with 'low' phonemes and morphemes – together with the language of the poor (when not utilized in the playful, snickering and cavalier manner of 'great literature'), the reality of a world which found difficulty in facing its harsh existence, what with 'storms' in the food supply, hygienic marasmus, servile conditions and precarious trades verging on beggary (costermongers, spinners, spirit-vendors, street-talkers, porters, latrine-emptiers, tricksters . . .), always on the point of sliding into the social temptation of vagrancy or beggary, when work – often unrewarding, always hard – did not guarantee even the necessary minimum, or when hit by unemployment and the cost of living.

And even more it pains my heart
to see my child
say to me often, from hour to hour,
'daddy, a little bit of bread':
it seems that my soul leaps out
at not being able to help

the little one, oh terrible fate!
A bad thing is famine.
If I leave my house
and I ask a penny for God
all say 'get some work',
'get some work'; oh proud destiny!
I don't find any, despite all efforts
so I stay with head bent low,
oh fortune, cruel and evil
A bad thing is famine.

I have no more covers in the house
the pots I have sold
and I have sold the pans;
I am clean through and through . . .

Often my bread is made from
the stems of plants,
In the earth I make holes
for diverse and strange roots
and with that we grease our snouts:
and if there were enough for every tomorrow
it wouldn't be so bad
A bad thing is famine.[2]

In the worst moments of the crises in the production and supply of food, when work (like bread) became scarce for urban labourers, even the mountain-dwellers descended into the city, driven by the mirage of better and easier living conditions, and ended up by expanding the not at all submerged mass of the underemployed and 'rogues' of the public square, of idle porters and begging youths. As noted in a sixteenth-century Provision for alms in Bologna:

> innumerable families from the mountains of Modena and Reggio come to live in Bologna, and the father of the family goes lugging things throughout the city while the five or six little children are sent begging: this causes a shortage of houses, bread, wine and other things necessary for survival, and above all, an overabundance of beggars.
>
> *Item*, as is true of the city, so in its country districts, many who would be capable of working and performing tasks throw themselves into this indolence, and one sees many young men and women of healthy appearance none the less begging, and, what is worse, they bring up entire families in similar filth.[3]

In the sixteenth and seventeenth centuries the rogue was experiencing his golden age, with his repertory of 'miserable frauds', his loitering and the 'fiction of broken limbs'. It was said in Bologna around the middle of the sixteenth century that 'the better one knows how to deceive, the better one succeeds.' In Genoa, begging, minor crime and roguery constituted a negative social model that worried the civil powers: the *garzonastri* ('young toughs') joined in with 'some of the vilest criminals, who – not having any trade and being sent on the hunt, it could be said, by fathers who cannot feed them, from around the age of ten to twenty-two, wandering through the streets of the city day and night – support themselves with thefts and vile deeds'. Rogues, on the other hand, represented 'a certain type of scrounger who, as enemies of work and resolved to live at the expense of others, go about asking for alms under various forms and pretences'.[4] The business of living the life of a swindler was day by day becoming an ever more subtle 'art': beggar-philosophers and wandering sages discoursed on their privileged condition and perceptive, disenchanted experts speculated on the penetration of fraud to all levels (like the Machiavellian Francesco Vettori), recognizing the primacy of the 'industry' of deception and theorizing on the universality of the 'imposture', its cosmic expanse, its infinite beauty and ubiquitous metamorphoses. Its indispensable pre-eminence in the formation of man and its unrivalled role in the techniques of expanding the intelligence were vigorously supported.

> And thanks to this variation the world becomes beautiful, the brain of one person is made more acute in the search for new ways of defrauding, and that of another becomes sharper in order to guard himself against it. And in effect, all the world is imposture; and it begins with the men of religion, and continues with the lawyers, the doctors, the astrologists, the worldly princes, those who participate at any time in all arts and trades; and day by day everything gets sharper and more refined.[5]

The public square 'is none other than the Theatre of worldly events', a much vaster stage than the ambiguous space which constituted the inn (the shrine of meetings, pranks and deceptions). But even certain hospitals, at night, were transformed into gambling dens and card rooms by unreliable types, as can be observed in a few pages of the *Speculum cerretanorum*,[6] where a group of vagrants – wandering pedlars of sacred images – are caught playing dice on the reverse side of a panel depicting the Virgin Mary; or in the *Serenata di Gian Pitocco* by Giulio Cesare Croce, in which the hospital becomes a safe refuge for wandering lovers.

The furtive shadows of dubious faces moved about on the stages of itinerant actors, sign of the uncontrollable osmosis between fiction and its representation. Nottola (whose name unexpectedly evokes the

nocturnal world of the street actor which Francesco Fulvio Frugoni portrayed with his neurotic and wild prose), 'the false count, cross-eyed and
hunchbacked', constituted the centre of attraction of *Lo schiavetto*, 1612,
by Giovan Battista Andreini (who played Lelio in the company of the
'Comici Fideli'). This foul 'prince of the swindlers' goes on his way,
'overturning the whole world', with Rampino and a band of eight hooligans, 'fit to populate the pest-houses, taverns, and to die on straw, the
food of fleas and lice'.[8]

The comedy of these ragamuffins makes its way into the territory of the
mendicants, turning the hospice and the hospital into an oasis of recreation for swindlers and a 'sanctuary' for the plotting of their organized
loitering. The strong presence of dialect and slang in this and many other
seventeenth-century comedies resulting from the contact with a variegated and polymorphic society confirms the invasion of the literate
theatrical tradition and its linguistic conventions. Here as elsewhere, the
'school of the trivial' becomes of great cultural importance and, leaving
aside linguistic expressionism (which none the less constitutes one of the
fundamental tendencies of popular literature), develops particular codes
of communication, often in jargon: a projection of linguistic corporativism which reflects the extreme specialization of trades, legal and illegal,
and the very heavy pronounced social fragmentation.

Rossa dal Vergato ('Redhead of Vergato'), who presents herself as a
servant woman, asking for work in her 'rustic language'; *Simona dalla
Sambuca* ('Simone of Sambuca'), who 'goes searching for spinning to do
in Bologna' ('in rustic mountain language'); *Filippa da Calcara* ('Philippa
of Calcara'), who tours the world in search of washing, all express (by
means of the reflected voice of the story-teller, intermediary on the border of orality and literacy, interpreter of the *civilisation de l'oralité*[9]), the
bitter and unpleasant request for a piece of bread, the tough condition,
shouted in the streets, of those who offer their services and work in the
precarious trade of their own two arms.

The migratory stream from the mountains and the countryside to the
city resulted not only in the increase of rents and the price of staple
goods, but also in the abnormal proliferation of sub-trades dangerous to
the economy of the city, and of uncertain and precarious occupations,
which were fundamentally unproductive.

The governor of Modena complained, just after the middle of the
sixteenth century, that 'no more day-labourers are to be found', and that
there was an increase in the prices of 'things which, because the peasants
are almost all given to the selling of second-hand goods, one could
no longer buy without them having already been resold two or three
times'.[10]

These semi-marginalized migrants, 'meandering between productive and unproductive work',[11] ended up most often by swelling the already over-expanded ranks of the army of beggars and mendicants, abandoning family and so creating new widows and orphans (the stereotype of the orphan or, better still, the boy abandoned by his mother, herself often already a widow, or by both his parents, constitutes a tragic figure in both oral and written literature, becoming evermore present from the sixteenth century onwards). 'The poor, in order to avoid seeing their children die of hunger [the scene is Modena in 1601] set out into the world of the vagabond.'[12]

When it is not the fathers who take the path of ruin into the world, it is the sons who go to beg in the city: 'They have allowed', wrote the chronicler Giovan Battista Spaccini of Modena in 1630, 'too many peasants to come and live who now work as porters or in other low jobs, and have a mass of children that they send off wandering, and the churches are full of them.'[13]

In Bologna, in the second half of the eighteenth century, almost a quarter of the population was unemployed; there were 16,000 beggars wandering the streets (out of a population of around 70,000), prolonging the severe manufacturing crisis. The 'portion of the populace vulgarly known as rogues' ('lowest class of the mob'),[14] made up, together with the porters, the lowest and most infamous social stratum. According to Giacomo Casanova, they 'valent moins encore que les *lazzaroni* de Naples'. In the eyes of foreign travellers this 'bas peuple' generally seemed 'peu laborieux',[15] little enamoured of work and resigned to the worst.

Vagrants and beggars increased the already overflowing numbers of the city's 'famished inhabitants', its permanent unemployed and its poverty-stricken established residents. 'The city and countryside,' one reads in a supplication sent to Pope Clement XIV in 1771 by several Bolognese senators, 'are covered with beggars, thefts are very common and licentiousness and loose living have become a means of subsistence, a product not only of the inclination to laziness and fecklessness, but much more the lack of opportunity to work and obtain even the price of bread.'[16] The streets of the city 'can be seen day and night covered with indolent people of every age and both sexes who look for bread, some asking only for alms, others stealing, others selling their own virtue publicly and scandalously. Thus from the beginning of evening to midnight a public traffic in licentiousness is conducted in the streets and squares.'[17]

When bread became scarce or absent in the great houses, if not in the courts themselves, it was easily remedied by accompanying meat with more meat, but when severer than usual hunger entered into peasant houses, they attempted to survive by resorting to surrogates for flour and by devoting themselves to the tiresome search for the herbs and roots necessary for survival. As Tomasino de' Bianchi, a chronicler of Modena in the second half of the fifteenth century, writes: 'they take hawthorn fruit, then *chaga* [the fruit of the hornbeam, as Gian Luigi Basini explains, which even today bears this name in the dialect of Modena]; they dry and grind them and they take three parts of this flour and one of wheat flour and they make bread . . . many children are sent to the woods to look for this fruit.'[18]

On a day in 1484 this same chronicler noted that a group of thirty women and children had entered one of his fields, 'gathering roses, patience-docks, persicaria, field thistle, poppy, rape leaves . . . and they mixed everything together with a bit of oil or fat and with vinegar, water and salt in the pot, and they ate it.[19]

In this way they were similar to those peasants of more-advanced Gaul who, during the time of Gregory of Tours, tried 'to make bread out of virtually everything, "grape pips, hazel tree flowers and even fern roots", and whose stomachs were grossly distended because they had had to eat field grass'.[20]

5

'They Rotted in Their Own Dung'

The drama of everyday life, in its tough existential reality, escapes historical writing which examines the *longue durée*; even more it evades quantitative evaluation and the computerized sequencing of numbers. The graphs, curves and tables serve only to quantify over a period problems and dramas whose troubled and hopeless sense needs to be grasped over the short term, or even reconstructed within the tense and vibrant arc of one solar day. Only in this way can we animate that *vissuto* ('lived experience'), undervalued and ignored by quantitative analysis, which remains one of the primary objectives tempting the most sophisticated historical writing regarding the knowledge of the past in terms of the 'science of lived experience'. Two of the major Italian representatives of this tendency have recently made their own an unequivocal statement of Steven Kaplan's, according to which the *longue durée* approach 'can generate an abstract, homogenised social history, devoid of flesh and blood, and unconvincing despite its scientific regulation.'[1]

If the reconstruction from the inside, *a parte subjecti*, of a poor man's day enters more into literary invention than the perspective of social history (the abbot Parini reconstructed the day of a wealthy man in minute detail,[2] to the point of suffering the subtle temptations of *la Notte*, 'the night'), the inner experience of a beggar's bitter existence has been inadvertently touched on by several heroic priests who spent almost their entire lives in the Christian consolation and aid of the poor, with an unending, fraternal motivation.

One of these extraordinary models of charity, not so rare in the annals of modern piety, was the Bolognese priest Giulio Cesare Luigi Canali (1690–1765), parish priest of Sant'Isaia and founder, among other things, of the *Ospedale degli Abbandonati* (Foundling Hospital). He lived in daily contact with the beggars of the city, the 'disasters of the wretched' (the words are his), the bitter frustrations of the alienated and exploited, and with those working for low wages, whose productive labour served only barely to distinguish them from the tide of real out-and-out beggars: a class more sensitive than any other to the changing prices and the diminished buying power of cash.

> Which is the bread that is not kneaded with bitterness for them? Which is the cup that is not mixed with tears? Which is the clothing that is not woven with thorns for them? They sleep, but they feel their sleep interrupted by the cold, the filth, the screams and infants' cries, and by a thousand other anxieties. They work, but see little or no fruit of their labours; they pray, but they are not heard; they utter complaints and appeals, but they are not admitted or believed. If they serve, they serve those who pay them only with insults and abuse; if they are right, they are held to be wrong; if they are innocent, with all this they must remain silent and hide themselves as if guilty. They are poor, and that is enough. The days pass, but their hardships never cease. The seasons change, but only to renew their troubles and suffering . . . for them it is never less than freezing winter, and a dark night of misery and pain.[3]

A dense, indignant eloquence, not unusual among those men of the Church who lived in close evangelical contact with the lowest and most deprived classes. Outside of the literary–ecclesiastical tradition of sermon, homily and preaching, the convoluted style of Canali hints at a socialization of writing in which is reflected a 'lived' knowledge of the crowd: a reflection on the 'collectivity', on the sad epic of privation, pain and evil. The pages of the preachers and the ecclesiastical treatise writers constitute an important source for the reconstruction not only of the popular psyche, but also of the culture, ideologies and myths of the lower classes. Sources too often wrongly unexploited even by the praiseworthy archival researchers who occasionally fall into the pseudo-scientific illusion that a series of facts, more or less correct and more or less comprehensible, is more real (and therefore more attractive) than a printed page, neglected not out of ignorance, certainly, but out of a disdainful and inexplicable programmed rejection of a text which is not a manuscript source quantifiable in figures and tables.

In the eighteenth-century Bologna of the poor, the Bologna of Benedict XIV, perhaps there no longer stirred the grim and bloody figure of the nark, a specialist in the repression of vagrancy and the war on beggars, like 'Tofalo zafo sbirro de poveri mendichi' ('Tofalo the runt, nark of poor beggars'),[4] whose memory lingers on in a song composed by one of the many story-tellers who wandered through the cities of Italy.

These *cantastorie* were precious messengers and intermediaries between the oral culture of the illiterate masses and the writing of the literate world. They represented the point where the word departed from the sea of the usual and the ordinary to become the lasting vehicle in the expression of sentiments, ideologies and mythologies often not welcomed by the dominant groups, and an instrument in the struggle – still fragile and precarious – against a power which used writing as a means of disciplining and controlling the masses. 'If writing did not serve to consolidate knowledge', Lévi-Strauss has lucidly observed, 'it was perhaps indispensable in order to affirm domination.'[5]

This Tofalo, whose death was received with exultation by the wretched poor of Bologna,

> Was large of stature,
> But full of bravura
> And he had one leg
> Longer than the other.
> Tofalo the runt has gone away.

This 'spy' and nark – gigantic and deformed, the image of criminal teratology – used a whip to scourge the poor who wandered throughout the city. The fear of the vagabonds of Bologna shines through the words of the Veronese story-teller who, a wanderer by necessity of his craft, must have had first hand knowledge of the professional wickedness of the narks

> He carried a whip in hand
> Which seen from afar
> Astonished all the people.
> Tofalo the runt has gone away.

> However many of the poor he found
> For whom he was looking, on the ground,
> Dog-lashes he gave to everyone.
> With that thong that he carried.
> Tofalo the runt has gone away.

A 'man so furious', specializing in treating the beggars to thrashings like those given to dogs ('Dog-lashes he gave to everyone'), 'And wronging the poor, / Finally on a pile of straw he died', abandoned even by his wife. Hunter of the poor and 'most atrocious' scourger,

> His hands without compassion,
> That were always giving floggings,
> Are now transfigured
> And no longer seem what they were.
> Tofalo the runt has gone away.

After the monstrous nark has died the Bologna of the poor heaves a great sigh of relief.

For the parish priest of Sant'Isaia the poor were not only the beggars, but also the non-paid servants, the poor women workers, scarcely remunerated, the 'wretched, cheated workers, with whose sweat you knead tastier bread and make your foods more exquisitely delicate.'[6] The 'owners of the land' (who in Bologna had imposed a controlled system, bent on improving their landed revenue by abolishing *de facto* the corn market and fixing the prices at whim according to a complicated system of price-control restraints) will one day have to fear the 'masters of the Kingdom of Heaven . . . the poor, the humble, the weeping, the hungry.'[7] Although not emerging from traditional Catholic interclassism, Canali's vigorous denunciation of the senatorial class and its pathetic call to solidarity, rendered still more touching and disturbing by the exemplary heroism of his life, leads us to reflect on the great balancing act performed by certain levels of the clergy regarding those human disasters provoked by a society based on authority and inequality, in which the privileged classes often pretended not to hear the 'grumbling, angry stomach' of the mob, or see the 'crowd of the wretched, wounded and hurt by hunger'.[8] One day the rich would have to answer for 'the food left to become wormy, the bread left to grow mouldy, the rotten fruit, the wheat kept in the granary and gone bad and, in short, for every type of food and sustenance left to spoil, rather than given to the poor'.[9]

As the biographer of Canali, the priest of the Oratory Giambattista Melloni, writes: the 'mournful sound of the workmen', that is to say, the laments of the paid workers, did not leave him indifferent. He also fought using 'political' means. In 1758, for example, he circulated a proto-mayoral letter to many of his merchant friends, calling their attention to the 'planned balance of wages on the one hand and of jobs on the other', since 'although the drudgery of jobs has increased notably, the wage has not gone up at all'.[10]

The imbalances of the economy reflected harshly on the working population of a city like Bologna where perhaps a fifth or more of the inhabitants were spinners and silk and hemp workers: industrial activities which from the second half of the seventeenth century had entered into a slow but inexorable decline. Here more than elsewhere the employment crisis had become continually more serious, and the picture of extreme poverty ever darker and more worrisome, with the loss of many lands in the plain reconquered by the waters. It was a dramatic situation, brought to light some time ago by historians, and one of the profound civil unrest, much worse than the Bologna of Giulio Cesare Croce. For Bologna, the Enlightenment of the eighteenth century coincides with a deep economic depression: a social and moral decay, reflected too in the canvasses of the greatest Bolognese painter of the period, Giuseppe Maria Crespi. In the brushwork of the 'Seven Sacraments', restless, dismal and gloomy, is reflected the drama of a city prostrate and without hope, for which the *lumi* (the 'lights' of the Enlightenment) was a word devoid of sense and outside the range of every imagination, even the most drugged and delirious. The matrimony of the poor is celebrated here, in a grievous atmosphere bereft of joy or laughter, by an elderly couple, worried about the dark and precarious future. Even love and precocious pleasure was a privilege of the rich who sought in every way to dissuade youthful marriages within the poor and impoverished classes.

In several of the pages penned by Canali, beyond those precepts of corporeal mercy like 'clothe the naked', there emerges an indignation towards the group in power of a city still rich despite the serious crisis of the silk industry, which during the frozen winters, with cynical insensitivity, allows

> a man to die consumed by the chill, whether for lack of something with which to cover himself or because bereft of a fire by which to warm himself. And this . . . in a city where the columns and walls of many houses and palaces are covered with tapestries and damasks, thousands and thousands of citizens, for themselves only, have shorn the fleece of more and more sheep and have cut the wood of more and more forests.[11]

'I want to clothe the poor and not the walls,' the Bolognese curate kept repeating *ad nauseam* (with the words of the Blessed Alessandro Sauli), following a viewpoint (which the canon Giovan Battista Segni also supported in his time) in opposition to the politics of ecclesiastical prestige and support of established power, which was not new for the post-Tridentine Bolognese Church. The curate of Sant'Isaia knew from close range the drama of the 'stomach of the poor': of their flesh, pierced by the chill and hollowed out by ringworm and lice, the intolerable annoyance of having 'to wear in daytime in the depths of winter the clothes of summer, and in the rage of summer those of winter'.[12] He had a first-hand knowledge of beggars, born of the daily mission to help them, revive them, clothe them, even with his own clothes, to find them shelter, even in his own bare presbytery, so that they did not end up as livid corpses, dying in the streets or under the frozen porticoes battered by the north wind. He knew well that terror of the helpless poor, announced, as in the poem by Giulio Cesare Croce,[13] from the beginning of November, by Gianicco, or the 'little man of frost', ambassador of the cold who until some decades ago was alive in the jargon of the vagabonds to indicate the season of inclement weather.

He sheltered the wretched in his own house, both foreigners and Bolognese, in every way unwell and derelict . . . He sheltered for some time a leprous foreigner . . . he put up a poor dying man at home and had him lie on his own mattress. I also read in the register of the Foundling Hospital [it is Giambattista Melloni who narrates] that on the 21st day of August, 1741, a poor old man by the name of Matteo – son of the deceased Paolo Fiorini of Montasio, a moun- tain in the Modena region – was put up at home by Canali. His legs were full of sores and wounds; the rest of his body was eaten up by numerous disgusting little animals, so that because of this and other foulness he resembled a monster rather than a man . . . On 24 January of the following year he piously sheltered in his own presbytery a poor young Savoyard, named Antonio di Giovanni d'Arbora, who had been found half dead under the portico of S. Maria della Morte. He was warmed and rested in bed, adminis- tered the last rites, and during the following night he passed on to a better life.

But since his presbytery was not large enough for his works of charity, he therefore often rented rooms and houses . . . and finally with the help of the Lord he founded the oft-mentioned Foundling Hospital.[14]

The people of the mountains, above all, continued to swell the ranks of Bolognese vagrancy in those years of serious dearth: that 'young Savoyard' who, dying, was taken in by Canali, was probably a seasonal migrant passing through Bologna. They fell on the city, rich and opu- lent – so it was believed – the 'numerous troops of mountain-dwellers . . . so that his presbytery and porch and portico, inside and out, was seen to be full of these wretched poor'. During the severest winters, the 'mountain-dwellers, who previously used to eat the roots of herbs, now, because of the snow that fell, died of hunger'.[15]

This curate, who lived in such painfully close contact with mendicity, also serves as a precious guide in an oppressive circumnavigation around the pitiless miseries of fallen humanity, shining the ray of his lantern's light on the most secret aspects of the beggars' lives. He also illuminates the insomnia of the poor, the recurrent and almost obsessive theme of stench, fetor, rags and lurid scarred flesh ('with foul sores, seething throughout the body', Luis Vives had lamented),[16] and the subject of dirty underpants, even more traumatizing and shocking for the 'good taste' of the eighteenth century:

And by the fact of not being able to sleep at night whether due to sleeping on a bed fouler than a rubbish heap, or not being able to cover oneself, who can explain how much harm is done? But then who could exaggerate the discomforts of the rubbish, the stench, the emaciation and the squalor whilst these paupers are forced to wear the same underpants for months and months? What Capuchin's most hirsute sackcloth, what penitent's roughest hairshirt, in comparison to these underpants, should not rather be considered the finest linen and delicate sea-silk, particularly given the insufferable troubles that this causes, sordidness which, so to speak, generates rotten flesh.[17]

The images which the implacable eye of the Bolognese curate forces us to smell more than observe, are those of the hell of the poor: a putrefied inferno, foul with bodily waste, stagnant faeces and decomposing urine. Whether in the gloomy interiors of their tumble-down hovels ('the shacks, hay-lofts, caves, dungeons, muddy pools, the semi-infernos of the paupers. Oh, spectacles of compassion and horror!' exclaims Canali, 'How many times I nearly fainted for the intolerable stench and fetor!'[18]), or in the total inferno of the prisons, perceived, carnally and viscerally, as the 'universal punishment of all the senses',[19] where the nauseating perception of stench and fetor which impregnates everything dominated obsessively, yet again.

That filth and those faeces, in which it is their need to swim and remain immersed, so that the prison nearly becomes a sewer! What tongue and what ink would suffice to describe the pain that they bear above all, that they would sooner lie on thorns or burning coals than on that rubbish? And yet they are seen reduced to such intolerable extremes of misery, that they could fit almost to the letter the words of Joel: 'the beasts of burden rotted in their own dung'.[20]

The descent into the depths could not fail to pass through the 'dismal, frightening spectacle' of the hospital: 'theatre of horror', 'residence of tears', 'home of spasms', 'dark region of death: *in regione umbrae mortis*'.[21] They stagnate in gloomy corridors, where the 'miserable diseased incurables . . . the helpless poor', lie amidst the 'stench and horror of their own disgusting sores' (Carlo Bartolomeo Piazza).

Stench and fetors assault the sense of smell, screams and laments the hearing, squalid and deformed faces under one's eyes. Some, because of burning fevers, rave and throw whatever is handy; others, also because of fevers, but of opposite type, shiver and clatter their teeth. Some have their heads split by unbearable headaches, others have their ribs broken and guts pierced by acute pleurisy. One who is about to be suffocated by excessive catarrh, and another who thinks a thousand times he is about to die from the incessant attacks of bad asthma, but never dies. There, as a result of a most bitter thirst, one suffering from dropsy struggles impatiently, and here, because of intestinal inflammation, a consumptive is heard to come to his end . . . [22]

There are the convulsions and the contractions of the nerves, that although without the ministry of the torturer, none the less cause one to feel the pain of the wheel and the wooden horse; there are aqueous hernias, false catarrhs, fistulated sores, tumours of such large size that there is no medicine other than iron and fire[23] . . . so that, doing the necessary both with iron and with fire, in a metamorphosis that is too difficult but otherwise inevitable, the infirmaries become Calvaries, the beds gallows, the doctors . . . executioners.[24]

Strange priests wandered among the pallets of the dying, the attendant fathers of the sick, called fathers 'of Good Death': servants of God who 'exert themselves in the gain and pursuit of souls', writes Marcello Mansi in the *Consigli per aiutare al ben morire*. Sinister, black as crows, disliked by the sick, they tried to convince them that since diseases were none other than 'a royal road to show us the way to heaven so as to rejoice in the Divine Essence, they should not decline our attention nor regret it, but should accept and endure with holy will'. Better dead but saved than vagabond and sinner, was their logic. In many the 'holy will' was late in showing itself, and this was a shame, because in fact the diseases could 'take away the opportunity', continues Mansi, 'of falling into some very grave sin'.

This Bolognese priest of 'fiery and most sour temperament', who circulated day and night among the 'most disgusting sick',[25] literally denuded himself in order to cover the neediest, such that the women of the house 'used to keep at least a pair of linen underpants hidden in order to have them ready in similar circumstances'.[26] This despite the fact that, especially in old age, this movement cost him stabbing pain, suffering as he was from 'a most frequent excruciating descent of the intestines', a hernia for which an iron belt, rather than contain, 'gave him a pain, or rather an anguish incomparably greater than all his penances',[27] and tormented unbearably in his last years by 'most troublesome scabies'.

The Bolognese beggars to whom the intrepid curate of Sant'Isaia, from admirable motives, donated his underpants – third-class citizens of a city whose economic decadence and mercantile decline during the mid-eighteenth century was felt more acutely than in almost any other city in the Papal States – are the still more desperate and fallen brothers of those *poveretti* who, from the last decades of the declining sixteenth century, are heard increasingly frequently with the help of the popular press. They emerge from the silence of nothingness thanks to the mediation of story-tellers such as Giulio Cesare Croce, Vincenzo Citaredo of Urbino, author, among other works, of the *Speranza de' poveri* (1588), and Giacomo Cieco Veronese, and many others, often anonymous. Among the latter there is the author of the *Opera nuova. Dove si contiene il lamento della Povertà, sopra la carestia dell'anno 1592 . . . ,*[28] in which the anxiety about bread that 'is in size / like a bird's egg', the feeling of being 'poor creatures' in the hands of monopolizers and usurers, powerless and wretched ('Poverty, surely you are a beggar, / We are with the pikes, the little fish'), is moderated by the acceptance of the unavoidable fatality of famine sent to those with 'evil phalluses', and in homage to the established powers.

> Pray take, poor creatures,
> this advice full of love,
> to those greater, be you subjects,
> yet let it please,
> do not serve till heartbreak
> false, boorish Christs.
> 　Patience, poor creatures.

The entire poem is punctuated by this obsessive call to patience and forbearance, the exhortation to be suspicious of false prophets and professional troublemakers, the shuddering call to the great journey to the Kingdom of Shadows, the appearance of old late-medieval motifs and the re-emergence of death's lugubrious triumphs:

> The end of all days shall come,
> and that sea of death;
> oh, pray and keep watch
> because at the time of departure,
> no one knows where they must go,
> the old, young men and women.
> 　Patience, poor creatures.
> It is worth nothing to be lords,
> nor patrons of great cities,
> since in this world everyone dies;
> power doesn't matter,
> lands and districts will remain,
> and the provinces with their castles.
> 　Patience, poor creatures.

In reality, the opinion that famine and plague were signs of divine wrath, caused by the corrupt and wicked habits of men, was widespread. Many held that famine was brought about by natural causes like the 'irregularity of the weather and the altered seasons',[29] but most, uninfluenced even by the political side of the unequal distribution of resources, believed that it was divine anger which punished excesses, 'debauchery, discord and lust'. A good portion of the population swore that it was not the 'corruption' of the air, 'the putrefied inferior elements', the eating of 'rotten fish', the action of 'wicked ministers' in the service of the Turk, or the coming and going of 'merchandise', but the angel of the angered God which generated the scourge.

The Bolognese druggist Pastarino was firmly convinced of this. In his *Preparamento . . . per medicarsi in questi sospettosi tempi di peste*, while he noted the frequent outbreak of the plague in the 'two most mercantile cities of Italy',[30] he swore that the 'many iniquities . . . that are performed in transactions, dealings and trading moves God to send some of his terrible scourges and, in particular, pestilence'.[31] Both herb vendor and preacher, he exhorted his fellow-citizens to dry out 'this our body full of grease and humidity'.[32] This is in accordance with Galen's precept, 'It is proper to dry up the body in this way, and keep it dry', and reinforced by the authority of Avicenna, according to whom 'The best treatment of them [those ill with pestilential fevers] is desiccation, and it is best that their foods be dried.' Preacher of sobriety and abstinence ('one lives better with little'), this singular and ambiguous spice merchant – citing Galen ('it is proper to open up the blocked pores')[33] – called for the opening up of the soul before the body.

And what are these blocked pores if not our own ears, deaf to sermons, and our mouths, closed to confessions? These should be opened, because by doing so the infirmities are discovered, the bad humours are revealed, we recognize our worst qualities and, better, they are more easily restored to health . . . Having done this, it is necessary to conclude with a good evacuation and make every effort to evacuate all the superfluities that are within us. Thus we have the rule given to us by Galen that 'convenit corpus superfluitatibus plenum evacuare'. And Avicenna as well . . . used these words: 'Purging and loosening is very useful as is the evacuation of the stomach in treating the plague'.

Let us now accept as a principle, my fellow-citizens, to evacuate from this our body every superfluity that is found here. Superfluous are the evil thoughts, dishonest reasoning and wicked designs that occupy the mind. Superfluous are the lascivious glances, malicious signs and curiosities that dominate the eyes. Superfluous are vain things . . . superfluous swearing . . . Superfluous are the things of others that we wrongly keep. And superfluous is still all that with which we could help the poor but do not . . .

Let us therefore protect ourselves from divine anger, and with this complete evacuation of the body . . . let us prepare to treat ourselves.[34]

It is not easy to say how much the voice of this Bolognese druggist was heard, seemingly bizarre in the play of extravagant comparisons between apothecary culture and pastoral ideology (it was said that he was a 'man of mature years, Catholic, very practised in the composition of medicines'); author too of an eccentric *Instruttione sopra la universal peste, e frenetico morbo d'amore*,[35] dedicated to 'young Bolognese lovers'. Perhaps Pastarino interprets the opinion of the intermediate classes of the 'city of doctors', in which the druggists were neither few in number nor of little account: a class tied by a two-way link to the doctors, the *Signori nobili* and the merchants for whom they prepared expensive electuaries, refined unctions and antidotes rich in the sought-after rarities of the vegetable, mineral and animal (man included) kingdoms. The *elettuario de sanguinibus* ('blood electuary') was a speciality of Pastarino's shop, to which the Senate of Bologna had conceded the privilege of publicly preparing, on the second day of August, the antidotes with which the city, *madre delli buoni studii*, prepared for the 'defence' of its citizens as if for soldiers 'enclosed in a strong and well-fortified castle', in order to resist the attack of diseases.

The turnover of cash around the druggists' shops was considerable. It is known that two pharmacopoeias existed, one for the rich – full of expensive rarities like 'ambergris', 'bezoar-stone', 'unicorn stone', rubies and gold – and one for the poor, much more modest, almost entirely vegetable. The *Fabrica de gli spetiali* by Prospero Borgarucci (1566), Valerio Cordo's *Dispensarium* (1554), Johann Schroeder's *Thesaurus pharmacologicus*, Osvaldus Crollius' *Basilica chymica* and Ludovico Locatelli's *Theatro d'arcani*, presupposed buyers with unlimited available finances.

The apologia for the doctors that Pastarino composed is therefore too suspect to be credible, even ignoring what Leonardo Fioravanti had written several years before in the *Specchio di scientia universale* regarding the odious arrogance of doctors and the vacuity of the robed physician:

Medicine being something divine, and in such a way created by the benign and powerful hand of God, so that because of this every day one sees the gentlemen doctors (although doctoring is an art) who however never assign any merit to their efforts as all other artists are wont to do; but they take without asking anything more than whatever courtesy is given them, almost as if by doing otherwise they could rightly be perceived as simonious and sacrilegious, as they would be vendors of the holy and divine thing that is medicine . . .[36]

Even Giulio Cesare Luigi Canali participated in this vision of the world – moralistic to the point of bigotry – that Pastarino had preached, not disinterestedly, in his own time. The parish priest–theologian of Sant'Isaia, on the other hand, lived this vision in perfect good faith and simple, spontaneous, naive adherence. It was something of a surprise to find this moralistic gloom in the spritely songs of the Arcadia, rhymed in easy little verses that the theologian–philanthropist Canali – child of his time in this – continued to draft, grafting on to the eighteenth-century forms a pauperistic idiom foreign to 'good taste':

Weep, oh Bologna,
   Weep for hunger,
   But more infamous,
     Your guilt.
And more than the evil,
   That surrounds you,
   That which abounds:
     Your iniquity.
Weep also for that
   Which is dealt out to you,
   Poor meal,
     Bread of suffering . . .
If bitter food,
   Hard and fetid,
   Breaks your teeth
     With grave horror,
From your faults
   Comes the harshness,
   Comes the bitterness,
     And the bad smell.
Profit it lacking,
   Work is lacking,
   Because dignity
     Was absent first . . .[37]

Death in Bologna during the eighteenth century has the same face as in other centuries: its style is the atemporal, immutable, liturgical one of fated events, outside of man's control. The Church had a full and total monopoly over death, and it made ruthless use of it. Even Canali, like all other priests, used the shadow of *thanatos* to terrorize the rich and the poor, with the obsessive constancy of the mournful men in black.

> Death you have always at your side.
>   Think about it my brother,
>   Stay close to your God, flee
>   from sin.
> One day you will be afflicted
>   With sickness and agony:
>   How will you fare among so much
>   distress and pain?
> All fleeting hope
>   Will then fade into oblivion,
>   The pomp, charm, vivacity,
>   pleasures, positions.
> The money will be put back,
>   Strength left behind
>   And all abandoned to
>   other hands.
> The last farewell to one's own brother
>   To one's sons, one's consort
>   Must be given at the gates
>   of Eternity.
> To grow pale, to pant,
>   To have cold sweat,
>   Delirious because of the pain and
>   the discomfort.
> Around the bed there are
>   Horrid irate monsters.
>   Break loose from there: oh you,
>   poor wretch!
> . . .
> The light of day is already out,
>   Night has already come,
>   The harvest has passed, the game
>   is over . . .[38]

In the 'Lamento della povertà per l'estremo freddo del presente anno 1587'[39] the voice of the deprived – the desperation of those in their 'holes' who suffered, along with the torment of the cold, the devastations of obscure diseases (the 'strange aches') – and the laments of the *poverini* ('paupers', who are habitually distinguished from the 'citizens'), 'wrap-ped up in the straw, / sighing, / with their hearts desiring that spring returns . . .',[40] and the 'poor scabbies',[41] all succeed in reaching us 'live' even today by means of the obsessive refrain. A flashing but essential fragment of a tragic and painful 'spoken experience' that strengthens the 'lived experience', without which real contact with the past would not be possible, and without which history would become a lifeless dominion of computer quantification.

> How many are there who have sold
> Even the feathers of their beds;
> How many more go searching
> At doors, under the roofs of others;
> How many shoeless little children
> Go around begging,
> Under the porticoes, shaking
> Because of this unfair cold.
>   Alas, God, what cold this is.
> Much harm is done to the citizens,
> And they suffer from strange aches,
> But worse off are the paupers
> Who cannot have any bread,
> And who die in their holes,
> Who have no one who thinks of them,
> Without help or relief,
> So they have sorrowful faces,
>   Alas, God, what cold this is.[42]

Even the cold was a 'scourge', complained Croce: one of the many scourges that tormented the living hell of the *poverini*, in the hard and ruthless winters of the past.

> How many burn their bedsteads,
> The chairs, and the benches,
> The hampers, and the baskets,
> The cases, and the boxes;
> How many poor women,
> In order to oppose the crude ice,
> With the pledge under their arms,
> Go to get a loan of money.
>   Alas, God, what cold this is.[43]

To the inclemency of the climate was added the harshness of social life and the drama of the rent which the less prosperous could not afford to pay, even if they lived in damp and squalid 'holes':

76

These poor wretches,
With wife and little children,
Have no fire to warm themselves
Nor bread to sustain them;
And in the evening and morning
They sit and shiver
On top of two coals.
    A bad thing is the rent.
He who has pawned his cloak,
He his hood, he his sheet,
He his wife's ring,
He who has sold the bedstead,
He his greatcoat and socks,
The shelves and boxes,
The chairs and cupboards.
    A bad thing is the rent.[44]

6

The World Turned Upside Down

If winter was always very difficult for the poor, existence became all the more trying in the years of famine, and the most defenceless found themselves 'lying on the ground, poor and wretched'. They sought refuge inside the straw, on refuse and manure. Tormented by chilblains, racked by coughs, infested by lice and ringworm and emanating intolerable smells – wandering dung-heaps, who in 'their own dung even grow fat / as if they were beetles or worms', unsatiated stomachs 'where the dung both leaves and enters' (Baldassare Bonifacio) – they slowly came back to life when the warm weather arrived and the pangs of hunger lessened; famine seemed in retreat. The exultation of the survivors fed the unjustified illusions of future health, strength and vigour. The discouraging images of prostration and starvation were put away.

> Never more will there be seen atop the dung-heap
>   So many wretched, afflicted and lifeless people,
>   Wrapped up in straw and refuse.
> In the future they will be the strong men,
>   Proud and robust they will gather vigour
>   Not weak and half dead like before;
> A healthy colour will return to their faces . . .[1]

The resurrection of the famished beggars – the 'half dead' with ashen and dried-out skin – and the abandoning of the bed of dung and the wrapping of straw, indicated the first part of a return to a more human social dimension. But the recovery of health (if it was ever possible) and the reappearance of a 'healthy colour', must have been uncertain and difficult for all, impossible for many. The disasters of a hunger epidemic, of a seven-year famine (like the one which raged in much of northern Italy between 1590 and 1597), left marks too profound to be wiped out from one day to the next. The 'triumph of plenty' (the verses quoted above are from Giulio Cesare Croce's poem of the same name) was just a literary *topos*: a triumphalistic hyperbole which bore little resemblance to the reality of things. The accelerated deterioration of physical and mental health during the years of stupefying starvation was for many people an irreversible process towards intellectual disorder and degradation that the return to 'normal' – to the low level of daily undernourishment – would not succeed in wiping out. As from a tormented physiological labyrinth, one exited with difficulty from this alimentary chaos; one re-emerged very slowly from the muddy darkness of the voyage through the realm of hardship and indigence. The harm caused to the sick body of this feverish society was often irreparable.

It is therefore not too daring to suppose that the culture of poverty (and therefore, in good measure, of almost all popular culture) could not represent the world if not under the form that its instruments of conscience had indicated. The cognitive statutes of a poor culture differ from those elaborated by the intellectual elites, even if the spheres of contamination, influence and overlapping between them could be manifold. The image of the world elaborated by the popular mental articulations of the pre-industrial age diverges from the classical model utilized by *clerici* and *literati*, much as the categories of logic (on a par with the aesthetic canons) appeared different. They avail themselves of reality in diverging ways. The beautiful, harmonic, symmetric and geometric do not correspond to the popular vision of the deformed, unmeasured, hyperbolical (or miniturized), monstrous, overflowing and formless. The image of the world, seen from below, appears uncertain, flawed, ambiguous, unbalanced and unhomogeneous, as in the visions of the drugged and the possessed. The images can be overturned, the figures turned upside down, the relations of time and space altered, the edifice of the world itself become illusory and shady. The natural and divine order is broken up and altered: chaos takes priority over a rational design that presupposes a centre towards which the whole immense periphery converges in unity. The 'expanded conscience' overflows everywhere. The same articulation of time changes the frame of reference: 'time outside of time' is posed as the anti-model of 'time that is within time'. The progressive is nullified in the regressive. The city of *Balordìa* (literally, 'folly'), kingdom of the idle, lives in a mythology of ebb and flow, unanchored in historical time. This compensatory dream projected from the popular utopia conquers ever more extensive territories in which 'superior' rationality no longer finds a place.

The cultural model founded on categories of logic does not have a hold on this society where laziness becomes the interpretative register of history: antidote to the poisons of a sickened, wicked and unidimensional social body. The pauper/slacker lives in the 'time of laziness':[2] the metahistorical time of predictability and insecurity institutionalized in security, set loose from working time, the risk of the future and the fear of history. The Land of Cockaigne, in the drugged logic of the impossible, becomes a driving image, able to penetrate the mental cosmos in which the natural (and the real) have been supplanted by the artificial and the unreal. In this dream universe, the mechanical and physical laws no longer make sense: macaroni falls from heaven like edible rain; the earth, no longer worked, miraculously produces pre-cooked foods; the trees do not toss down buds and leaves, but hams and clothes; the animals, their own butchers, spontaneously roast themselves for the comfort of men's stomachs. Work is abolished, time suspended, fatal old age staved off by the fountains of youth, and the women, in their bodily splendour, are triumphant over their straddled and subjected husbands.

But this dismal land of idleness – from which risk has been banished, untouched by the storms of history, without fear and without future – appears sunk in a perspective that is not only dream-like but positively funereal, in a world where plenty is reflected in the negative face of sterility: where nature, overturned, forms inhuman and monstrous landscapes, beyond every possible logic and far from every perspective of life. A 'nature' where the artificial has destroyed the natural, turning it upside down, altering its biological laws, the periods for the maturation of produce and even the time of animal gestation.

A nature unhinged and crazed, which re-aquaints us with the sinister memory of the Polynesian atoll where, after the atomic Big Bang, the tortoises lost their innate sense of orientation, and instead of directing themselves towards the water and life, turned their backs to it, setting out towards death.

As in the words of the Catalan archpriest of the fourteenth century, Bernart Metge, 'there [on the island of Cockaigne], there was neither God nor nature, since there was neither order nor measure, nor anything rational.' Cockaigne comes to correspond to the desolate island of the dead and to the sad, mournful landscape of things outside time, in an eternal suspension of the laws of existence.

> Here most of the trees were naked of fruit and leaves, and the rest were adorned with fruit and rich clothes; and the oldest and most important trees were less tall than those of humble origin; and the pine competed in splendour with the myrtle; and the willow did not tire of bearing fruit, while the pear tree did not have any, nor the apple tree; and the olive tree was all dry. In this place the

nightingale did not sing, but with a clear voice the cuckoo sang laments, as it is wont to; and the cicada with the nocturne bird that accompanied it; and those birds made displeasing song which normally make it pleasing. From this wood there originated two rivers, different in colour, movement and taste, each of them having its own nature; and the water of the river that had the most pleasing aspect and taste, after I had tasted it, brought me close to death, because drinking gave me stronger ardour and thirst, the more that I drank.[3]

In the Land of Cockaigne – revelation of the *mundus inversus* ('world turned upside down') – the happy time returns; indeed, it is blocked in. It reappears in an immobile circle, just as the rhymed and obsessive words of the propitiatory lullabies, spells and litanies compose bits of repeating, calming, sedating and drugging words. In this verbal dimension, the consoling word of the minstrel is utilized by the poor as a surrogate for the frustrations of psychic and bodily miseries: as an opiated word which, even across the anaphoric techniques of repetition – the wheel of words returning like the wheel of time – tears itself from the ordinary, opening fleeting but necessary parentheses of consolations glimpsed in dreams, of phonic and verbal surrogates for existential sadnesses and bodily miseries. The dream of plenty magically suspends, subdues and soothes the pangs of unsatisfied bowels.

Many people, in the fifteenth and sixteenth centuries, were reduced to living mainly on *beau langage* and feasting on names instead of tasting things. For them, these 'succulent' enumerations were like a little compensation for everyday poverty. But let us note well: this compensation obtained by force of words is only possible if a certain intoxication first attenuated the feeling of distance which separated the dream from the reality, and intoxication cannot here be but the fruit of verbal accumulation. Each term in these enumerations, taken in isolation, is nothing but a desire or a lie; it is the magnificent abundance, the uninterrupted flow of words charged with captivating flavours that create the illusion. In this state of euphoria provoked by the juggling of words, one ends up believing that one has played with things.[4]

The artifice of the word opens up consoling horizons to the starvation and catatony of the listener. The *histrio turpis* ('deformed actor') – man of filth, contaminated mediator – assumes the mask of consoler and therapist. Not by accident the minstrel, at a certain moment in his historical course, is attributed with demonic characteristics, to the point of almost perfectly resembling the lunatic.

81

He who has money
Is called a gentlemen;
He who has none
Is treated like a lunatic.

Poverty and madness eventually coincide, in the way that the face of a child struck by athrepsia (a diseased condition caused by malnutrition), undernourishment or the *mal dal simiòt* ('monkey disease', as it was known in Modena), his worn-out skin all wrinkled, appeared similar to that of an old senescent monkey.

The double face of *puer/senex*, dear to the mystic religions, was utilized at the popular level as the concrete image of the overturning of the natural order. The tiny malnourished senescent was placed on a baker's peel, put in the lukewarm oven and taken out three times with the incantation

Into the oven you go, and out you come, so that the monkey may remain inside.	A t'infôren e a-t desfôren che al simiòt al rèsta ind-al fôren.

The ambiguous, enigmatic, entangled and reversible logic of popular mental stereotypes presents itself as a cultural anti-model which, because of its subtle attraction, also contaminates the rationalistic, Aristotelian culture. In the folk vision of the world, preceded by ingenious anachronism, space is presented as a dimension of time and the universe as a place of ordered chaos, where the possible and the impossible dwell together in the same percentage of probabilities. Time is either still or is measured with the unabstract metre of sweat and toil. The land that can be ploughed with a pair of oxen from dawn to sunset becomes a day: a unit of time substitutes for a unit of surface area. The years are counted in terms of empty and full, the seesaw of famine and plenty. The 'year of hunger' is placed in the centre of the calendar of the poor. The 'longest day' is the one during which one does not eat. Time becomes an expandable and shrinkable variable, articulated by the stomach's pulsations, the gut's thinning out or filling up and the fatigue of labour. The popular ceremonial of eating also reproposes a different use of time, alternating long days of the most frugal nourishment – a regimen of survival bordering on starvation – with interminable ritual excesses, dietary orgies and colossal feasts, disorder and drunkenness: quite different from the noble banquet based entirely on the aesthetic values of food, a visual cuisine to be displayed.

In this perspective, where the paradoxical and the impossible dominate, every aspect of the world can be turned upside down. Every series can be interpreted contrarily, every beginning can start at the end (as in the reversed *Pater noster*). The universe itself becomes reversible. Paradise disguises itself as hell and vice versa. The 'miracle' becomes a revelation of another system, a submerged order that can come to the surface. In the two-faced world of things turned upside down, the impossible is always on the point of becoming possible. It is the logic that appears in visions and nightmares, in the system of the absurd and those *cose pazze* ('crazy things') which Machiavelli mentions in a famous letter of his. But it is the same overturned universe that this 'peasant' of Molise visits in a dream where he takes refuge in the impossible fancy of the 'world head over heals', raving of improbable delights after having filled his stomach with 'bread and spittle'; when he thinks he had seen a procession pass in which the donkeys marched in front and the horses behind.

The common people of Calabria cast their own, useless, spells against poverty:

> Damned poverty,
> go to the sea and drown yourself:
> this is blessed flesh
> and you don't belong here.
> Loading and unloading, appetite and misery
> scabies and ringworm
> when you see me, dead you fall.

In the land of hunger even the dearest sentiments are turned upside down. One weeps over the donkey's death, since it is useful for carrying wood, not over that of one's old, useless father: 'If only dad had died and not the donkey; the donkey was useful and dad isn't'.[5]

> Our land is called poverty
> where one does the dance of hunger.

So went a cradle song of the peasants of the Salentine peninsula.

It is in this social panorama, traversed by profound anxieties and fears, alienating frustrations, devouring and uncontrollable infirmities and dietary chaos that adulterated and stupefying grains contributed to delirious hypnotic states and crises, which could explode into episodes of collective possession or sudden furies of dancing. The forbidden zones, those most contaminated by the ambiguous, ambivalent magic of the sacred, seemed to emanate perverse influences and unleash dark energies. Psychological destitution, together with the torment of an ailing body, acted as detonator of the epileptic attacks and tumultuous and surging group fits, in which men were attracted and repelled by centres of powerful fascination and places of sacrifice, like the altar. The

pathological trance into which entire groups fell – as appears in the
episode related by the fifteenth-century chronicler Giovanni di Maestro
Pedrino – forms the alarm call originating from a feverish world: a social
body altered in its physiological and psychic equilibrium, where 'marvel'
could be confused with 'miracle', which in its turn could appear as
'trickery', 'enchantment' or 'diabolical invocation'. The horrible dances
of the sick inside churches, where the troubled presence of the contaminated and the impure was united with the consecrated and the supernatural, resulted in spectacular, bewildering performances:

> There was a rumour going round Romagna in 1383 of a miracle
> which had taken place in Faenza, in the church of San Piero, near
> the end of May. It was in this church near the square of the same
> name that a painting or crucifix performed miracles and healed the
> sick; and several men are said to have seen it. And when its fame
> spread, many of the city's sick went to this church. They then
> wanted to go to the altar, and there men and women started to
> tremble and dance like madmen, hurling themselves to and fro
> inside the church, and they went into ecstasy three or four times
> before being able to approach the altar; and whenever they reached
> the altar they went back and fell, and did not get up without help,
> and no one was liberated. Finally it was seen that it had been caused
> by some evil person's spell, some diabolical incantation. And the
> flow of people ceased.[6]

At Ferrara in 1596, according to the Modenese chronicler Giovan
Battista Spaccini, 'it is believed that the cause of many illnesses, of which
numerous people even die, is the bad breads which the people eat,
namely that of beans, cabbage and plain oil'.[7] The dark spectre of food
poisoning and the crisis (even fatal) of 'evil' breads weighed heavily on
the cities of the Duchies and Papal Legations. Because of the criminal
intervention of cynical speculators, 'vulgar' bread could sometimes hide
destructive traps. Or else, as happened at Modena in 1592, it could lead
to a dangerous slide into the dull and delirious senselessness of intoxi-
fication. Adulterated breads had been put into circulation by the *untori*[8]
of the Public Health: criminal attacks orchestrated by the 'provisionary
judges' who were supposed to oversee the well-balanced provisioning of
the public-square.

> On the 21st, a Sunday, with Monday approaching, Master . . .
> [blank in the manuscript] Forni, Judge of provisions in the square
> of Modena, was arrested, along with the bakers, for having had
> forty sacks of bay leaf ground to be put in the wheat flour to make

bread for the square, where it caused the poverty to those who bought it to worsen, so that for two days there were many people sick enough to go crazy, and during this time they could not work or help their families.[9]

Temporarily losing their reason or permanently weltering in hunger, many peasants preferred to leave home and turn to begging rather than helplessly witness their children's agony. Changed into a 'house of death', the hut becomes a murderous trap and tomb for the least protected:

a few days ago [April 1601] in the town of Reggio . . . a peasant, along with his wife, so as not to see their three sons perish from hunger in front of their eyes, locked them in the house and set out in the name of heaven. After three days had passed, the neighbours, not having seen them, decided to knock down the door, which they did. And they found two of the sons dead, and the third dying with straw in his mouth, and on the fire there was a pot with straw inside which was being boiled in order to make it softer for eating.[10]

7

'Famine of Living' and 'Times of Suspicion'

City wage-earners, often on the edge of unemployment, and peasants, continually wrestling with the unresolved problem of insufficient agricultural produce, were among the first victims of the famine's advance. The peasants in particular saw their hunger, it could be said, literally grow from the earth. They, who in order to survive had to be attentive planners and schedulers anxious for the future of their cereals, lived continuously with the 'obsession of dearth'.[1] The caprice of the seasons was enough to send them to the brink of catastrophe. The fear of the future weighed perennially on these workers of the fields, 'de-socialized' with respect of the workers of the cities, fortunately closed in their archaic, protective and, in a certain sense, reassuring magical universe.

During the great famine of Emilia, and particularly in Bologna, the sinister effects of which were first felt in 1590–1, and which raged as in the Biblical famines, for another seven years,

> one could no longer find anyone who had wheat at home with which to make bread for his family [noted Pompeo Vizani, friend of Giulio Cesare Croce and spokesman for the senatorial class]; and despite everything the Senate and many individual citizens did to find and bring in foreign wheat, not enough could be done to prevent up to 10,000 paupers from dying of hunger in the city, even in the public streets; and in the entire countryside, even in the fields, over 30,000 peasants, for whom the rich could not provide with their vast almsgiving because of the all too serious need. The wretched were often forced by hunger to the necessity of eating not only bread made of every type of pulse and bran, but of roots and

herbs and every type of refuse, though greatly abhorred by human sensibility.[2]

Perhaps it would be better not to attempt to discover what lurked beneath the term 'refuse'. However, it is certainly not easy to forget a passage written by the Bolognese cleric Giovan Battista Segni (the most attentive and sensitive treatise writer on hunger and its horrible excesses): a passage, everything considered, not new in its series of varied, heterogeneous evidence strung together, but from which a sullen light shines upon the non-ritual cannibalistic practices and the cruel and desperate dietary excesses frequent in times not so far away and in places neither mythical nor remote.

Hermano Contratto writes in the year 890 that there was a famine so cruel that it reduced men to eating one another. In 1396 Matteo Palmieri writes that there was a famine so great that the crowd of beggars lived on human food, and that they barely sustained themselves. Martino Cromero in the eleventh book of the *Histories of the Polish* says that in the year 1315 such a bitter famine afflicted Poland that men did not abstain from the corpses, and even from dung, and fathers turned against their sons and vice versa. In 1359, writes Matteo Palmieri, there was such great hunger in Italy that they ate human flesh. In the year 567 there was likewise such great hunger in Italy and especially in Liguria that, as related by Paolo Diacono, several mothers ate their own sons . . . In the year 1006 Sigisberto writes that there was so much hunger and at the same time so many deaths that to save the tedium of carrying the dead to burial oftentimes the living buried themselves along with the dead.[3]

In the general marasmus of this shattered human condition, the descent into dung-eating (man is not a complete omnivore), brutalization and physiological inversion unleashed latent hatreds and hidden conflicts. Fathers turning against sons and the revolt of sons against fathers within the sacred (or damned) domestic space causes the bright flashes of lightning that are sinister carnivals of blood, cruel dethronings and violent inversions within the micro-society of the family, which explodes like a crazed cell. Aberrant frenzies ignited by hunger on the flowing of blood which has suddenly become its own enemy: lacerations of the human and domestic fibre not dissimilar to those provoked by the plague, dissolver of every emotional and social bond.

Hunger is crueller than the plague, because man is in need for much more time, but the plague is more abominable because as soon as it gives us time to catch our breath, it takes away our memory, removes every thought of repentance, and causes the confessors to be absent; the notaries no longer come to write the testaments, the doctors flee, the fathers are sick and tired of their sons, who turn their backs on their fathers, the mothers abandon their daughters and they shun their mothers, one relative does not recognize the other, friends become enemies.[5]

The testaments to which Segni refers pertain to the death ritual of the rich: they were the 'passports to the world beyond' (Jacques Le Goff) which foresaw vast endowments to churches and convents, so that the dying passed away with a peaceful conscience, socially and religiously relieved of every misdeed. The poor amused themselves, in the absence of goods and the difficulties arising because of them, by enacting parodies of testaments, in order to laugh a little at this act sacred to the religion of 'things', indispensable instrument in the transmission of the 'household effects'.

The bitter comparisons of the Bolognese priest delineate a hierarchy of pain and horror, as well as depicting human blindness not unlike the frenzy of death mysteriously induced by several elusive pathologies of the past. Like the sort of frenetic and hallucinating attraction towards dissolutions, for example, which was translated into a flight into nothingness: a race to collective suicide transmitted by the so-called *mal mazzucco* ('frenzy') which, 'by causing the sick to lose feeling, led them further towards their final end, and oftentimes they gave themselves up to voluntary death'.[6] That same *maal mazuch* (in the dialect of Friuli) whose course the anger of the sixteenth-century Friulian peasant would have liked to transfer from the workers' hovels to the lords' palaces, together with all the other depressive and convulsive syndromes:

Rabies, fury, poison, frenzy,	Raibe stizze velen el maal mazuch
Splinter and flashing sickness, anguish, neurosis,	Mal di sclese e di sclop lancuur foiaal
Hysteria, hypochondria: all the diseases	La madreule el madron e ogni maal
To the Lords, and throw them into the hovels.	Ai Signors e in tiri in t'un scrusup.[7]

A disease difficult to identify (as obscure as the 'brick sickness', that of 'the ant' and many other pathologies indicated by terms incomprehensible today) that seems to have had different causes from those epidemic hysterias, not infrequent in the past, like the one described by a French doctor at the end of the eighteenth century: 'A melancholic disorder also prevailed, mostly among women, the principal symptom of which was a bar of fire which the sick women said they felt across the coronal bone. They all desired to throw themselves into the well'.[8] Those who had been smitten, observed Leonardo Fioravanti, 'speak a sea of madness and do a thousand crazy things'.[9] The universe of fear seemed to extend indefinitely towards ever more uncertain and indeterminate confines. For example, the sources agree in attesting that fear of the plague reaped more victims than the plague itself: 'More are those who die of hunger, fear and suffering than of disease'.[10] The terrifying dreams of the collective unconscious during the pre-industrial period, like the one of the cart for the dead – which in the *ancien régime*'s well-stocked storehouse of terrors had a multi-dimensional fullness of meaning that cannot be felt today – collaborated powerfully in opening the way for the 'pasture of death' (Ludovico Antonio Muratori) among uncontainable fears and horrors:

> The strong *passions of the heart*, ruling Contagion, can be called the first grave-diggers of man. All the doctors proclaim with one voice that especially Rage, Melancholy, and Terror are cause for flight as much as the Plague itself . . . Thucydides recounts that in the very serious plague which he describes, the melancholic and fearful fell dead more than the others. Various doctors have observed likewise in their own times, and among others Sennerto attests that not a few have been taken by this disease from just the *Terror* conceived observing from afar, or even without seeing but only hearing that the funeral *Cart* was passing under their windows, on which were carried the corpses of the dead.
>
> Others, frightened only by a funereal *Dream*, have so lost heart that, once fallen ill, they have eluded all treatment . . . Once the imagination is wounded and the spirits and humours put into disordered movement by some frightening spectacle, the pestilential poison is all too easily taken, and even without the plague people sometimes die of pure Consternation and Black Humour.[11]

But in times of Suspicion – when one hears of 'cases of the plague far away, yes, but which necessitate the precautions of health observances, and of railings or gates, when one must force out of the City as from the State, within a few days, the beggars, vagabonds, gypsies, mendicants, lepers, invalids and similar sorts of people not engaged in some trade and without the will to procure their bread, if not by the all too confortable begging for it'[12] – the entire variegated universe of those on the margins of society, always and everywhere watched with suspicion and fear, became the potential vehicle of contagion and carrier of epidemics.

And on the twelfth day of May, 1498, the Officials of Disease went around the hospitals, chased out the poor, and wherever they were found throughout the city they sent them out of Florence; and they did a still crueller thing: they stretched out a rope with a pulley at the Cuirass-makers guild to catch those who came back. It was held to be a cruel thing and an adverse remedy.[13]

The pestilential disease reaped most of its victims from among the poorest people – labourers, small artisans, urban beggars; among those who did not have the necessary means to leave the inhabited centres rapidly.

Where the cities are of a large population and the families, mostly of the poor, live in close and crowded houses, the plague causes incredible slaughter . . . [F]or this reason in the quarters most crowded and overflowing with poor inhabitants, when the disease has entered therein, a frightening desolation is seen in a short time.[14]

The conditions of those who were forced by indigence to remain in the city (the peasants would have pushed them back there in any case) became most difficult; the 'poor people' risked 'the manifest danger of dying then from hunger and hardship'.[15]

The beggars, artisans and many others used to earning their bread day by day, remaining then in the city . . . and, on the other hand, only the well-off being able to seek refuge in the countryside, every-one can understand that the poor of the city are without those people who could give them alms or provide them with work, and as a result every day they receive less from the granary and storehouse, so that they remain exposed to the daily risk of dying from hunger, not less than that of the plague.[16]

In the 'afflicted city', dominated by the nightmare of the 'lazaret/slaughter house',[17] smokey and malodorous from the vapours of sulphur, pitch, animals' horns (especially birds' beaks), old shoes, hair, nails and cattle manure,

it is too easy for one to lose courage and die of fear, on seeing and hearing the ministers of the lazarets and grave-diggers go around with horrible faces, odd clothes and frightening voices and carry away the sick and the healthy, the dead and the living, as long as there is something to pilfer. Nor can it be said what horror is inspired by the frequent sound of their bells.[18]

In a world where the sad winds of Insecurity, Fear and Suspicion blew, the terror of the plague – multiplying the 'antidotes', internal and external 'preservatives', 'pouches', and 'amulets of arsenic', poisonous or innocuous – had as an unfailing consequence the realization of the 'great Chaos of Pharmaceutical Preservatives'.

In this dance of prescriptions containing arsenic, sublimate, quicksilver, and of 'curative or preservative aromatic pouches', magic, superstitious practices and apotropaic astrology re-emerged – if ever they had been renounced – with unusual popularity and desperate impetus. The 'archaic attitudes' of the popular world and the magical base of its culture shattered even the inconsistent rational barriers of a medical science more unsteady and contradictory than ever, groping in the dark.

> The astrologers and the superstitious have inverted many seals, medals, bulletins, rings, cards and similar things with figures, signs, numbers and even sacred words. Some, and mostly in Germany, exalt and call a marvellous preservative the wearing of a dried *toad* hung from the neck – or burned and reduced to ash and enclosed in a pouch – during times of contagion. Others in the same manner recommend the wearing of *Quicksilver*, well closed and sealed with wax inside a walnut . . . and they tell of its wonderful effect. According to others, Emerald, Sapphire, Hyacinth and other gems hung from the neck, in such a way that they touch the external regions of the heart, so frightens the plague that it dares not approach.[19]

8
Night-time

If a reasoning and cautious thinker like Ludovico Antonio Muratori also dwells at length on the 'medical management' of the terrible disease (he wrote his treatise on the plague in 1710), it is because even in the first half of the eighteenth century the general mentality was imbued with magic, occult beliefs, unreal suggestions, 'voices' and 'rumours' (the *untori*, for example), 'errors' and 'prejudices'.

The popular *Giardino fiorito di varie curiosità, diviso in due trattati* ('In the First Is Included What Are Ghosts, Visions, Goblins, Enchanters, Sorcerers, Witches, Charmers . . .'; 1667) still met with favour. Giovanni Maria Vincenti had just investigated the *Mondo infestato dagli spiriti* (1667) and Henningus Grosius had just collected a myriad of entries and evidence in the *Magica de spectris et apparitionem spiritum* (1656). Apparitions and strange noises foretold the deaths of great personages (cf. the late sixteenth-century treatise by Loys Lavater of Zurich, *De spectris, lemuribus et magnis atque insolitis fragoribus, varrisque praesagitationibus, quae plerumque obitum hominum, magnas clades, mutationesque imperiorum praecedunt*, 1570). The *Discours des spectres . . .* by Le Loyer dates from 1586; the *Traicté de l'apparition des esprits* by Taillepied came out at the beginning of the first year of the seventeenth century, and the *De miraculis morturorum* by Christian Garman in 1709.

'Terrible noises', 'violent and repeated' and 'unusual' rumblings were said (and written) to have come from the sepulchre at Ferrara of the Blessed Beatrice d'Este II, born perhaps in the third decade of the thirteenth century, and who, with the passing of years, became devoted to the 'preservation of her most serene nobility'; diligent in

> predicting the events of the family and in warning of the calamities which struck her city. Private oracle for the family and public barometre, anticipator of calamitous history, the rumblings of 1709

and 1711 for the arrival of foreign armies was considered notable
. . . as for that of the famous inundation of all her lands, or for the
death of the animals; or, finally, for several famous fires which
occurred in recent years.[1]

Occasionally the tombstone of the *Beata* was not content to produce the
'usual clamour' but, as took place in 1504 and 1505, 'for some time its
colour changed and it became red and everywhere exuded liquid in great
abundance.'[2]

In the *Vita* of this glorious saint of the house of Este (mentioned by
Ludovico Ariosto), reprinted in Ferrara in 1777, the vocal messages of
the Benedictine virgin are carefully selected and interpreted.

She was wont to make this clamour heard in different ways, according to the gravity of the cases that were predicted by her. At times
she is heard by all the nuns, other times by many, and sometimes
by a few of the nuns whose rooms are close to the altar. Whoever
happens to view the said altar when it is rumbling will see its stone
move and tremble as if for an earthquake; and those who see or hear
it feel no fear at all, but rather a sudden jubilation, accompanied
by some wonder, and by this they understand it to have been the
clamour produced by the *Beata*, and not something accidental or
fortuitous which produces that tremor. If it were something else,
like what is usually created suddenly, it would certainly frighten
them all.

Although it is not really known what event it is that she predicts
with such crashing, none the less by the diversity of ways of beating
(by means of the ancient practice and tradition of the nuns), it can
usually be conjectured without mistake. If the misfortune is deadly
for the Este family, or if some great death is about to take place in
the city or convent, and especially if the blow is to strike some
superior, the clamour is like an overturning of stones, in the way
that a cart, hurrying along filled with them, overturns everything at
the end of the run. If she then wants to announce some common
gladness, whether to her family or to the convent, a sort of violent,
rattling explosion of artillery is heard in the air throughout the
entire convent. And finally, if the pre-announced accident is not of
a death, just a roar and shaking is heard which causes the earth to
tremble like a running cart, but in the end no other rumbling occurs
similar to the overturning of stones. This appears on the most
remarkable occasions. At times for long periods, and repeated
often; at times, three or four days before, and only once; and
finally, on some other occasions she makes herself heard on the day

just preceding the event, now by day, now at night, but most often during the hours of matins, nones and compline.[3]

Another 'clock' marking times of death was the wooden coffin of the Blessed Eustachia preserved in the convent of Monte Vergine at Messina, where, as Antonino Mongitore warned (in his *Della Sicilia ricercata nelle cose più memorabili* of 1742), 'when a nun of that place is close to death, the coffin in which the *Beata* is enclosed is heard to rattle, giving a warning; nor has any nun died in that convent when the rattling has not been heard, so that the warning helps in preparing oneself for death'.[4]

All it took was a ghost – a supposed masked apparition – to throw a city into confusion and fear. It could happen that the fear of a spirit, put in motion by another deeper anxiety, provoked a collective trauma – so immense was the power of the imaginary – not in some remote Apennine village, but in a ducal city of the plain: Modena. Not in the 'barbaric' centuries of the 'dark' Middle Ages, but in the 'modern' eighteenth century, almost rational, on the path of the pre-Enlightenment.

The spirits – igneous, acquatic, earthly and subterranean – concealed themselves everywhere. Some of them

> prevent the passage of nourishment and food, others alter the humours of the body, like the spirits of fire that infect the blood, those of the air the choler, of land the phlegm, the underground spirits the melancholy; and so with their continual discord they cause headaches, stomach agonies, nerve contractions, tremors, suffocations, kidney ordours, fevers, catarrhs, plagues and similar diseases.

'Jovial', 'mercurial', 'saturnine', 'lucifugous' and 'meridian' spirits knew 'where the riches, the treasures, the books and every other hidden thing was concealed'. With 'visions, illusions, disguises and frights', apparitions of 'phantoms', 'jacks', 'loom frames' and 'little devils' caused 'much inconvenience to human life'.

Eurynomus, prince of demons, 'armed with long and protruding teeth, with a livid and putrid body like that of a dead man, dressed in a fox skin', was 'wont to feed on the flesh of corpses, with such voracity and greediness that he devours flesh and bone all at once'.

Bearers of 'bad tidings', the spirits were also 'signs of pestilence, ruin and every calamitous adversity', like the earthquakes caused by subterranean goblins. These wicked beings – 'awful spirits of the death and ruin of men' – often took the form of black dogs, wolves, monks and old women.

In Parma there is a family of the most noble Torelli, who are lords of a castle, in whose fireplace for over a hundred years now it is usual to see one of these spirits in the form of an ugly old woman; and every time this spectre appears, someone of the said Torelli family dies.[5]

'Dark spirits . . . make noises in the houses at night, in the church cemeteries and other places where men have been buried or killed or where corpses are to be found.' And: 'When the world is most covered with darkness', the spirits are wont to 'make noise in the houses during the silence of the night'. They could change the bodies of the animals and men they had extinguished into statues of salt.

Fincelius, the German doctor and scholar on the plague, collector of marvels and *Wunderzeichen* (1556), related that in Padua there had been caught a 'werewolf in the form of a wolf, whose paws were cut off . . . and at once it became a man without hands and feet, to the very great terror of those involved'.[6]

In the present year 1713 we have seen with our own eyes in our city that outcries, fears and blood-lettings have been caused by the rumour that a ghost wandered about the streets at night. Oh, many saw it, but they showed only the former Apprehension and Fear, which is an industrious deceiver, especially at nightime.[7]

'Nightime' drew an impalpable but very clean line between Apollonian, virtuous, luminous and active time, and demonic time, which dwelt under the sign of the divinities of the night, disorder and the protector of thieves, Mercury. As Sabba Castiglione apprehensively warned in his *Ricordi overo ammaestramenti* of 1554:

You will be on your guard when walking at night, if not out of extreme necessity, firstly against scandals, inconveniences and dangers which lurk there continuously; then against the various and diverse infirmities which are often generated in human bodies by the night air . . . It is certain that going out at night without need is nothing other than disturbing nature's order.

The night realm belonged to ruffians, low-lifes and those in a bad way; to the dubious presences which the darkness covered in its deep, faceless anonymity; to ghosts, spirits of the dead returned among the living, incubi, goblins, and witches, who silently glided to suck the blood of children or, atop brooms and pitchforks, went to the witches' sabbath.

Certain girls, slaves of Satan, seduced by the demon of illusions, believe in and are promised during the night hours to Diana, goddess of the pagans, or Venus, to ride among great numbers of women, and to perform various wicked deeds . . . to pull away children from their mothers' breast, to roast and devour them; to enter into houses by the chimneys or windows and disturb the inhabitants in various ways.[8]

In the darkness of the villages, at the setting of the sun, the mother's prayer/incantation was uttered 'so that . . . no night-owl would have children in the shadows, nor would there be ghosts at the crossroads'.[9]

Certain furtive women went 'naked at night on to church roofs to turn over the tiles, so as to overturn men's hearts'. On the evening preceding Sunday peasant women did not permit 'anyone to drink water out of his bucket from above or below, saying that if water is drunk in this way, the dead come at night to drink, and finding the water drunk in this way they curse . . . On Saturday evenings during winter the women leave the fire lit so that the dead, as they say, go to warm themselves at night'.[10]

The peasants, who saw in the dark like cats, loped along silently, feeling the articulations, divisions and fragments of the nocturnal hours almost physically, measuring them by the stars with an awareness so precise as to appear astonishing today.

After sunset they wandered along footpaths shadowed by the night, living almost a second life, finally free of every control: hunting with a reflecting lantern (an activity prohibited them), of the kind used in night fishing. The anonymous author of the *De natura rusticorum* speaks of them in terms of nocturnal animals, children of the devil, 'cursed dragons', mobile like birds in their movements.

'Vagabundi sunt ut oves' ['They are vagabonds like the birds'], stirring in the shadows and softly breathing, with their cloaks hovering like owls: 'Nocte vadunt ut bubones' ['At night they make their way like owls'].

They went to secret enclosures in order to abandon themselves to forbidden games and dances. 'They are to be found at licentious threshings and prohibited games,' anathematized the members of the curia, obsessed by that ghost of the agrarian orgy, the demonic sabbath (the 'licentious threshings'), and its lunar variant, entrusted to the authority of the Lady of the Night.

The promiscuous night-time orgy and formless burial ground of lust endured, so it seems, into the heart of the modern age. The humanist Francesco Panfilo da Sanseverino reconstructs in heroic metre the nocturnal meeting (the pagan *sacrum*, or sacrificial rite) which took place in the depths of the caves in the ancient Massaccio region (modern Cupramontana):

They run to the Goddess Venus (oh, wicked debauchery!),
Having deposited the sacrifice, here they perform the
    bacchanalia . . .
They go into the cave-dwelling by the friendly stillness
    of the night . . .[11]

The nocturnal wind of cruel sylvan sacrifices penetrated even the
Cinque canti of Ariosto. In the secret world of the caves, or the 'dark
shadow' of the forest – the wood 'full of fear' – where 'evil spirits and
troublesome / religion are dominant',

. . . of human blood, unknown to the gods,
impious sacrifices and vows are made.
                    (canto II, verse 102)

In the Kingdom of Medaea, Queen of herbs ('. . . by virtue of herbs
and spells, / she was made one and immortal with the Fairies'), the
ancient ritual of the propitiatory orgy of fertility and fecundity was
repeated six days out of ten. The great director of the sacred fertility rite
was the Italic goddess Melusina, the serpent-woman of the popular legends and songs which speak of lizards: *eguane, aiguane* and a 'hole of the
anguane' (the latter being the mouth of one of the caves inhabited by these
fairies or nymphs); the fairy-witch who every seven days took the form of
a serpent (animal of the earth *par excellence*, guardian of the treasures
hidden in the earth's dark depths), custodian and priestess of the tree of
life (at Ferrara and Parma an image of the *arbor vitae* protected by the
dragon is depicted in the most sacred places of the two cities).

The oration finished, they formed two groups,
on one side the one sex, on the other side the other;
then, having put out the lights, in leaps and flights
they formed that most wicked embrace;
and mothers mixed with their sons,
brothers chanced often with sisters:
and this custom, which began at that time,
seems still to exist among the Bohemians.
                    (canto II, verse 112)

Obscene and repugnant rites, moreover, were often attributed to rival
sects by orthodox apologists. In the fourth chapter of the *De daemonum
operatione*, Michael Psellus reproaches the Eutychians for ritual banquets
of excrement.[12] According to Flavio Biondo, the Fraticelli sect of the
Marches often met at night in certain hidden caves around the town of
Fabriano, where they abandoned themselves to a most licentious and

incestuous 'mixing', the fruits of which – the babes born of this wicked embrace – were roasted and pulverized: 'all the priests assemble together and they roast them on a spit, and having made a powder of it, they put it in a pitcher with wine, which they make the novices of these wicked sacrifices drink.'[13]

Similar accusations were made against the Gnostics, according to a fundamentally identical stereotype, varying only in the particulars. An example is a passage of Gaudenzio Merula's where, through Flavio Biondo's filtering, the ancient accusation reappears.

> And having made certain sacrifices, putting out the lights, they join together carnally, he with his mother, he with his sister and he with his daughter, without taking regard of or making difference over consanguinity or kinship. Then, at the end of nine months, they return to the same place with the violated women, and taking the children that they bear, they wound them in different parts of the body, and with the blood, which flows out from different parts, they fill several pitchers; and together they burn the babies' bodies, and taking the ashes of those burnt bodies they mix them with the blood, and they make several cakes out of it, which they carry hidden wherever they go.[14]

Diabolical-criminal witchcraft, heretical rites, fertility orgies and 'congregations' of witches and wizards are all mixed together – as in a complicated palimpsest or the multiple geological stratifications of a cliff – into an iconographical stereotype where the witches' horde, the sabbath, the infernal cavalcade and the games of Diana are all consumed by the 'silence of the dead of night', to use a literary *topos* common to many rumours. Nocturnal was the charivari which, preceded by the mournful sound of horns, on the vigil of St Martin's Day, roused the foggy villages of lower Romagna for the *festa dei becchi* ('cuckolds' feast').

The night, experienced as a time of anguish, was held in sharp contrast to the solar day: a kind of day *à l'envers*. It was a criminal time that filled every statute, and which jurisprudence (medieval as well as seventeenth-century) took into consideration in order to stiffen the punishments for certain crimes perpetrated after sunset. 'It is not by chance that medieval legislation punished crimes committed at night with an extraordinary force.'[15] For nocturnal *stercoratio* ('defecating') on walls and doors the 1567 statutes of Ferrara provided severe punishments.

Fear was a child of the night and the world of the dead ('Metus Noctis et Erebi Filius', wrote the jurist Polidoro Ripa), and Deceit too had sprung from its breast. Fraud had been given birth by the night as well ('Fraus Noctis filia'), in the same way as Poverty, Misery, Hunger,

Disease, Pallor . . . The *Tractatus de nocturno tempore* is one of the many indications of the attention given to day's opposite by a culture descended from a land of nocturnal shadows and apprehensions.[16] It is a complex certification of the influence of folk mythologies, along with that of 'erudite imagining', on jurisprudence and its doctrinal ghosts: profoundly contaminated by magico-witchcraft rituals and popular legends, so as to make it appear closer to an imaginary science of dreams than to a societal norm.

God's sorcerer – the divine wizard – imposed the restoration of the troubled order on this whole obscure, ghostly world, vomited from the clammy and dark stomach of the night. Great hunter of satanic spirits, flawless expert on their strategies, deceptions and tricks, he re-established the sovereignty of the Word by means of the doctrine and power of the magical litany.

In presenting the *Compendio dell'arte essorcistica, et possibilità delle mirabili, et stupende operationi delli demoni, et de i malefici*,[17] the famous work of the Franciscan Girolamo Menghi of Viadana, Giulio Cesare Croce composed two sonnets unknown until now which give witness both to the popularity of this 'art', and to the long presence in Bologna of this famous scourger of demons and nocturnal spirits.

> The Abyss trembles, and with infinite pains
>> The daughters of Cheron and the night
>> Weep with dark spirits, and the City of Dis
>> Resounds with interrupted voices.
> For their impious forces united in evil
>> Fall dead, shattered and broken;
>> And there is no longer shadow in the black caves
>> That could give mortals bitter wounds . . .

Terrifying apparitions, ghosts, goblins, spells and collective hallucinations, spread by uncontrollable rumours, disturbed the nights (difficult and uneasy like the days) of 'modern' age men: un-sought-after supplements of shivers and frights that were added to the terror of plague, hunger and war ('a bello, peste et fame libera nos Domine'; 'from war, plague and hunger, deliver us O Lord').

The spirits of evil were the masters of the elements: arbiters of the meteorological and climatic mysteries. The subterranean goblins conspired to increase human anguish with earthquakes. Demons, spectres and angels roamed about the streets of the city in the heart of darkness: 'All the people,' recounted Strozzi Cicogna, 'saw every night with their own eyes one of these spectres who wandered about the city at midnight with an angel.'[18] The angels who brandished swords were threathening signals of imminent calamities. Several of Pompeo Vizani's pages offer a not exhaustive yet strongly indicative sampling of the natural scourges and imaginary fears that tormented the existence of other times. A page of the Bolognese chronicle relating to 1504 told how

> already a great living famine had begun . . . where cries and laments were heard everywhere. Furthermore, the citizens were sorrowful because they oftentimes saw several fearful signs, which indicated impending ruin: since there blew strong and violent winds which destroyed many houses and uprooted quite a few trees; and from the sky descended water and storm in such quantity and accompanied by so much lightning, thunder and flashing that everyone was left dumbfounded. Still another amazing thing appeared in the so-called 'Sala' fields twelve miles from Bologna: at midday in those fields several shadows were seen from afar which, caused by meteorological impressions, seemed to be eighteen or twenty men dressed in white, red and black, and they seemed to be fighting among themselves. And when anyone approached to try and see them at close range, they saw nothing at all; and to those who remained far away it seemed as if those who had approached were conversing with the ghosts, which appeared for a good many days, during which time many curious citizens went to see them. It was during this time that certain Observant Friars, who lived in the monastery of Saint Paul of the Observance, located in the Apennines two miles from the city, related that they had seen an Angel, who, situated above Bologna, threatened the people with his unsheathed sword in hand. While the citizens were full of bewilderment because of these things, Giovanni Bentivogli was waiting to celebrate.
>
> During this year in the month of December it seemed as if sweet spring wanted to appear, since the weather was so pleasing and the air so mild that the trees began to bloom and send forth their flowerlets, and everywhere was seen roses, lilies, violets and other flowers and many fruits that usually appear at the beginning of spring. But prudent men did not have a very good opinion of this; in fact, they doubted whether this unusual novelty did not threaten some great ruin. Nor were they exactly misled in their thinking, because on the last day of that year the earth began to tremble during the night, and that trembling lasted for around a quarter of an hour, causing much damage and ruin to the houses throughout the whole city, where the citizens were very much afraid. And so with everyone frightened of the coming of the year 1505 and the

earthquake often becoming stronger, it lasted for forty days, so that every hour there were seen new ruins and ravages of churches, towers, palaces and finally, of almost all the citizens' houses, who, in attempting to escape death . . . lived outside the houses, in gardens and other uncovered places, under awnings and canopies, and many even in wine barrels . . .

At the same time the living famine continued to grow in such a way that many poor men died of hunger, not being able to find nourishment for themselves. And when some bakery occasionally made bread to sell, the magistrates had to supply an armed guard for its defence, otherwise it was put to the sack by the famished populace. Even the peasants, who suffered the same hunger, were forced to eat the roots of herbs, and other less nourishing things . . . With the oats beginning to ripen in the month of June, the famine began to let up little by little; and finally, because of the very good harvest, there was an abundance of everything. But, since the plague had been discovered in many cities of Italy, and in the end in Bologna as well, the citizens could not live without much difficulty, because of this as well as another disease called the hammer sickness . . . Of this disease died not only a very large number of commoners but sixteen doctors as well, all of them important.[19]

Murderous wolves in winter, and in summer swarms of mosquitoes, flies and fleas (spreaders of the plague) tormented the *poveri homini* of the Apennine villages like those in Friuli. At least until the eighteenth century the image of the wolf as slaughterer of children and assassin of men (other than of sheep) was a fairly common nightmare everywhere. Numerous Friulian *preenti* ('spells') survive in Inquisitorial trials begun against those who searched for a magical defence against those beasts and, in general, against the hostile forces of incomprehensible nature. The plague was continually lying in wait, along with cholera and intestinal fevers. Medicine and magical practices (hellebore root cut and applied to the extremity of the limbs) confusedly attempted to keep away the diseases of unknown aetiology. One of the pages written by Dr Spinelli in 1598 offers a striking picture of the merciless harshness of living.

At Cividale del Friuli wolves had killed abandoned animals, children and men during the winter; in summer, with the heat and dryness at their worst, along with many apricots, there were gnats, fleas and many flies, and recurring fevers with rashes grew strong and continuous, as well as diarrhoea and cholera which were soon treated with minor cutting of a vein [blood-letting] or purgation. With summer and the real heat increasing, burning fevers, rashes, worms, diarrhoea and vomiting raged, although veins were repaired surgically. Children marked by rashes and spots, despite having bad symptoms, were almost all saved. At the beginning of autumn the plague appeared, with its agonizing and putrid fever, accompanied by worms and abundant diarrhoea. Those whose pulses were strong at the beginning suffered from watery urine and most severe headaches: looking like owls, their pains were always assuaged in cavernous gloom. Hellebore root had to be cut and fixed to certain peoples' extremities before the flesh benefited. Suffering from urine on the third day, as from most disorders, on the fourth day one finally died, pulse indistinct and weak: neither bezoar nor Armenian stone was of any use. This plague was milder at the beginning; the meaner and viler of the oppressed were afflicted.[20]

Bracketed between the brief and rare moments of anxious and astonished tranquility, as soon as one scourge let up or disappeared, another still more terrifying punctually made its appearance, in a perverse alternation of illusory mirages of calm followed by pitiless gusts of horrible calamities. The demonically wicked direction of human events added the extra of an almost permanent social marasmus to the tangled situation. To the 'brawls, disputes, [and] killings' in the cities corresponded exactly the 'continuous killings, burning down of houses, rapes, thefts and thousand other sorts of despoiling' in the countryside, tormented by the bloody struggles and feuds of peasant gangs and clans: by 'evil killers', 'ruffians', and by 'cutthroats, by thieves and by bandits'.[21] The *douceur de vivre* of the *ancien régime* was a myth enjoyed solely by a few privileged aristocrats,[22] or by the *scemi del villaggio* ('village idiots'), luckily graced with the sad privilege of insanity, the only one available to the wretched poor.

9

Ritual Battles and Popular Frenzies

With unintentional but certainly bitter irony, many went on saying and repeating that the one and only treasure of the poor – the *thesaurus pauperum* – consisted in the maintenance of their health. None the less, many of the poor preferred sickness and death to a state of health which forced them to live an insufferable life and bear the intolerable torment of hunger. In any case, the course of peasant illnesses was very rapid, apparently so fast as to enter the sad 'wisdom' of the Sicilian peasant: 'The peasant's illness lasts twenty-four hours: in the evening the doctor, the next day the Lord.'

The *medicina pauperum* (medicine of the poor) attempted to apply inexpensive therapies which made use of preventive and curative remedies, the composition of which did not require rare and costly ingredients. On the one hand, the two-way medicinal path led to the complicated and very expensive *triaca* (theriac) for the rich, believed to be a powerful remedy for almost all sicknesses, a universal panacea; and, on the other hand, to the 'theriac of the poor', composed only of herbs. For those with 'strong stomachs and used to hard work', like peasants and porters, the great preserver of health was garlic, the 'theriac of the rustic', suited to rough and work-weary people, those selected in reverse, from whom – according to the science of the time – could only be born rustic and obtuse offspring, since 'no son is born who does not obtain his quality and temperament from the food which his father ate before he was conceived.' From this presupposition, which seems to have been widely shared, it was deduced that

the meat of the cow, steer and pig, the bread of red wheat, beans, cheese, red wine and other heavy foods cause strong semen and bad temperament: the son that is conceived will have great strength, but will be wild and of animal wits. From this results that among men of the countryside it would be a miracle if one turned out to be of acute intelligence and prone to study, especially where such coarse foods are eaten. The opposite occurs among city-dwellers, whose sons we see have more intelligence and ability.[1]

Fortunately for the peasants of the plain and the *cacamarroni* (literally, 'chestnut-shitters') of the mountains, popular medicine was less poisonous and probably more effective than the medicine of the rich. Nevertheless, the most effective therapy – the diatetic – was as impracticable for one group as for the other. The poor of the city, in fact, were very often forced to devour foods that were 'fetid, putrid and verminous . . . [filled] even with mice, worms, snakes or other most disgusting and abominable animals'.[2]

The rich, on the contrary – of 'exacting stomach . . . insatiable beast', for whose delight it was necessary 'that the cooks wear themselves out more by studying than by the heat of the fire in order to tickle their appetites' – killed themselves at table, seduced by the 'shameful enchantment' and 'impostures' of the 'subtle philosophy of our gluttony'.[3] Excess on the one hand and privation on the other drew an impassable line between health and illness: the monstrously hypercaloric diets (7,000 to 8,000 calories daily) were just as deadly as those of the poor, chillingly inconsistent, who did not even manage to reach a minimum ceiling of 1,000 calories.

'Plenty' was the great absentee; rare were the days when songs could be sung to praise its return and the defeat of 'Famine' (a literary exercise as well, modelled on the very popular theme of the struggle between Carnival and Lent in which, as in all the forms deriving from folk rituals, archaic apotropaic virtues were obscurely presented). In 1597, Giulio Cesare Croce – after the good summer harvest which seemed to spell an end to the seven years of tribulations during which he himself had been heavily hit ('. . . the past scarcity, which not only shook the branches of my slender plant, but knocked to the ground much more solid and gnarled trees than mine, pulling them up from the roots') – exalted the return of plenty to Bologna, praising the vice-legate Orazio Spinola for his decisive and victorious intervention during the years of dearth. In the excited dialogue between Plenty and Famine, Spinola's intervention is described as fundamental to the safety of the community for which Croce presented himself as intermediary and spokesman: a bard assigned to the expression of the city's collective conscience. Victor at last, Plenty can let its ringing voice be heard:

The bread has grown in size, just as your insolence
   Had so lowered and diminished,
   That with difficulty its presence was seen;
And if it was black, badly cooked and, worse, dense,
   Now all the bakers have the order
   To make it good, white, large and with care;
And all the granaries are wide open
   And what was worth sixteen is now worth eight,
   So that misers hang themselves from the pain;
Bread is no longer seen on display
   Already spoiled, as it used to be,
   But bright as snow, and well-baked;
The bean, which sat on the throne,
   And which seemed like sugar to the artisans,
   Is now little appreciated or valued;
Now, in these plains, thanks to God,
   Goods abound, and all the countryside
   Produces abundant grains in great plenty;
Such that Bologna will once again
   Be glorious and great, and neither
   Will there ever be heard laments and complaints:
Never more will there be seen atop the dung-heap
   So many wretched, afflicted and lifeless people,
   Wrapped up in the straw and refuse;
In the future, they will be strong men,
   Proud and robust, they will gather vigour,
   Not weak and half-dead like before;
A healthy colour will return to their faces,
   Strength will be put back where it belongs,
   And natural warmth to its rightful state . . .[4]

This portrait painted by Plenty corresponds to the octaves of Girolamo Accolti, the 'Allegrezza de' poveri sopra il crescimento del pane'[5] ('Cheerfulness of the poor over the growth of the bread', in which is written 'Of wheat we have great plenty', octave 1,5), and 'Il gran lamento fatto da Nicolotto Fornar da Pesaro. Per non poter fare il pane piccolo e nero come prima. Con il grandissimo pianto della Carestia nell'uscir di Bologna'[6] ('The great lament made by Nicolotto Baker of Pesaro. Of not being able to make the bread small and black as before. With the very great weeping of Famine on leaving Bologna'. Newly composed by Alessandro de' Monti),

Since the bread has increased in size,
White and beautiful and even well-baked,
Fancy breads, twice baked,
And no one can be satisfied.
　　We poor bakers.
Scottish-style and side-table breads,
With the finest flour,
From evening to morning
We are forced to make . . . (fol. 1v.)
Even the husk and the pollard
Are not sold, but are thrown away . . . (fol. 2r.)

The bakers, much hated by the *poverelli* ('little poor') and singled out by everyone as profiteers and creators of hunger, frequently saw their shops attacked and plundered by the mob. Together with the usurers and tax collectors they were the first to face the popular fury, as in the attack on the oven of the Casse district of Bologna in August, 1677.

It was Taccon who, with six boys, started
　　the scuffle at the oven and frightened the court,
　　it was Tagliatella who unhinged the doors
　　of the baker's shop and caused such an uproar.
It was Mattarel who, with great efforts,
　　caused chaos, ransacked pitilessly,
　　and caused the death of the cavalryman
　　by throwing the mattresses from the balcony.
Blessed be the Borgo delle Casse
　　that dispensed flour to woman and children
　　without a porter bringing it to their doors.
If the wine-keg carrier had sounder help
　　he would catch in heaps in his keg
　　thirty or forty of these cuckolded peckers.[7]

Anonymous verses, obviously, created during the wave of plunder and motivated by a coarse and defiant enthusiasm, like a miniature popular epic, with the leaders of the revolt indicated by the nicknames by which they were known: 'Tagliatella' and 'Mattarel'; a laudatory sonnet put down in the heat of the action, in the rush of the sudden rebellion instigated by a keg carrier, already convicted, suspected of sodomy (Gherardo Tacconi was a carrier of wine kegs, who had been hiding for several months in the basilica of Santo Stefano, having already been condemned to exile), and also an example of a 'wild variant' on the sonnet of the classical tradition, a *sonetto-canaille* (or 'rabble-sonnet'), restated in pragmatic–popularistic terms.

The popular furore had entered some time ago into the 'museums' of realistic literature, whether it examined the immense reservoir of human activities and appearances with regard to trades and professions, or specialized in the typological analysis of the various faces of famine. In this excited atmosphere of social tensions, uprisings and looting, it is not surprising that G. B. Segni rifled a page by Garzoni (even more sensational plagiarism was committed with casual frequency during a century when copyright was an unknown expression), replacing it in a real-life scenario of social disorder and disintegration, even though it remains essentially an *exemplum*: a rhetorical model of the abstract theme of human frenzy.

Whoever would like to see the misery of this present famine and starvation in its most wretched form should go to certain cities and lands that are tyrannized, where the taxes could not be higher, and see bread put in the warehouses and storerooms which is as black as coal or as grey as a donkey's hide, and of such a mixture that even hearty eaters could not stand it, and so small it seems like the balls of *zarabottana*, and so expensive that those responsible are wished a thousand evils, and sold with such an appearance that it seems to come from the executioner's hand, and so often contested that clubs, daggers and pikes are necessary in order to possess it, and brought out in such low quantities that many poor families die from hardship and hunger, cursing the traitorous usurers, the villainous rich and the murderous tax-collectors who are to blame for such a wicked and cruel famine.

He would then hear all the people scream; he would see the common people rioting, with good reason; the poor crying into the wind; the peasants from outside claiming greater power; the hospitals filling up; the doors of the rich echoing with miserable voices; the square full of acts of rage; the warehouses and storerooms surrounded by calamitous and unhappy people; the earth crying out and the air sighing, the sky weeping for so much dearth and such an unbearable famine. He would witness many thefts, much stealing, much plundering of granaries, many virgins raped for a piece of bread; many husbands become voluntary scoundrels for a penny, that he would recognize as true the saying of Regnicolo Foretano, 'In times of famine due to lack of bread, there is no better foodstuff than human flesh.' What Quintilian also meant when he said 'Non habitant simul pudor et fames' ['Shame and hunger do not dwell together'].

He would see many rich people murdered, so much clashing of arms that everything would exhaust itself. The customs-houses would be ransacked, the warehouses emptied, the banks broken into, the bakers beaten or pilloried, or forced to walk the rope in public, or hanged by the neck, for behaving like gluttons and scoundrels.[8]

10
Medicina Pauperum

The strategy adopted by the political powers of the seventeenth century to prevent the tumultuous revolts of the very poor – the 'door-knocking' mendicants, the 'rabble who only eat and shit', the beggars 'born only to transform mouthfuls / into turds', like a 'putrid grub / oh, sordid slug' (after the 'most atrocious peasants' war . . . what would happen if we had to make war with the mendicants?', asked Baldissare Bonifacio in 1629) – and to prevent blind uprisings of beggars and the 'insolence of all the rabble', was clearly delineated by the second half of the sixteenth century. It consisted of expelling from the city mendicants coming from the countryside: peasants induced by hunger to pass the city walls and search for help in the 'city, where they somehow hoped to find a more human sustenance' (Manzoni). This was to be followed, immediately afterwards, by the internment of these so-called 'agrarian poor' in controlled areas. For the poor of the city this meant mass hospitalization in open hospices and the re-launching of the Congregation of Mendicants, so that with the birth of a small city of paupers inside the city the urban space was considerably modified.

The alarmed concern of the ruling classes and the Church, master *ab antiquo* of poor relief – a Church which in poverty had invested the maximum pietistic and theological capital – is presented, at least with regard to Bologna, in a page (referring to the year 1590) of Pompeo Vizani's, writer and 'gentleman' (much closer to the ruling groups than the Modenese chronicler Giovan Battista Spaccini), who with lively and informed attention described the cross borne by the lower classes:

The Regiment, desiring to provide for the necessities of the poor, ordered that the peasants, who had converged in great numbers to beg throughout the city, be sent away; and that every day in different designated places in the countryside there be dispensed four ounces of rice [an even scantier ration than the hunger rations so frequent today in South-East Asia] for each of them, so that they could defend themselves from hunger until spring arrived. And then they had the curates of the parishes give them in writing all the most wretched poor of the city, and had drawn up in a list up to ten thousand people. It was decided to maintain them with great piety for eight months, that is, until the next harvest. And because they had made a good provision of wheat, beans and other various kinds of pulses, it was ordered that they be given, for those who showed a certain copper token as a sign, four loaves of bread made of one-third wheat and two-thirds other kinds of corns and pulses ['black bread of commoners . . . of rogues and peasants', wrote Tommaso Garzoni during those years]. And it was likewise ordered that an infinite number of poor creatures, who, because of the hardship suffered and hunger, find themselves sick and weak, be gathered together and looked after, with an infinite increase in the number of beds, not only in the hospitals where the sick were already cared for, but also for those places allocated for the lodging of pilgrims and in many others that – since those already in existence could not satisfy the need – were then put in order for that purpose only, inside as well as outside the city.[1]

When they could, the peasants of Emilia fled from their fields and migrated to the lands beyond the Po River: 'because it is said that there the loaves of bread are big'. 'They left with all their things and family members, and went to settle in Lombardy, and most of them around Pavia, because it is said that they prepare *gnocchi* covered with cheese, spices and butter; that they hoe in May, and furthermore, that they tie their vines with yellow sausage . . .'[2] So noted with sarcasm and irony the Modenese chronicler Tomasino de' Bianchi, who did not believe in the image of Lombardy as 'the land of promises', the land of plenty just beyond the Po, or in the dream of the 'big bread' and the well-seasoned *gnocchi*, which one does not know whether to attribute to the visionary imagination of the starving peasants that induced them to leave in search of the phantom-bread, or to the sarcasm of the urban chronicler who makes fun of the wondrous inventions of the undernourished masses. The sarcasm of the chronicler was justified. Bread and peace were rare and unreliable goods for all, and in particular for those most at risk, in the countryside. The waves of fugitives belonged to a habitual human landscape. Even in Lombardy, naturally, people fled. In 1483 – one case among the many – thousands of these dispersed peasants passed through Florence on their way south.

109

And during this time, for fear of hunger and the great war in Lombardy, many families left from there. Many families passed through here and were heading for Rome fifty or one hundred at a time, so that they made up several thousand people; and many of them also passed through Romagna and other lands. It is said that there were more than thirty thousand people.

It caused great compassion to see so much poverty pass by: with their haggard donkey, wretched little cooking pot, pan and other similar miseries, so that they caused those to weep who saw them, shoeless and without clothes.[3]

The war distributed famine and misery with great generosity. Over the Apennines an observer from Cesena, less easily moved than the pious spice merchant Luca Landucci, noted that 'the famine was very harsh this year [1483] in Romagna and Lombardy because of the said wars. Around 1,200 families left Lombardy in this year because of hunger and went to the Marches.'[4] In that same dark year, Giuliano Fantaguzzi indicated in his *Occhurentie et Nove* that 'because of the famine, the outsiders and the poor from Rimini, Cesena, Ravenna, Faenza and Cervia were sent away, and many of them died of hunger'.[5] The immune defences of the towns and cities forced out of the social fibre all outsiders, those not integrated and those on the margins of society. Vagabonds and 'poveri homini' – when they had died – were once again tossed over the margins: their corpses were given burial outside the city boundaries, beyond the walls.

The 'food assistance' during the 'tightest and leanest'[6] times, and the 'dietary materials'[7] (as expressed by Ovidio Montalbani in his shrouded and whimsical language), devised by an ultramillenial practice geared to the meanest and most difficult survival, included a vast range of wheat surrogates invented in order to produce that foodstuff which constituted the 'principal foundation of nutrition, and the chief grain in the conservation of life, bread', as Nicolò Serpetro wrote in *Il mercato delle meraviglie della natura, overo istoria naturale* (1653).[8] Human ingenuity was indulged in the infinite variations and innumerable combinations of ingredients involved in 'bread-making': from the 'prescriptions' of Giambattista Della Porta's *Magia naturalis* ('in which ways various types of bread can be made', 'various types of bread made from roots and fruits', and 'on how to make varieties of bread from grains and pulses'),[9] to the 'secrets' revealed by Giovan Battista Segni in the *Discorso sopra la carestia, e fame* (1591) and the *Trattato sopra la carestia e fame* (1602), to the eighteenth-century works of Giovanni Targioni Tozzetti, the *Istruzione . . . circa le varie maniere d'accrescere il pane con l'uso d'alcune sostanze vegetabili* (1767) and the *Alimurgia o sia modo di rendere meno gravi le carestie proposto per sollievo dei poveri* (1767), and to Saverio Manetti's 'memoir', *Delle specie diverse di frumento e di pane* . . . (1766).

The following made up the incredible reservoir of ingredients that – boiled, dried, crushed, sifted, reduced to a flour and variously mixed – could become an uncertain and approximate form of bread, vaguely resembling that of wheat: water brambles, acorns (from which was also extracted oil for dietary use, a process which persisted until the first decades of this century with beechnuts), turnips, dog grass, lupins, parsnips, wild radishes, pine-nuts, fir seeds, laurel berries, wild asparagus, hazelnuts, sorb-apples, pumpkins, elm leaves, broad beans, various pulses (not to mention the mixtures of inferior cereals like millet, 'panic grass', rye, barley, vetch and sorghum), and in general, all the 'most harmless and tasty roots'.[10]

Along with the *medicina pauperum*, one can imagine a cuisine of the poor: both useful in locating 'easier materials and of lesser cost, just as good and efficacious as the most precious', as authoritatively advised the 'Gratianesque' doctor Ovidio Montalbani,[11] versatile and polymorphic palace intellectual, who also held the office of 'Tribune of Commoners' in Bologna.

'Regularly shared food' and 'medicines proportionately distributed',[12] together with the balanced joining of 'pharmaceuticals' and 'dietetic formulas', would have resulted in a 'more fruitful economic artifice', monetary savings and rationalization of the city's resources, according to the opinion of Montalbani. Dietetics and pharmacology had to work in close collaboration, giving preference to local products rather than 'foreign ingredients'. The earth – the 'Great Mother of Life' – had thought of this too, sagaciously distributing its antidotes within reach of everyone, without needing to have recourse to the 'great forest of foreign medicaments'.

A programme of municipal autarky, leaning towards the saving of 'coined metal, which must not be squandered rashly'; the only exception being senna, a herb of multiple prodigious virtues, which inspired the unconditional and raving admiration of Montalbani:

a most simple medicinal herb, very liberal of itself both for its great plenty and for its very low price, and yet as greatly beneficent and healthy as the others. Discovered in the world not more than six hundred years ago, and therefore unknown to Hippocrates, Galen, Avicenna, Theophrastes and the other ancients, the miraculous efficacies of which are well known by all the learned . . . This herb . . . cleans, expurgates and digests the dried excrements,

111

extracted from as far as the brain and all sensory organs, as also from the regions of the heart, lungs, liver and spleen, helping greatly in the aches of those parts. It is not a little contrary to melancholy and obstinate fevers and obstructions, as mother of the happiness and prosperity of the entire body, to the point that the Arab Serapione commended it as a sedative for delirium, calmer of agitations of the mind and healer of shaken nerves, scaly, itchy and pimply scabies, and of epilepsy; and finally, very friendly towards our vital principles. Nor do they finish here the praises and honours for such a desirable plant, the very great gift of Divine Mercy . . .[13]

It 'extinguishes the choleric fires and drives away mucous laziness'. 'Every scabious, serpiginous and elephantine impurity, however large it may be, is swept away by senna'; it expels the 'morbific materials'. 'Erba sena, sana' ('the senna herb heals').

This eighteenth-century pharmacology produces a skilfully delirious prose, drugged by the penetrating aromas of the spice vendors' dark workshops. Even the frenetic love for senna was stimulated by one of the many toxicological deliria of the period.

The *Formolario economico cibario, e medicinale di materie più facili, e di minor costo altrettanto buone, e valevoli, quanto le più pretiose* (1654), dedicated by Montalbani to the 'Most Illustrious Congregation Next to the Government of the Most Merciful Institute of Poor Mendicants of Bologna', serves as a glimpse at the pharmacopoeia of the poor – used to cure the most wretched levels of the Bolognese population and, in particular, the mendicants – in a brief sampling of a magical pharmacology that leads to the witches' laboratory.

The collection of remedies, 'hospital decoctions and infusions', antidotes, powders, oils and amulets, opens with praise for the very economical senna and a recipe for the 'way of making nutritious and healthy bread in times of the greatest wheat famine, with an increase of 100 per 30 and more still'. It was offered to the 'economical President' and Treasurer entrusted with the 'conservation' of the 'very vast place' and 'unendingly ample Hospital for Poor Mendicants'. To the 'maximum theriac of the poor', immediately active in all its substance against every poison and malign quality' goes the place of honour, followed by the 'little theriac of the poor', 'juniperine apples', made from the 'berries of mature juniper plants, from which is extracted by pressing the juice to be condensed in the sun'. Nor could a 'hypnotic cooling electuary' be absent, made from poppy and lettuce seeds and syrup, which would 'induce sleep and assist in the vehement ardours of fevers'; an 'asthmatic electuary' ('proven and secret of the poor'), and a 'safflower syrup' (safflower seeds), similar to that described by Jean Provost ('Prevozio' in Italy) 'in the book *De medicina pauperum*'.

The miseries of the beggars and the torments of their scarred and ravaged flesh can be understood by examining this mid-seventeenth-century prescription book, abounding – for the present post-Victorian taste – with disgusting filth. The 'vagabond's disease decoction' was meant to combat lice, 'animals most harmful to man', by washing 'all the parts of the body from which excrements are generated'. The 'altheric decoction' was used several times a day to clean a 'head afflicted with ringworm'. To the plaster used to treat 'people injected with this filth' others added pigeon droppings. And a 'healing water or decoction' was prescibed against 'malign ulcers, especially of the legs, wolf sickness, cancer'.

A 'restorative juleb' was used 'wonderfully and very quickly to restore lost strength'; 'lung ulcers' were fought with 'pulmonary syrup'; and plasters of ivy were used in the attempt 'to heal tumours of every sort'.

Melancholic afflictions, depressive syndromes of the poor and their 'scummy humours' were treated with 'hellebore pills'; the gloomiest melancholy and the 'darkest humours, troubling even the speech' were repressed with an 'anti-biliary electuary'; and with an 'anti-biliary oxymel' one could purge 'efficaciously melancholy and phlegm of the head'. A particular oil was reserved for lepers. For the 'delirious', the so-called 'oil of seven flowers' was used; and for scrofula sufferers, 'goitre oil': a mixture made from 'living rats, recently born, that is, without skin, and small lizards . . . suffocated and ground up, exposed to the sun on dog days'. There were perfumes against deafness, anti-venereal perfumes, perfumes for 'hopeless fluxes' and 'intestinal hernias'; ointments for scabies, chronic fevers and burns; powders against gout and stones ('Prescription: powder of millipedes, in other words, those little animals vulgarly called woodlice which are found under earthenware vases . . .'). A powder was made with a 'large living toad and several living shrimp . . . to be roasted in the oven in a glazed cooking-pot', against 'cancers particularly of the breasts . . . miserable disease'; oil of 'frogs and earthworms, boiled . . . to soothe the pains of joints, nerves, and for wounds, punctures and malign ulcers'; 'syncopal plaster . . . to apply above the right breast, to re-awaken lulled strength'. St Basil's plaster, made of hemlock, was 'applied above the uterus or above the genitals for uterine furies [nymphomania] or satyriasis, since it extinguishes every venereal fire'; 'destructive plaster . . . to place above the hardest tumours to make them mature and break'; and 'fistula plaster . . . for fistulated ulcers'.

Then came the gallery of amulets: the one against the swelling (tumour) and pain of haemorrhoids, consisting of the 'green roots of dropwort worn so that they touch the flesh and dry up on it: the secret of a certain Sicilian doctor who practised it in Rome'. There was 'vervain herb worn from the neck, on the head and on the joints' for chronic head pains and those of gout; and vipers' heads 'which have been strangled with a lace of crimson silk. These, after having been well dried and replaced inside a crimson headdress, must be worn from the neck', in order to dispel angina, the *scaranzia*. Against quartan fever: 'Prescription: a living spider enclosed in a hazlenut worn from the neck. Likewise, several worms that hide in the herb *dissaco* or Venus's lip, namely dyeing sedge, which must be tied up in a little piece of this cloth and worn from the neck of the quartan ague sufferer, will work wonders.'

These were the pharmacological tools which were used against the most widespread diseases in one of Europe's most learned cities during the mid-seventeenth century. 'Secrets' and amulets that from times beyond probing, popular culture and medicine had practised and which continued to be reproposed by official medicine: insistent nevertheless in requiring severe sanctions against those who exercised the 'art' without permission, like the charlatans. The invention of printing, contrary to the prophecy of Leonardo Fioravanti, had not in any way given new instruments of control to the lower classes (at least in the brief middle period); instead, it had accentuated the cultural imbalances rather than alleviate them. The ignorant doctors continued to judge as in the past, 'out of stupidity and vileness', and the 'kittens' had not yet begun to open their eyes:

> Since this blessed printing has come to light, books of every type have multiplied so that everyone can study, and even more so because most are printed in our mother tongue: and so the kittens have opened their eyes, because each person can see and understand on his own, with the result that we other doctors can no longer corruptly chase the people as did our earliest predecessors, who made the sick believe that donkeys could fly.[14]

Almost a century after Fioravanti's over-optimistic dream, the poor of Bologna continued to wander about with spiders and vipers' heads hanging from their necks. The invention of printing had given free rein to the most savage charlatanism, and the 'science of medicine' had arrived 'little by little . . . at the bordello'.[15]

11

'Tightness of Purse'

In years of great economic depression, during which the agrarian humour of the *Compagnia della Lesina* (literally, 'Company of Stinginess') had codified a style of life that many people had to observe from stark necessity, there continually surfaced the warning voice of Parco, who saw in man 'the blindest of all the animals . . . an insatiable fury, a mathematical body without points, raw material without power, and finally, beast of burden with no control'.[1] In fact, in his great imperfection, contrary to the animals (in a parody of Ficino's *homo quidam deus*, or man as a reflection of the divine), man had to clothe and warm himself, find shelter and eat. Therefore, 'Since privation is not only a principle, but the cause of our every delight . . . it must be joined with parsimony in all things'[2] and, naturally, with Temperance, justly interpreting the hidden laws of nature, 'which also gave man two ears, two eyes, two nostrils and two hands, and only one mouth, so that he might hear a lot, see much, breathe and touch plenty, and speak and eat little: as in, "Shut the mouth, and despite the rumbling keep the buttocks closed" '.[3]

The animal emblematic of the idealized perfection of 'stinginess' was the chameleon: 'I should say that man must nourish himself with air, in the manner of the chameleon, since breathing is the source of life, and one breathes by reason of the air: who does not know that air has the role of nourishing . . .?'[4] This eater of air, citizen of the 'noble City of Parsimony', populated by the 'shyest, stingiest and especially most blundering gentlemen'[5] – who save not only on eating (one egg per family), but also on clothes, footwear and heating – is the perfect satirical opposite of the citizen of the ideal city: a parody of the happy islands of the sixteenth-century utopian reformers, of the City of the Sun and the wise and just communities, since 'whoever is not stingy', wrote Giulio Cesare

Croce, 'cannot amass goods'.[6] It was a city of avid maniacal bourgeois accumulators, brought up in the techniques of saving according to 'guild principles', in which the 'master' passed on to the 'novices' the secrets of the art (of making do); whose 'articles' had 'to be inviolably observed by all the brothers', even in wifely matters, since

> If you can stay chaste it is better: but if you want a wife and cannot do without one, whence that Roman called her 'a necessary evil', take a small one so as not to have to spend even to dress her, and so as to make the mattresses, sheets and bedcovers with which to cover her smaller, if the size of the dowry should not, like a gleam, check the darkness in this respect.[7]

It was a city where even the nuptial banquet was celebrated under the direction of 'Our Lady of Parsimony, bestower';[8] where Master Tiratutto Gaffatosto (literally, 'Stretch-all Quick-blunder'), in a generous mood, could afford to lend Rampino, servant of Our Lady of Stinginess, 'a plum stone to suck on in order to quench his thirst' (on the agreement, however, that he give it back),[9] or invite him to his house to 'sniff a quince'.[10] A city of 'the dullest and most niggardly' men,[11] well described onomastically too: like Pitocco Rastrelli, Coticone de' Coticoni, Tanghero Villani, Lesiniero Finetti, Uncinato degli Uncinati, Brancazio Spilorcioni, Quomodocumque, Taccagnino da Carpi, Tiraquello Rasponi, Truffaldino da Graffignano, Gabbinio de' Gabbini, Semprecarpi, Brancailtutto, Prestaniente, Taccagna, Sottile, Formicone, Mettintasca, Pignastretto, Scorticante, Carpione, Aprilocchio, Gramignante and Stringiforte, all masters of a certified 'conscience of stinginess'.[12] In the case of illness, an article of the Company ordered that

> when one of the brothers becomes ill, do not suddenly send for the doctor, so as not to inconvenience him, but wait six or eight days, following a good diet during that time, to see how the illness proceeds. You could nevertheless let the Lord Inspectors of the Company know of his illness, and they will not be lacking in their service; and it would not be a great event that with this good warning and detention, this brother, without spending a penny, was freed of the disease, as has happened many other times, and like this: 'Rest in peace.'[13]

With extreme ease this conscience of stinginess made use of an knowledge of 'snatching', astutely roguish, borrowing from the world of knaves and scoundrels, the tricks, expedients and techniques that belonged to the repertoire of the art of hunger, great inventor of swindling subtleties. In the manuscript *Galeria de Lesinanti* (or 'Gallery of Misers') almost the entire Italy of hardship is emblematically portrayed by the most close-fisted figures: besides a Bolognese doctor (Master Gramignante, or 'Weeding') and a baker (Master Sottile da Pisa, or 'Sharper of Pisa'), there appear a 'Milanese alchemist' (Master Grifagno, or 'Rapacious'), a cloth merchant from Gattinara (Master Anurino, or 'Anurine'), a 'false mendicant' (Master Corriadoni de Trabacchi, or 'Street-beggar'), and so on.

The inventions used 'to thicken the broth' – to do the shopping without paying, to steal the cheese with dexterity, to assemble the vegetables without spending a penny – shed light on a starving and picaresque Italy, inhabited by people who, with 'marvellous ingenuity', worried about getting by at the expense of others. The mirror of an impoverished society where ingenuity (even criminal and fraudulent) was a necessary artifice in the hard struggle to survive. Out of this situation emerge pages where this daily improvization is transformed into roguish comedy, performed under the masks of misers, such as the 'Veronese pedant known as Master Vadibene ('Go-well')': it is a prefiguration of the 'school-nightmare', that temple of youthful hunger, diabolically run by the ineffable Doctor Capra, in the *Historia de la vita del buscón llamado Don Pablo ejemplo de vagabundos y espejo de tacaños*. In the comedy Coticone de' Coticoni describes the Veronese pedant:

Coticone: This man not only kept boys at school but as boarders too, and he had many and was well paid by them. Now, Master Vadibene, knowing that boys are always hungry, since they never snack or breakfast, thought of filling their stomachs at lunch, and he served food that had to be digested, since every time he bought a belly of an old ox, he had it cooked so little that it could not be quickly digested, and as a result their appetite did not return between meals. And if someone complained that it was not cooked, he responded that meat should be like this, saying in French 'fish cooked and meat raw'. But first he had it filled with carefully ground herbs, then he cut it rib by rib from one tip to another as one would do with a melon or pumpkin, and one slice he would give to four boys, saying, 'boys, notice my generosity, for I could take out the bone, and yet I leave it for you so that you can linger; besides, this piece of food represents a globe for you, since in eating you can still feed your intellects'.

Rastellante: In what manner could an ox-rib resemble a globe?

117

Coticone: In this way. He would say: 'You see, boys, the bone of this rib is the height of the world, these membranes wrapped around the bone are the two tropics, this strip of skin that encircles the insides is the equator, these nerves are the other zones, the insides are the core, and the zodiac which touches both tropics where the solstices are found you could say is the meat attached to the membranes'.[14]

A burlesque phase in Giulio Cesare Croce's work, represented by *La vera regola per mantenersi magro con pochissima spesa*,[15] becomes a fitting element in the climate of penury (or of dearth) during perhaps the most difficult and miserable years which Bologna had ever known. The 'science of saving',[16] and the sublime ideal of fasting that reaches as far as the heroic theology of non-generation, also indicate a palaeo-bourgeois form of accumulation founded not on the expropriation of other social groups, but on the privation, abstinence and fraud necessary to gather, conserve and increase those 'goods which are acquired with much hardship and sweat'.[17]

> Don't boast of having too many talents,
> But always act the poor man, and the beggar
> So that people won't bump you off.[18]

So warned Croce, mindful of the Company's decisive admonition which prescribed that the wise householder 'with just and honourable industry, thinks, attempts, tries and proceeds to make himself rich' simulating limited means and poverty in order to escape 'every sort of trap and deceit' set up by 'a large number of begging and lazy men'. 'Rather, that with all ingenuity, he should take the opportunity, in public and in private, to complain of his misfortune, misery and calamity: this is said so that neither thieves, sharpers, suppliers, pimps, vagabonds, failed relatives, nor police, court, spies, hypocrites or greedy men will have designs on you'.[19]

The attempts to substitute herbs for wheat flour could not but be praised by the misers' bible. In fact, herein lies the proposal of a Viceroy of Naples – never realized – to have bread made which was 'mixed from certain roots reduced to a powder, of an herb that is found in abundance, so that grain, being much less consumed, would greatly abound'.

> But those people completely opposed to our praiseworthy profession, instead of recognizing its notable benefit and being thankful for it, began to be recalcitrant and cause an uproar, so that the Viceroy imposed silence and waited patiently. Then he thought, if matters went well, how advantageous it would be to both sides: to

him infinite earning and to the people inestimable saving and abundance. Since by having that bread, exceedingly bitter and displeasing, less of it would have been eaten, and so it could have been made bigger and cheaper. But the insatiable squanderers, used to swimming in fat, did not want to listen.[20]

Although the Company cruelly joked about it in this way, for the 'insatiable squanderers, used to swimming in fat' (the famished urban poor and the undernourished peasants) the 'bigger' bread was a dramatically urgent dream that, as we have already seen, forced the rural folk into a search that was problematic – not to mention dream-like – for the large, white, good loaf of bread.

The poor of the South certainly did not need the improbable suggestions of a viceroy in order to attempt survival by means of an artificial bread, a bitter surrogate of blended ingredients that constituted the norm for the country and mountain population (inferior cereals, broad beans, acorns, chestnuts, and so on), because such mixtures in the bread of the poor was widespread even in less troubled times. Persecuted 'by a morbid and tiresome hunger', as the witnesses to the terrible Neapolitan, or more generally, southern Italian famine of 1764 narrated, they attempted to survive by having recourse to desperate deceits ('with every most abominable method and evil art they took away the necessary food from whoever was languishing'), all the same ending up 'lying in abject poverty on the bare earth; visions of emaciated sadness, ragged and breathing wretchedness'.[21]

12

Collective Vertigo

The hierarchy of breads and their qualities in reality sanctioned social distinctions. Bread represented a status symbol that defined human condition and class according to its particular colour, varying in all shades from black to white; that is, before the introduction of maize to breadmaking, which modified – with regard to colour as well – the tyranny of cereals that for thousands of years had persisted among the populations of the West and of all those lands where grain constituted the primary foodstuff.

In a society such as that in Italy, substantially without dietary taboos, nourishment represented a socio-economic (not to mention political) rather than cultural fact. One does not hear of people preferring to let themselves die rather than touch forbidden foods. If anything, it is possible to measure the seriousness of famines by the food substitutes which people allowed themselves to bring to their mouths. Everything, as we have seen: even the most incredible and repugnant substances.

The eaters of bean bread (the people of the countryside) were socially inferior to (and different from) the consumers of wheat bread (the people of the city). The age-old city–country conflict was also represented *sub specie alimentaria*, resurrecting the hostility between peasants and city-dwellers and the permanent guerrilla war, in a sort of food-supply variation on the satire against the peasant which reached a temporary armistice only in time of famine.

'I reside in the cities,' indignantly retorts the 'wheat bread' in Giulio Cesare Croce's *Contrasto*, which takes its title from the dietary disagreement between the two types of bread. The wheat bread thus refuses the help of the 'bean bread': 'brownish' in colour, nourishment for the 'wretched' and 'humble poor', 'coarse to the palate' and digested with difficulty, but more 'sweet, and flavoured' than wheat bread.

Thus go back to dwelling in your lairs,
    Since I don't pay heed to such help,
    Your forces being weak and vain.
In your appearance you are so dark,
    That everyone flees from you, being by nature
    Wretched to digest, coarse and hard . . .
And whoever still persists in tasting you,
    For three days seems to have a rock on his chest,
    So much does your food irritate and harden.
And in passing through, and dropping out below,
    He who knows says so, whether or not there is suffering,
    And if one remains weak and weary.
And, nevertheless, I return to you to repeat
    That you go back outside, among the peasants,
    For you don't belong in an urban place.[1]

Necessity none the less forces the proud city bread to put aside its aristocratic arrogance and accept the (temporary) help of the county bread after the latter promises to return to its lands whence it had generously come running to the assistance of the city-dwellers, once the emergency is over.

Wheat bread:
    . . . I know in truth, that the dearth
    Of the bad harvests was the fact
    That caused you to run with such fury.
And yet until the new season
    We shall remain together in perfect love,
    Perhaps the grain harvest will be better.
Bean bread:
I promise you to remain within my borders,
    And come no more to mix with you,
    Because I feel much better among the peasants.
The peasants know how to knead me better,
    Nor are they like your bakers
    Who can't wait to mangle me.
They, instead, make me big, fat, round and even . . .[2]

The scarcity of precious grains resulted in bread-making that paid little attention to the quality of the mixtures, into which entered grasses with stupefying seeds such as darnel, and a related variety, known in the Bologna region as *ghiottone* (literally, 'glutton'), and elsewhere as *gittone* or *ghittone*, a herb with black grains, used as forage or feed for chickens and capons, for whom, rather than being harmful, it sped up the fattening. 'The bread that has this [darnel] in it, besides disturbing the mind by making people act as if drunk, causes much weariness and nausea'.[3] Vetch grains, which produced melancholic humours, also often found their way into the blends. However, it often occurred that its seed pods, like those of the broad bean, had not even ripened. As Pietro Andrea Mattioli recounted:

> The peasants lay out the pods together with the whole plant for the livestock, although I have sometimes known those who, because of hunger, have eaten the seed in spring still unripe in the pods, as it is the custom to eat broad beans and chick peas. But in reality, not only are these seeds disagreeable to the taste, but difficult to digest and constricting for the body.[4]

One of the side-effects of famine, which has not been paid its necessary due, was a surprising fall in the level of mental health, already organically precarious and tottering, since even in times of 'normality' half-wits, idiots and cretins constituted a dense and omnipresent human fauna (every village or hamlet, even the tiniest, had its fool). The poor sustenance aggravated a biological deficiency and psychological equilibrium already profoundly compromised (syphilis, alcoholism, etc.) and visibly deteriorated. If the devastating effects (beginning around the middle of the eighteenth century) of pellagra on mental equilibrium and the damage caused by a maize-based mono-alimentation are recognized, the effects produced by estranging and stupefying herbs and grains unknown, or almost unmentioned. The phenomenon appears extraordinary and in many ways upsetting. It is as if a spell had been placed on entire communities, bewitching and benumbing them; as if the masses had become victims of a colossal somnolent vertigo induced by a drugging herb growing wild in the countryside, victims of a collective stupefaction that – even if temporary – resulted in their deserting work and habitual occupations. Unsuspected artificial paradises were opened up to the undernourished and the starving: the sleeping, dreaming, torpor, relaxing and incoherence of the bodily functions took hold of whole strata of the population, not only the marginal, but the active and productive. If the absenteeism in the workshops and in the silk and hemp manufactories is not quantitively demonstrable, indications and examples are nevertheless sufficient to initiate research into a new controversy of great topical interest. It is as disconcerting to come up against a society not far away in time, and very close in space, extensively enveloped in a narcosis induced by adulterated bread, as it is to discover the world of the urban workers subjected to frenzies or torpors. These were even more frequent in the countryside, especially in the lowlands where the cultivation of hemp, in all its various phases – from field to maceration and the domestic spinning machine, producing aphrodisiacal effects – helped to feed an agrarian sensuality of which the mechanization of the countryside has erased every trace.

The effects of darnel (the French *ivraie*, from the apparent etymology *ivre* or 'drunk'), blended in excessive quantities with grain, have been known from the most remote times. The result was a 'dazed' bread (the term is Croce's) with devastating consequences, well known to botanists and herbalists.

> The bread, which has significant quantities [of darnel] in it, causes men who eat it to become dazed and like drunkards, taken by a deep drowsiness, and yet we in Tuscany [these are the considerations of Mattioli from Siena] extract the darnel from the corn with great diligence, in order to escape the harm that it causes to the head, intoxicating and causing sleep.[5]

When bread was made in this desperate way with the most impure and heterogeneous mixtures, every pernicious adventure was possible, and the 'evil' darnel, 'often causes people to beat their heads / against walls'.[6]

The masses of the pre-industrial era – suffering from protein and vitamin deficiencies, poorly protected from the attacks of infectious diseases by precarious and inadequate diets, tormented by shingles (particularly widespread in the areas of rye consumption), subjected to sudden attacks of convulsions and epilepsy, the deliria of fevers, the festering of wounds, ulcers which ate away at the tissues, unrelenting gangrene and disgusting scrofula, the crazed patterns of 'St Vitus's dance' and other choreographic epidemics, and the constant nightmare of worms and choleric diarrhoea – also suffered the harmful effects of 'ignoble' breads (Mattioli), the toxic deliria of impure flour mixtures, and the stunning, demented stupidity and dullness of food poisoning. A hallucinating scenario, in which the feeble-minded and demented, the insane and the frenzied, 'dazed' and 'drugged', the chronic and temporary drunkards, tipsy on wine or – most incredibly – on bread, wandered about alongside cripples, the blind, scrofula sufferers, fistulates, those with sores or ringworm, the maimed, the emaciated, those with goitre, abdominal pains and dropsy.

Hallucinogenic and sleeping drugs derived from the poppy – distilled opiates, rough and dangerous, used as sedatives and pain-killers in the medicine of the poor – and hemp pollen or fibre (the peasants of the Emilia and Romagna lowlands lived in a close, familiar symbiosis with this plant), outline a dramatic human landscape: delirious or catatonic,

123

inert or epileptic, castigated by the conscious or involuntary use of drugs and toxic products.

Even the youngest children were not exempt from this tide of narcotics. The anonymous author of the *Istruzioni mediche per le genti di campagna* wrote:

> When children appear a little restless, when they do not sleep, and when it is a comfort to mothers and wet-nurses, there is the custom of having quick recourse to remedies that put the children to sleep. Once this usage has been adopted, the boiled poppy mixture will be given to them for every little complaint, and this remedy becomes almost habitual. It is therefore necessary to warn such people that the over-frequent use of sleeping drugs is quite harmful. Medical observations teach us that the most robust people, because of the too-frequent use of these remedies, contract a weakness, and sometimes a paralysis of the limbs, and a sterility of the spirit.[7]

This was a custom practised for quite some time, recorded in the *Erbolario volgare* as well: 'Some give poppy powder mixed with milk to the children so that they sleep better'.[8]

Herbalists, spice-vendors, apothecaries, druggists and alchemists paid close attention to the collection, distillation and manipulation in infusions and decoctions of the herbs of which the *donnicciuole* ('humble women') of the countryside were just as wise and knowledgeable experts. From opium, used to deaden pains, calm coughs and induce sleep, to other stupefying and drugging herbs such as henbane: powerful in causing one 'to sleep and rave',[9] known also as the 'Apollonian herb' because of its hallucinatory and visionary properties, arouser of prophetic spirits, frightening dreams and terrifying nightmares; black nightshade, whose root, drunk in wine in the measure of one dram, 'deceptively presents images of really joyous things to the intellect, while a doubling of the weight causes others to remain in ecstasy for three days';[10] and 'deadly nightshade' (or dwale), which 'by the eating of its fruit, causes men to become crazy and wild, and similar to those possessed'.[11] The vegetable kingdom offered its green deliria to the people and to those particular experts on nature's secrets who were present in the great 'pharmaceutical theatre', with the slyness of the alchemist and the measured shrewdness of the druggist, master of the knowledge that made up the great 'dispensary or pharmacopoeia', and learned manipulator of the science of herbs, 'occult virtues', precious stones and 'secret herbs' (as Osvaldus Crollius wrote in the *Tractatus de signaturis internis rerum*).[12] It cannot even be ruled out, as has been thought, that witchcraft itself was linked to hallucinatory processes reached by the use of certain herbs (the 'witches' herb', or deadly nightshade, foxglove, the herb of folly, and thorn-apple, known in France by the name *herbe aux sorciers* or *herbe des démoniaques*), while the relationship between witchcraft, undernourishment and hunger goes without saying (and the 'madman' Girolamo Cardano guessed it). In the chapter dedicated to the *striges seu lamiae* ('witches or soceresses'), the great Lombardy doctor traced an identikit of the witch that corresponds to the appearance of a poor old woman, malnourished and maniacally absorbed in moody hallucinations:

> There are these little women, wretched, living in valleys on herbs and wild vegetables, and if there are no intestines around, they cannot live at all. So, being decidedly thin, deformed, with eyes discharging, pale, and rather indistinct, with their black bile and melancholy they display a strange intuition. They are taciturn and dazed, and they hardly differ from those who are thought to be possessed by the devil; fixed in their thoughts . . . What is affecting them, however, is the sickness of black bile, plus the getting of food, lack of money, not to mention the very shape and likeness of the face and body, plus the words themselves of folly . . .[13]

From the world of hunger, privation and frustration, in the illusory attempt to compensate for existential alienation, there spring herbs with upsetting effects, diffused hallucinogenic techniques, dream manipulations, fantasies overexcited by myths, fables and stories filled with wonders; voyages into the supernatural, imaginary cosmographies, lands and kingdoms made of the same material with which dreams are made, such as the Delian paradise, the Land of Cockaigne and the islands of bliss; visionary fantasies, millenaristic hallucinations, religious fables and demented stammerings; the sublimation of the idiot and the respect/terror for the madman; witches herb distillations with strange powers, philtres and spells; goblins and werewolves, 'lizards', fairies and 'queens of the game'; Morgana and Mayglory, Queen Mab, Harlequin and his gang, the incubi and succubi, enchanters, sorcerers and soothsayers, the nostalgic recalling of the mass orgy and the great banquet of the witches' sabbath; cannibalism and vampirism, the nocturnal flight and gathering of witches; and the collective demonic and nocturnal fancy of the generations belonging to the pre-industrial era.

The most effective and upsetting drug, bitterest and most ferocious, has always been hunger, creator of unfathomable disturbances of mind and imagination. Further lifelike and convincing dreams grew out of this forced hallucination, compensating for the everyday poverty, the bleak view point of reason and the continual outrages prepetrated on miserable existences and infantile personalities by psychic diseases characterized by convulsive and hysterical tendencies, typical of a society crushed by the weight of the social pyramid's layers, unchangeable by command of divine law and royal will. The deliria, hallucinations and frenzies experienced by the protagonist of Knut Hamsun's autobiographical novel *Hunger* (1899) can help us to understand what the mental health of the *ancien régime*'s starving people might have been.

By conquering hunger (at least temporarily), Western society has destroyed the reservoir of dreams which nourished that broadening of conscience, fundamentally irrational and visionary, which certain North American Indian tribes often used to reach by fasting, even before the use of mescaline. With the prohibition of hallucinogenic herbs they have been deprived of the advantages of a 'fundamentally visionary image of the world',[14] as well as the features of a consciousness and a science which differ from those – in one dimension only – of reason.

'Dazed' bread also gave its contribution to the voyage to *Lubberland* in the 'Land of Folly':

. . . whoever eats you, then, remains
In much distress, so that he well and often goes crazy,
So overburdened is he with misfortune.[15]

No longer fit to work, staggering and stupefied, the labourer, workman or apprentice had to abandon the shop for his bed, to sleep at length, pursuing his fantastic dreams generated by the bread which intoxicated him and caused the loss of his wits.

The paralysing and narcotizing effects of this adulterated bread are effectively described in the exchange of sallies between a 'master' and 'shop-boy' in the *Dialogo fra un Maestro e un garzone sopra il pane alloiato* by Giulio Cesare Croce:

Master:	What's the matter, that you're not working, you clumsy oaf?
Shop-boy:	My dear master, I cannot work.
Master:	Why not?
Shop-boy:	Because I feel my head going round like a whirl.
Master:	Are you perhaps wearing a ship's shadow: why do I see you all a-staggering?
Shop-boy:	Oh, were it so, that I could give up half a wage and have all my senses.
Master:	So what's the matter, that your eyes are so changed?
Shop-boy:	Now don't you see, that if I am shaking so much it's because I'm dazed?

126

Master: Oh what a great thing this is, that from now on whoever eats this bread appears beside himself, crazy, drunk and stupid. Oh, we unlucky men! Go ahead, if you want to get better, go and sleep, since this is the best remedy for such an illness.[16]

A society so profoundly involved in close and inextricable contact with herbs, berries, roots and tainted grains – on which, in addition to the abundant libations, fell lasting alcoholic balms – constituted a world in precarious mental equilibrium especially for those groups devoted to these drugs, for whom the night-mare of schizophrenia was always lying in wait. In this visionary society, the quality of the visions was not subject to liturgical control, as occurred by contrast among those populations who made ritual use of hallucinogenics, but – on the contrary – could explode into sudden and furious crises: excesses induced by collective intoxications and the deliria provoked by hunger. Lysergic acid, a narcotic derived from ergot, was probably the agent responsible for the motor crises and neuroses known by the name of 'St Vitus's dance'. And it is known that the chemical composition of this acid is related to mescaline, the narcotic which the Indians of the New World extracted from *peyotl*, derived from a cactus root.

It is difficult for us to understand what profound changes of consciousness struck the undernourished populations of the past. But if one considers that hunger, like mescaline, produces hallucinations and the tremors of dementia, by inhibiting the formation of enzymes which serve to co-ordinate the ordered working of the brain and by reducing the level of glucose necessary to this organ which absolutely needs it in order to be able to function, we can make some assumptions – even without bearing in mind the poisons of vegetable origin: that a huge stratum of the poorest part of the population, suffering from a profound deterioration of will, socially demoralized and without interest in the highest and most human 'causes', lived in a world of squalid intellectual and moral apathy, altered in the relations of time and space: a universe of completely unreal extrasensory perceptions. 'When the brain runs out of sugar,' wrote an intellectual who had a deep knowledge of drugs, 'the undernourished ego grows weak, can't be bothered to undertake the necessary chores, and loses all interest in those temporal and spatial relationships which mean so much to an organism bent on getting on in the world.'[17]

The popular riots, in fact, represented the convulsive jerks of an epileptic kind that had not the slightest probability of organizing themselves into revolutions, existing as they did outside of time and space, and beyond any social or political strategy.

Oscillating between narcosis and neurosis, the poverty-stricken society of the past sunk into a fantastic universe of high potential. The nocturnal deliria were piled together with the daytime intoxications and obsessions in order to build a particularly adaptable dream machine, which still awaits a visit from social psychoanalysis in order to penetrate a bit more lucidly into the *ancien régime*'s intricate labyrinth of dreams.

A tiny dream biopsy – a sample of aerial tissues woven out of nothing, of 'chimeras, oddities and fantasies' – can, however, be carried out on the *Sogni fantastichi della notte*, in which Croce pours out a not indifferent sample of his generation's dreams, suspended between collapse and levitation, aerial flights and abysmal, tortuous journeys.

> I have sometimes gone out of doors,
> And have lost myself in caverns and caves,
> And have talked several times with Death.
>
> I have had my nose cut off and my hands maimed,
> My feet deformed, and have crawled on hands and knees,
> So that I thought I had only half my legs.
>
> One moment I ride on the back of a ram,
> Another I seem to mount a dolphin;
> Now on an elephant, or a lion.
>
> Almost every day I dream I am flying . . .
> Last night I sailed through the air,
> And on top of a high mountain I was captured,
> And was put inside a cloth sack.
>
> I have even dreamed that storks
> Carried me to some dark cave
> And buried me along with the carrion.
>
> Sometimes I have been lifted up
> And carried inside a well, and the well became
> A lantern, and myself a burning taper . . .
>
> Sometimes I have fallen to the bottom of a river,
> Then I found myself in a barrel,
> And I slid around down from a mountain . . .
>
> I have heard from many people that they have had
> Certain dreams, so horrendous and frightening
> That come morning they have remained demented . . .[18]

The 'herb *ophiusa*', wrote a visionary of the 1580s, a contemporary of Croce's, 'when drunk, induces such terror and fear by the great number of serpents that appear before the drinker, that he is induced to kill himself because of the fear of being devoured by them . . .'[19] By then increasing the dose, he added that the 'herb *potamantina*, which is found near the Indus River, causes men to go crazy when drunk, presenting before their eyes things beyond nature.'[20]

Lazaro Grandi, self-styled doctor, in turn divulged a 'secret', foolishly improbable, for keeping away 'frightful dreams': 'Make sure you do not have an onyx stone around your neck when you go to bed, because this stone has natural powers which stir the worst humours so much and upset them altogether, that by then sending corresponding qualities to the head, it stimulates similar forms and causes frightening dreams.'[21] The emerald, on the other hand, if placed inside the mouth, brought about liberation from disease, forgetfulness and long intervals of stupor, according to the evidence of Girolamo Cardano in the *De propria vita*. A donkey's skin hung above the crib kept night-time fears away from the children, according to Albertus Magnus in the *Libellus de mirabilibus mundi*: 'And if the heart of a hoopoe, or an eye or brain is hung from one's neck it confers oblivion and sharpens man's intellect.'

The bad humours were the carriers of 'queer and horrible' dreams, which threw into anguish those who suffered most from intemperance of the humours, the victims of black bile and the lamp-black hypochondriacs.

Finding oneself among the dead in graves and among the limbs of quartered men and not being able to get out; seeing oneself in the hands of the ministers of justice, condemned to execution; seeing the sky burst, and from it pour down fire and lightning with the most frightening appearance of strange figures; being deep inside very high and dark towers, with no way of finding the exit, and being restricted and distressed between two walls and not being able to breathe for the suffering; beholding oneself immersed in mountains of mud or other dirt and filth; finding oneself placed on some terrible precipice with the inevitable danger of falling; being surrounded by a multitude of serpents ready to devour one; or seeing oneself chased by very fierce and mad dogs or by other most ferocious animals, waiting from moment to moment to be lacerated and devoured by them; seeing oneself before one's dearest friends, either dead or in death's agony, or to have lost them and not be able to find them ever again. These and a thousand other dreams, of which more frightening cannot be imagined, are so disturbing to suffer and such horrors to see that man would rather choose death, or at least to never close his eyes in order to sleep.[22]

The 'strange thoughts', 'follies' and 'strange convictions' that during the daytime tormented the saturnine spirits fallen into an everlasting hell of obsessions and deliria without respite, corresponded perfectly to the nocturnal nightmares.

Many, judging themselves to be dead and because of this not wanting to eat or drink, have run the very manifest risk of dying; others not only think they are dead but, in fact, condemned to hell; there are those who believe themselves to be pursued by great potentates, and for this lock themselves in their own houses, and do not want to move for any reason; others think they have some animal living inside their bodies, and others [think they have] an illness or a putrid and incurable wound on some part; others [think] their heads [are] of the most fragile glass or clay or stone, or have been transformed into some kind of animal.[23]

The boundary line between life and dream, reality and hallucination, had practically disappeared: the 'things beyond nature' had introduced themselves into the corrupt nature of man. The stupor and terror of drugs had turned into the dark angels of neurotic insomnia.

13

Hyperbolic Dreams

The underlying hysterical tendency that occasionally exploded into collective epidemic hysteria, culminating in convulsions and paralyses, characterizes the restless inward character of the common man of the pre-industrial era, 'psychologically linked', as Jean-Pierre Peter has noted, 'to a sort of infancy': a man who 'no longer belongs entirely to himself' and cannot 'choose his own social condition'.[1]

The 'hysterical components of popular behaviour',[2] at least in France, began to subside following 21 January 1793 and the execution of the 'father', according to the same scholar. But in Italy, even if no father or pope was guillotined, the psychological morbidity improved slowly but continually with the global evolution of society in all its aspects, from hygienic to political.

Every age knows its own diseases, even if the one with which we are occupied seems a veritable incubator of monsters:

> Raging most mercilessly
> Erysipelas, with its sacred fire
> Flowing, and nothing less than inflamed
> Schinansy, and the stinging and painful
> Pleurisy, and biting Tenesmus,
> And likewise, Hectic fever and the voracious
> Malign ulcer; and grim Nephritis;
> Plagues terrible to see,
> And Scrofula and Ulcers, that gnaw away;
> And the cruel torment of Lientery,
> And those inflammations of the glands,
> Tuberculosis, which later suppurate,
> And Cancer, swollen with mortiferous

Rust, and the pain of Sciatica,
Which gives no peace, and, not lastly,
The affliction of Asthma, in which the precordium
Twists and knots with the intestines.
Then, too, with the very first time,
Appeared Syphilis, horrible for its foul
Abscesses, and for the indecencies
Engendered and deformed appearance,
And burning Carbuncle, and the ignominy
Of Piles, and the breaking out of the Stygian
Cavities, detestable Elephantiasis, or Polypus,
Or that, which is deformed by its sores,
Of Impetigo; and the 'Ant sickness',
That erratically develops, little by little . . .[3]

The hysterical components – to which must also be added the very serious phenomenon of epilepsy, known also as the *mal caduco, mal benedetto, battigia, morbo sacro, morbo erculeo, morbo comiziale, mal maestro, grande male* and *mal de lunatici*[4] – represented a pathological fact affecting all classes, which cannot be correctly limited to the common people. It was primarily the more prosperous classes who suffered from melancholic and hypochondriacal disorders, accompanied by crises of depression. But it would be arbitrary to connect even the tendency to hysterical and convulsive attacks with the nervous morbidity of the lower classes. The convulsions were not only a reaction to the social malaise, but the pathological response to a type of authoritarian and hierarchical suffocation.

None the less, if one examines the detailed history – laid out by Giambattista Moreali – of the malignant fevers which hit Reggio Emilia in the years 1734–5 (fevers accompanied by vomiting and the 'expulsion' of worms, fainting spells, nausea, torpor, delirium, diarrhoea, nose bleeding, heavy breathing, cough, whose warning signs were failing strength, restlessness, mental confusion, headache and heaviness of the eyes), one becomes aware that the fantasies of the diseased often presented themselves in the form of a compensatory megalomanic dream. Visions of a hierarchy that removed social frustrations, one could say: 'hyperbolic dreams, adapted, for the most part, to the character of the persons; if religious, then with mitres, hats, abbeys, patriarchates and similar dignities; if laymen, with principalities, kingdoms and such things'.[5]

This delirious apparatus of splendour, experienced entirely in terms of social and hierarchical advancement, was accompanied by visions of ghosts, horrible spectres, and a thousand frightful dangers, especially at night; these were things that still occurred after the end of the fever, that is, during the convalescence, when in the fury of pain everyone can imagine things that seem to be happening. And the images they formed were so clear that it was very difficult to persuade the people otherwise . . . In my above-mentioned illness [Doctor Moreali, having also been taken ill, had by this time arrived at the jaws of death], of great comfort to me was the Reverend Father Michelangelo da Reggio, ex-Provincial of the Capuchins . . . who, with the greatest love, pretended to keep armed men away from me, or the wild beasts which I said I saw in the corners of my room, about to make an attempt on my life; and my seeing the charitable priest wave his arms, billow out his cloak and venture to fend off those who wanted to attack me . . . Mr Gian Antonio Barbieri . . . during his delirium, kept screaming that the people walking about the room were stepping on a great quantity of diamonds scattered on the floor. I arrived when those present were striving to convince him of his mistake; but, with them still shouting, I had him show me the place where he saw the imagined jewels, and by forbidding anyone to approach that place, I calmed him down.[6]

Men's visions and deliria, resulting from feverish, queer and melancholic dreams, belonged to a society with a high level of dream potential where the nocturnal spirits, 'frightful and horrible',[7] maliciously disturbed men's sleep. A visionary society, that during the watches of long shadowy nights had constructed an entire pharmacopoeia of herbs and antidotes, decoctions, electuaries, syrups, juleps, fruit preparations, tablets, medicinal morsels, manuscristi ('pastilles'), pills, lozenges, and broths, 'to dispel melancholic and displeasing dreams'[8] and induce 'clear and joyous insomnia' (Giambattista Della Porta): balm-mint, comfrey, lemon balm, borage, aniseeds soaked in distilled water, or 'comforting and supreme preserves like those of roses, violets, comfrey, borage, orange flowers, betony, rosemary flowers, sage . . .',[9] in addition to the powders of 'deer-heart bones, pearl, emerald and coral powders . . .'[10]

Such herbs could subdue and 'alter even frightful and horrible spirits, and present them to nature in a welcome and pleasing form', it being improbable 'what is told about the Egyptians and the Indians: that they have several medicines, both simple and compounded, which have the virtue of creating cheerful and pleasing dreams, such as whoever takes them wishes his dreams to be'. The seventeenth-century obsession with ointments kept pace with the techniques of dream control: experiments

133

and attempts to direct the images of the unreal towards attractive and pleasing forms, and away from the terrors of the night-hours. Paolo Zacchia, a seventeenth-century specialist in melancholy syndromes, physician to the pope and pioneer in legal medicine, wrote:

> Much less would I trust those who, by making a few ointments, or by putting something under their pillows, are convinced that they cause the dreams they want, as relates a curious author about the blood of a bird called the hoopoe, which if one anoints one's temples with it before going to bed, he believes will create dreams of marvellous things; and this same person [Cardano] relates that by putting a monkey's heart under someone's pillow while he sleeps, it causes him to dream of a multitude of beasts, which seem to be about to tear him to pieces. Other authors [Della Porta] suggest other ointments so as to see welcome, lovely and pleasing things in dreams; like the one made from lovage juice, tender poplar leaves, sweet flag, black nightshade, thorn-apple and aconite, spread on the temples and neck. It is certain that there are others, not without their effects, and especially those among the Indians and other barbarians, which are used by the false priests, convincing the simple people that they see the gods and paradise in their dreams; and like those that are also used by witches, who, due largely to the properties of these ointments, having fallen into a deep sleep, see a few dreams similar to their imaginings and falsely think (at least most of them) that they have attended feasts and weddings with demons and their favourites, and have banquetted there and enjoyed the most infamous pleasures.[11]

The image of the witches' sabbath as a toxicological delirium is the most alarming clue to the visionary disorder of an age which combined the ravings of the imagination with the torments of obscure and incurable diseases, and which mixed ointments (*lamiarum unguenta*, or 'witches' ointments') and demonic philtres with exorcisms ('terrible, very strong and effective' in eradicating devils/worms 'and pressure of the body', and infallible in the 'destruction of demons'), spells, poisonings, and similarly bewitching and magical prescriptions. These included oils, electuaries, lozenges and pills with the powders of doctors, spice vendors, herbalists, druggists and sacred and profane charlatans: obscure amalgams drawn from the mortar's multifarious womb. The anguish of the twisted spirit embroiled in the sufferings of the flesh inspired an almost universal lament:

It would be better to be entirely extinguished
By fire, than to lead a life like this,
Between continual moans, if that which
Drags men amidst slow deaths
Can be called life. How can one say
That it has any resemblance to life,
That which lies torpidly idle; and torn
By diseases, is subjected to troubled
Ravages?[12]

Is it any wonder that among so many catastrophes and troubles, so much 'destruction' and 'fatality' (sad words that fell like a funereal tolling on the blood-curdling hexameters of the Jesuit Eulalio Savastano), so many 'slow deaths' and anxious lives, and in the desolate perspective of the expectation of that 'great day of final terror' (Torquato Tasso), men dreamed – and wanted to dream – of a land without death and pain?

As Keith Thomas has noted, 'The men of the time did not need complicated demographic studies to perceive how short life was and how adverse were the circumstances of their survival. In 1635 a writer observed: "We shall discover that those dead between thirty and thirty-five years are more numerous than those who have exceeded this age", and even those who continued to live beyond this limit could foresee an existence marked by continuous physical suffering'.[13]

For so many obscure, painful, inexplicable and incurable diseases – confronted with which the medical learning of Galen staggered in the dark of academic speculation – the prescriptions and 'secrets' of the old hags and other women, the manual remedies of the blood-letters, surgeons and 'butchers', the 'jars' and ointments of charlatans and herbalists, and popular and domestic medicine, often brought some relief, and were without doubt more efficient than a non-experimental, abstract, theoretical and deductive science. The peasants and people of the countryside 'have so much experience in natural things and know the virtues of so many herbs that they know how to treat many types of illness'. And the women – once again it is Leonardo Fioravanti speaking – 'have so much practice with medications that they know a world of health-giving remedies'. The poorer 'rational medicines', with all their impotent and unsteady doctoral hauteur, groped in the dark, often supplanted not only by empirical doctors, but also by the simple experience of illiterate people, old hags, poor women, peasants and artisans:

The health of men depends on so little! In fact, it is enough to make
all the other doctors go crazy and send Hippocrates and Galen to
the whore-house and never let them out again, since those diseases,

for which they prescribe almost desperate treatments, can be cured with much ease and brevity by means of a mere herb unknown to any of them.[14]

Perenially living an 'unsettled and uncertain life' (Tasso), prey to diseases and on intimate terms with death, the generations of the past, notwithstanding everything, were used to cohabiting with illness and frequenting the antechambers of nothingness, realizing that any hope of longevity was scarcely justified. Nevertheless, fear of the night did not prevent them from enjoying with total intensity the pleasures of a life known to be brief and, in any case, troubled and bitter. Being used to the idea of death not being far away and the familiarity with its symbols had made people immune to fear of physical destruction, if not indifferent to the status of their souls *post mortem*. On feast days, which were numerous and frequent, people ate and danced in front of the churches, in churchyards and inside cemeteries, next to the tombs. Many diocesan synods (to quote from the Ferrara synod of 1612) prohibited 'gluttony, drunkenness, dances and vain and obscene shouting' in the countryside.[15] An ordinance of a Bolognese synod of 1566 prescribed that on the 'vigil or days of festivity of any church, you shall not hop or dance or play publicly in the streets, squares, meadows or fields near the said church . . . That inside it or its cemetery, you shall not eat, drink, sleep, nor carry grain, wine, firewood . . .'[16] 'Such were the *potationes*, ritual drinking bouts of alcoholic beverages,' Georges Duby has noted, 'aiming at one and the same time to half-open the gates of the unknowable and to reinforce group cohesion for mutual protection.'[17]

The dark and mournful figure of the priest was perceived and interpreted in the twin valency of 'that which is charged with divine presence' and of 'that which is forbidden contact with men' (Emile Benveniste). The ambiguous and feared presence of the priest was exorcized by putting 'a stone on the table at the place-setting of the new parish priest, the first time he goes to their house, so that no one of the house or that place dies'.[18]

Then, when pestilences and epidemics raged, the country women 'drag a hoe on to the top of the church, so that the mortality of the people ceases, saying, ''death to the priest and long live the people'' '.[19]

The obsessive idea of illness and the impending and uncheckable threat of death were commonly received by everyone, permanently accustomed to the acceptance – sometimes dramatic but never neurotic – of imminent and inevitable catastrophe. It would therefore be a serious methodological error to measure the fear of the last day according to the perceptions and mental parameters of our own time. In this era filled with guessing, no one – not even for a moment – forgot that

Our life is scurrilous and fleeting,
Death has its forces proud and ready.[20]

14

Artificial Paradises

It would be wrong to suppose that one must wait for the arrival of eighteenth-century capitalism, or even of imperialism, in order to see the birth of the problem of the mass spreading of opium derivatives (first of morphine and then, today, of heroin) used to dampen the frenzy of the masses and lead them back – by means of dreams – to the 'reason' desired by the groups in power. The opium war against China, the Black Panthers 'broken' by drugs, and the 'ebbing' of the American and European student movements (supposing that hallucinogenic drugs were involved in the latter, as some believe), are the most commonly used examples – we don't know with what relevance – to demonstrate how 'advanced' capitalism and imperialism have utilized mechanisms which induced collective dreaming and weakened the desire for renewal by means of visionary 'trips', in order to impose their will.

The pre-industrial age, too, even if in a more imprecise, rough and 'natural' manner, was aware of political strategies allied to medical culture, whether to lessen the pangs of hunger or to limit turmoil in the streets. Certainly, we could laugh at interventions which are so mild as to appear almost surreal, amateurish or improvised; but we must not forget that both in theory and in practice the 'treatment of the poor man', cared for with sedatives and hallucinogenic drugs, corresponded to a thought-out medico-political design. The most interesting attempts and unlimited experimenting were directed towards the preparation of disguised breads, somewhat hallucinatory and mildly stupefying, like the 'poppyseed bread' praised by Ovidio Montalbani,[1] which, known by Galenic medicine as a hypnotic drug, calmer of hacking cough and catarrh, ends up by taking an unusual and disturbing place among the surrogates proposed for wheat bread. The problem of bread surrogates could be resolved in part, according to a theory formulated by science in harmony with the political powers, by practising an alimentary policy based on the massive use of milder hallucinogenics, as we would call them today. The *pane alloiato* ('dazed' bread; literally 'darnel bread') logically ended up by furnishing the model for *pane alloppiato* ('opiated bread'). Better a city populated by dunces than one shaken by riots and uprisings, hostage to the constant fear of angry and blind revolts, seems to have been the inclination if not the strategy of some ruling groups.

The nineteenth century also knew proposals similar to those advanced by the seventeenth-century Montalbani. A contemporary of Karl Marx, a humanitarian-philanthropist friend of the lower classes, university professor and senator, and eminent representative of the official 'science' and politics of the Kingdom of Italy, the doctor and anthropologist Paolo Mantegazza (1831–1910), was deeply convinced of the social necessity of introducing the habit of sucking on coca leaves among the destitute classes, and especially the working class, the effective benefits of which he had personally observed during a trip among the *Indios* of north-western Argentina.

The intellectuals of the Baroque age, learned but taking note of social realities – doctors, mathematicians, philosophers, churchmen – had for a long time pondered and meditated on an imaginary 'natural, relief-giving bread': a wild bread of heath and moor that could substitute for that of wheat with ease. Unaware of the political mechanisms of hunger and not even discussing the principle of inequality and the subject of the distribution of goods and resources, they fantasized on this unresolved theorem of hunger, hallucinating this impossible dietary unknown, with a stupefying seriousness. The only thing missing in this chimerical strategy for the invention and location of probable surrogates for wheat bread (or for inferior and 'ignoble' cereals) was the advising of locust bread as an alternative, which the peoples of Arabia 'kneaded', making use of a simple recipe which consisted in killing the locusts, drying them in the sun, and then grinding them into a flour. Canon Giovan Battista Segni, the greatest treatise writer on hunger, commented on this in all seriousness:

> At this, I am not shocked at all, having read that Moses, in diligently selecting foods, permitted the Jews to eat those which were healthy. And the Holy Precursor, John the Baptist, ate them in the desert with wild honey. It doesn't shock me, I repeat, because, dried as they are, they are easily ground into a flour, and have a light weight and contain liquid fats common to all animals. Wherefore, ground, kneaded and baked, they must make quite a good bread – excellent, in fact – for those regions, and for those

untamed and bestial men who have nothing else worthwhile. Isidorus relates that in some regions salted locusts are the food of the poor.[2]

In the event that everything came into short supply, there was nothing to do but hope for supernatural intervention: the 'help given miraculously by God to His faithful'. Faith and trust in God could be the last desperate surrogate. The Omnipotent had satisfied the hunger of his people with the manna which he caused to fall from heaven, and had nourished the prophet Elijah on Mount Oreb with bread baked under the ash brought to him by an angel. To his solitary prophet he was wont to send a crow, evening and morning, that refreshed him with bread and meat. Another prophet, Elisha, was able to feed one hundred people with a few loaves, thanks to supernatural help. God's servant Elijah was sent by the Most High to multiply the flour and oil belonging to the widow Sarettana, and the Son of God in person had turned the water into wine and multiplied the loaves at the wedding of Canaan.

For those who did not nurse an unlimited faith in supernatural interventions, the Bolognese doctor–philosopher–mathematician Montalbani waved the mirage of a mythical herb, remote and all but untraceable: that of the *radice Hipice*, used by the Scythians, which 'when put in the mouth, keeps hunger away for twelve days'. Its effects were quite similar to those of the herb from the 'Western Indies known as *Cacahe*' (the Freudian 'coca'), prized by the natives 'more than gold', which 'when brought to one's mouth, kills hunger and thirst' (Giovanni Maria Bonardo); and to those of *negotiana*, with which the Indians of North America 'delayed hunger and thirst', or *spartanta*, which causes one not to feel either hunger or thirst when kept in the mouth. 'And the hemlock ever blunting / represses a ravenous hunger', as recounted in the *Mondo Creato* (III, 1091–2) by Torquato Tasso, who was fascinated by the marvels of the 'green cloisters', and was a scholarly and bookish examiner of 'wild and unfruitful plants', 'horrid monsters' from the 'world of wonders'. Montalbani, too (a precursor of Paolo Mantegazza, who was obsessed with the search for prodigious roots and leaves, and the natural remedy able to blunt the pangs of hunger), believed in artificial paradises that magically emerged from nothing by the use of thaumaturgical herbs. Like all the cultured minds of his time, he was not untouched by the suggestion of an imaginary cosmography and the attraction of herbal magic (the witch was forever the great Mother of herbs). This magic spoke of strange breads made from wood by the peoples of the North, or from fish flour (common among fish-eaters), or lotus seeds (a hallucinogenic herb), customary foodstuff of Egyptian shepherds; and it exhibited the wonders of sago bread (used in remote islands to the east of Malacca), or tartar bread, eaten in a land located 'beyond the Nile'.[3] A society in closest contact with its gardens, fields and pastures – accustomed to expecting good and evil, health and sorcery from herbs – read and listened to such *mirabilia* with voluptuous pleasure and thoughtful sensitivity.

According to the *Moriae encomium* of Erasmus, the 'May of Adonis', in the far-away Fortunate Isles, cradle of Madness, was fragrant with herbs, 'moly, panacea, pitcher-plant, marjoram, mugwort, lotuses, roses, violets': plants for the most part rich in stupefying and hypnotic qualities. The herbs of the pleasure kingdom corresponded to the 'medicinal herbs' (*semplici*) of madness, oblivion and laughter.

The ancients praised the powers of elecampane, the dispenser of serenity and gaiety: that consoling *nepenthes* which the beautiful Helen (instructed in the secrets of the Egyptian pharmacopoeia by Polydamna) had mixed for Telemachus, dissolved into the sweet wine. 'She drugged the wine with an herb that banishes all care, sorrow, and ill humour' (*The Odyssey*, book IV).

Opium was a 're-agent' that 'induces oblivion into melancholy things' (Bonardo). The Syrian sorcerers drank the herb *theangelis* in order to prophesy. And the Homeric *farmacon* had such power that 'Whoever drinks wine thus drugged cannot shed a single tear all the rest of the day, not even though his father and mother both of them drop down dead, or he sees a brother or a son hewn in pieces before his very eyes (*The Odyssey*, book IV).

The tribes of the Eastern steppes inebriated themselves with the effluvia of Indian hemp, according to Herodotus in his *Histories* (IV. 7):

> The Scythians take the seed of the said hemp plant, and, creeping under the carpets, enter into the enclosure, and then throw the seeds on the flaming stones. The seed burns immediately, and spreads around such a vapour and so much of it that there is no Greek tepidarium which produces a greater effect. And the Scythians meanwhile, as they are beside themselves from the effects of that most powerful sudorific, shout with joy.

The *Naturalis historia* of Pliny the Elder told in turn of herbs dispensing 'hilarity': they were the *gelatophyllida*, *hestiateris* and *oenothera*, friends of revellers like borage, whose virtues were praised in a precept of the School of Salerno:

Experts say that wine drunk in which borage has been softened
Preserves the brain's memory power.
It is said that the decoction restores gladness to the feast.

It was a remedy for melancholy, recommended by Arnaldo di Villanova,
like saffron, also enemy of sad humours. In the *Tesauro de' rimedi secreti*
Evonomo Filandro advised, for those tormented by black bile, 'wine
tinged with saffron, which brings joyfulness and chases away
melancholy'.

Effective remedies for spells and poisons, as well as for demonic possessions, could be found in herbs. The entry of the devil into the human
body was the most terrible of poisonings requiring the application of
antidotes and 'medications . . . which are not only remedies for poisonings, but also drive out evil spirits'.[4] The image of the exorcist tended
to blend with that of the toxicologist, and the herbalist made his knowledge available for the professional involved in the expulsion of demons,
for the purging of the polluted spirit, and for the witch who cast 'spells,
very powerful and effective in repelling evil spirits and driving out possessions of the devil . . . in exorcisms'.

In the third book of *La minera del mondo* (1589), in which Giovanni
Maria Bonardo put together dense layers of fanciful botany in the style of
the vegetable mythologies drawn up by Pietro Andrea Mattioli, he mentions in his letter to the Archduchess Joan of Austria that 'St John's wort,
placed above those possessed, liberates them immediately . . . It is so
hated by devils that when it is burned and smoke is produced with it in
the houses where they are sensed, they immediately leave. For this reason some call it *cacciadiavoli* ['devil-chaser'].'[5]

Rosemary flowers were also considered powerful amulets. Whoever
wore them over 'the area next to the heart, would always go forth hap-
pily, and devils would flee from him'. And 'cyclamen, in the house where
it is kept, does not allow any spell or sorcery to cause harm.'

There was a herb known as the *morsus diaboli* ('devil's bite'), 'since
according to some the devil, being very desirous of the virtues of this
herb, goes around eating and nibbling its roots'.

Even the most orthodox exorcists of the Holy Roman Church – those
who reaffirmed the primacy of the formula recited in the name of the
Most Holy Trinity, like Girolamo Menghi – recognized the usefulness
of 'syrups . . . and other potions . . . in order to draw out the harmful
frenzies from possessed and bewitched bodies'. It was admitted that
'demons can be chased out by medicines', even though 'they do not have
bodies in which they can receive the effects of the medicine'.[6] Thus,
Menghi held, the argument constructed by Raimondo Lullo in the *De*

quinta essentia was quite valid: that the boundary between demonic possessions and the hallucinations induced by the *male nero* was as uncertain as ever. Those suffering from melancholy, obsessions, manias, deliria or possession, overcome by the deceitfulness of phantoms originating from the miasmas of rotten and upset humours, or penetrated by the spirits of evil, were distinguished with difficulty, shrouded in the mists of a double ambiguity.

> Most often demons unite with human bodies because of the bad disposition of the rotten and infected melancholic humour, which forms certain dark, horrible and frightening evil figures in the imagination and troubles the intellect. The demons, then, are wont to take such forms as these and dwell in dark places, solitary and without light. When, by virtue of the quintessence and other things, this humour is chased out of the body, which is sometimes the cause of demons going in that body, then they leave along with that humour . . .
>
> So use these medicines [advised Raimondo Lullo], and you will cure anyone who is possessed, frightened, melancholic; and especially if you add to the said medicines the herb known as *ipericon*, otherwise named *fuga daemonum* . . . since the smoke of its seeds chases out every demon so that it does not approach the body or habitations.[7]

Alessio Porri's *Antidotario contro li demoni* (1601) indicates by its own title ('Book of antidotes against demons') the convergence between the art of exorcism and the science of herbs. The doctor from Imola, Battista Codronchi, himself investigates 'the way natural yet notable things can act against evil spirits';[8] and in the treatise *De morbis veneficis ac veneficijs*, a work – he writes – useful both to doctors as well as to exorcists, he reserves a chapter 'on medicinal herbs, and also on some compound medicines and their venomous faculty for treating and expelling demons'. 'Our exorcists,' writes this expert on poisonings, 'when they force demons to appear and when they expel them, occasionally make use of rue . . . Between hypericum and rue, commonly called perforata, and demons there is such contention that when used in fumigation they frequently leave, wherefore our friends call it *fuga daemonum* . . .'[9]

In turn, the French doctor Pierre Boaistuau, who in the *Théâtre du monde* (1558) had described the monstrous excesses provoked by hunger, in his *Histoires prodigieuses* discovered in the *baara* root the herb able to cure 'madmen, demoniacs and others possessed by the devil'. While with regard to rue, Jean Taxil, more perceptive than Codronchi, maintained that 'since this herb is quite strong against the melancholic humour,

consuming the gross and slimy humours, removing the being or instrument which the devil makes use of or lessening their effects . . . he cannot
do what he would like to, and gives up quickly, until the humour is once
again fit for its task'.[10]

Against the attack of elusive and obscure diseases, the defensive techniques – the therapeutic responses – remained principally entrusted to
the Virgilian 'power of herbs' and 'their use in treatment', the art of
which was practised 'not only [by] doctors, but kings and heroes'. The
'perfect knowledge of herbs' remained the chosen bulwark in an
unending war that repeated itself in ever new battles with altered forma-
tions and tactics, since new pathologies allied themselves with those
already known. Therefore it was necessary to act 'as in war, wherein,
since every day we discover new stratagems and new military tactics, so it
is always necessary to discover new remedies for the new cases of disease
which are born every hour.[11]

It was believed, however, that herbs too 'fail because of great age and
become feeble',[12] and that they, like everything, were 'subject to muta-
tions, and if they are not cultivated, lose their potency and form'.[13]

The 'mysteries' of medicinal herbs were investigated by means of
signaturae ('signs') which interpreted the virtues offered. For this reason
herbal science was linked with astrology, and a perfect simplicista ('medical herbalist') had to bear in mind the constellations and the 'sites and
aspects' of the stars. Some referred to the corresponding astrological
figure for each herb. The poisonous herbs, like aconite, hemlock and
hellebore, were subject to the unfavourable influence of Saturn, a planet
known metaphorically as the malignus. The pharmacological properties
of herbs were closely connected to the influence of the sun and moon, and
the medications themselves were divided into solar and lunar.

The moon, in particular, was the vitreous and brooding queen over
medicinal herbs, whose power conditioned the entire pharmacopoeia.
Gifted even with the property of causing a lizard's liver to expand or
contract according to the rhythm of its phases, the moon inescapably
ruled over the preservation or decomposition of herbs:

All the things that the apothecary does in order to preserve them at
length, he must do during the waning of the moon so that they
don't spoil quickly, as in the gathering of roots, herbs, flowers and
seeds. The taking of parts of animals to preserve them, the making
of sauces . . . to preserve and season them so that they don't simmer or spoil . . . So too with syrups and electuaries and all the other
preparations, and principally theriac and mitridato, which, even
though they require fermentation (which is a simmering caused by

the motion of the inner spirits), occasionally simmer with violence. And we warned that liquid syrups and preparations simmer and expand when the moon waxes.[14]

In 'gathering his herbs' the really good herbalist therefore had to take into account the 'aspects of the stars', the 'state of the moon', the 'constitution of the air', 'the time of day most suited for the preparations', 'the places where the plants are gathered' and 'the company and proximity of the plants'. He had to evaluate the best method of collecting the 'celestial liquids' like manna and honey, and the right season for trapping the animals which possessed therapeutic powers. A detailed ritual of hours, days and months had been formulated in order to delve into the fragrant heart of the vegetable 'basilica', and probe the marvellous secrets of the *hortus sanitatis* ('garden of health').

Above all, the moon was the mandatory and inescapable guide for those going in search of herbs. It was a concentration of cosmic power, a miniaturized sun, a

little sun, that does in a month all that the sun does in a year and has its own four seasons. It has its winter from its birth to the first quarter, when it will make the air cold and humid, and likewise all things subject to it. Then it will have its spring from the first quarter to the full moon, making things hot and humid and fermentative. Then it will have summer from the full moon to the second quarter, with more heat and drought than the sun bestows. And finally, it will have its autumn, cold and dry and without moisture, from the second quarter to the new moon.[15]

None the less, a medicinal herb with the definitive and complete power of defeating death had not yet been found. As in the popular *Contrasto che fa un ignorante semplicista con la morte*, if the fear of God could also be overcome when one was resting in peace with him, 'herbs, juices and ointments'[16] could not postpone – or if so only briefly – the triumph of death: 'Gegen den tod ist kein Kraut gewachsen' ('No herb has grown against death').

The culture *de re herbaria*, the knowledge of botany, the taste of flavourings, spices and drugs, empirical experience and erudite meditation, had, on the one hand, produced a legion of great botanists, and on the other, a host of very able herbalists, apothecaries, spice vendors and alchemic distillers. In an age when just the composition of a salad required a great knowledge of herbs, their flavours and combined tastes, it was commonly said that 'In herbis, et in verbis et in lapidibus sunt virtutes' ('There are powers in herbs, words and stones'). The syncretic character of late medieval cuisine, as Jakobson has noted, finds a mirror-like reflection in the taste for farce and linguistic blending, and in the interweaving and overlapping of words. Farce, whether 'stuffed' or 'mixed', makes up the combination of seasoned ingredients which conspire to please the palate; it is the dietary archetype at the origin of linguistic structuring and presides over the stuffing of vocabulary and locutions. The mixing of a salad required subtle dosages of smell and taste of an alchemistic sort: thought-out sophistications, heavy with wise meditation and creative inventiveness. These vegetable panoplies, these 'panoplies . . . or foods of every mixture' (as Montalbani expressed it), were emblematic signs of an age that sensually took in 'odorous vegetable deliria', to the point of reaching the most rarefied aromatic light-headedness with Lorenzo Magalotti's maniacal and obsessive sensitivity to odours and distilled essences.

The marvellous creation of the salad – a jewel box in which the mysterious virtues of its interlaced herbs were mixed – constituted a small treasure for hedonism and pharmacology: a miniaturized masterpiece of ephemeral art, over-elaborate and affected, which, like the apothecaries' prescriptions, required shrewd experience in the 'art of manipulation' (Francesco Formica) and the *ars combinatoria* ('art of arranging') of infinite variety. Salvatore Massonio (1559–1629) composed a treatise of 426 pages on this precarious and delicate *poetica* of vegetable arrangements, the *Archidipno, o vero de l'insalata e de l'uso di essa* (1629). And Costanzo Felici da Piobbico attempted to penetrate the intricate 'labyrinth' of edible herbs used in salads with the naturalist's tools, in order to satisfy the 'taste', 'cuisine and table' of Ulisse Aldrovandi.[17]

At the same time, Giovan Battista Ferrari's *Flora sive de florum cultura* (with etchings based on drawings by Pietro Berrettini, Guido Reni and Greuter) and his treatise on citrus fruit, *Hesperides* (1646), broadened the empirical and therapeutic knowledge of the 'wonderful powers of herbs' (Castor Durante) towards ever more rarefied botanical horizons. In the process, he revealed not only the secrets but also the delicate beauties of that 'vegetable kingdom' (Emanuel Koenig) which the two Indies, East and West, continued to expand with 'medical drugs and other very rare medicinal herbs' (Cristubal Acosta), and that the *Tesoro Messicano* (1651) was to encapsulate within the fascinating shrines of its mathematical herbal icons.

15

Poppyseed Bread

The Bolognesi were 'admirably long-lived', according to Ovidio Montalbani, and from their origins ('thousands of years ago') had kept themselves alive up to a century and a half, thanks to the parsimony of their cuisine and the frugality of their food. However, it would have been a very difficult task in the year 1648 to convince the descendants of those austere patriarchs to revert to being root and mice eaters, despite the fact that hunger – 'the disease of wretchedness' – rendered the times exceedingly 'penurious', and the 'general shortages of wheat and crops around' became every day more acute. The 'memoire', or *Breve discorso teorico e prattico* that Montalbani addressed to the 'Signori Senatori di Bologna' in 1648, besides being an exhibitionistic display of uncommon erudition, was meant as a valid working tool in alleviating 'the oppressed and degraded of their major need'.[1] It was intended as a concrete instruction able to provide relief for the starving and, finally, 'teach the poor' the strategies necessary in the desperate struggle and long-lasting war against hunger. Apparently, in times of superheated economic cycles, the entire rigid regulation of the bread market and the whole complicated 'Tariff or perpetual price-control of grain'[2] (the so-called 'Justinian Tariff' of 1606) went up in smoke, and with it all the artificial mechanisms of the controlled bread market. *Il pane sovventivo spontenascente . . .* indicated for the famished citizens of Bologna not just the way to the ovens but to the fields, in a collective hunt for the mythical 'wild bread': from controlled market to desperate march (or diversion) towards the vegetable chaos of edible herbs and roots.

Montalbani, a Baroque 'tribune of the people', having become 'both successful doctor and surgeon for those most needy and famished', showed himself as a flogger of loafers and idlers, inveighing against impudent beggars who, inveterate loungers, dreamed of easy and sure bread: 'In time of plenty poor men become lazy, all of them thinking that they have become rich and that bread must run after them, and not they after the bread.'[4]

As for the peasants of Ruzante, so for the beggars of the cities – Bologna's 'myriads of mendicants' – life and physical survival took on the appearance of a vain and often murderous pursuit of perennially elusive bread, amidst private hallucinations and collective dreams, existential frustrations and imaginary compensations which disappeared into myth and fable. Consumption had taken lasting possession of 'weakened', 'hungry', 'destroyed' and 'poorly fed' bodies (Croce). It was the sinister agent in an everlasting battle between physical preservation and destruction waged by the flesh in order to try and repair the daily breakdowns inflicted on the bodily machine and its ever-precarious equilibrium by the continual deterioration of the human substance, ensnared by the internal oven that preserves life with its heat but that also dries up, dehydrates and speeds up senescence, according to the merciless law and unavoidable tendency of the breakup of energy, irreversible entropy.

> One must repair daily the mortal stings, which in the continual battle of the elements tests our composition, *quotidie morimur, quotidie commutamur* ['daily we die, daily we change']. Our substance is subject to flux, like running water, and can dissipate like a shadow, in the way of escaping smoke. Food is the thing that withholds water, that lights up the darkness and reconciles the inimical intestines.[6]

Morbid words, of an irreparable, fated sadness, almost Shakespearian in style, spoken by the melancholy of the Great Baroque. The years of hunger appeared on the scene of poverty's theatre, bleakly mournful, brandishing the felling scythe, like some Grim Reaper.

> This year I see more gloomy tragedies prepared than anything else, where paleness and terror will be the most conspicuous characters, that the funeral dirges will be performed by *illic habitant, pavorque, terrorque, et ieiuna fames* ['yonder inhabitant, and panic, terror and barren hunger'] . . . But in order to close one's mouth as best as one can to such monsters, pray God, that he be willing to concede *escam in tempore opportuno* ['food at the right time'] to our poor.[7]

The great puzzle – impossible task of squaring the circle – remained that of finding 'sufficient sustenance' (Montalbani) for survival, adequate to fight a millenary war which from the beginning had seen the poor succumb and their 'collapsing and woeful lives' cut down. It was necessary to disguise the bread, prepare *pane papaverino* (poppyseed bread), as Montalbani suggested, or at least mask what Manzoni would call *pane adulterato*. 'Hundreds and hundreds of different roots, buds, fruits and seeds of herbs are edible and can very well pass into the diet with a bit of artifice.'[8]

The camouflaging and metamorphosis of flavours, the denaturing and recycling of herbs – even the most unpleasant – through operations of simple natural magic, provided for the neutralizing of poisonous herbs and the technique of rendering pleasing the taste of those which were repulsive. The artifice derived from 'natural magic' would extend bread miraculously: a saving demon for the starving populace. The *trouvaille* was certainly not new. Previously Valesio had noted that the prophet Elisha neutralized the bitterness of colocynth by mixing it with other flours. Even the great Galen, in the *De alimentorum facultatibus*, had given instructions to 'remove all medicinality from the most intractable [medicinal herbs], that is, green dragon and wild arum, or what our people call "snake-bread".' In the *Magia naturalis*, Giambattista Della Porta had dedicated a chapter to the techniques necessary for making 'various kinds of bread from prepared roots and fruits',[9] and Montalbani himself noted that the Neapolitan magician 'teaches to make bread not only from lupins and asphodel bulbs, but even from arum in times of famine'. None the less, 'poppyseed bread' did not enter into the almost limitless number of surrogates and additives proposed by the emergency food shortage, for the use of poppyseeds in flour (at least in certain regions) was not a novelty but a regular culinary convention. Bread was seasoned and enriched with sesame, anise, fennel, cumin and wild and cultivated poppyseeds. 'The poppyseed can be usefully mixed into bread as a seasoning',[10] reminded Bartolomeo Boldo in the *Libro della natura et virtute delle cose che nutriscono*. Pietro Andrea Mattioli observed that

> the peasant women in the mountains of Trentino use the wild poppy herb abundantly in foods . . . the poppies they sow are of three species. The white one, the roasted seeds of which were eaten by the ancients with honey at the end of the meal. The peasants eat this by spreading it on crust of bread which has been dipped in beaten eggs . . . The white one is very abundant in all of Tuscany, and both species of the black one in Lombardy and the mountains of Trentino, where very extensive fields of it are sown amongst the broad beans. From whose seed they make several dishes of pasta, that they call 'pavrato', which they eat until they are full.[11]

The principal varieties of poppy were cultivated on an 'industrial' scale for dietary uses. Both kitchen and pharmacy, household cook and apothecary made massive use of them. Wet-nurses and nursing infants consumed it in abundance. Sleep and euphoria had to be available to everyone, even the youngest. Pap made from hemp and the fritters of flax flour (*linosa*, or linseed), with 'apples and pears, stimulate the sensual appetites'.[12] As for linseed, 'the poor peasants use it like bell flower, crushed and fried, with apples added'.[13] Sensual dreams and arousal available for the eros of the peasants as well.

Giambattista Della Porta, at once scientist, experimenter and inventor of the most incredible secrets, capricious and moody in the manner of a good theatrical strategist, brought into play the extraordinary duel between the great Glutton (*Leccardo*) and Hunger, in which the cruellest of all the diseases capable of attacking man ends up routed on the field, destroyed by the gladiatorially ravenous hyperbole of the supreme devourer. This during a period when science and military language had almost become a fact of mass culture, and the metaphors of spoken language imperceptibly followed the path of the seige, clash and duel.

> We challenged each other: the enclosure was a lake of rich broth, where capons, chickens, pigs, calves and whole oxen swam. We dove in here to fight with out teeth. Before she managed to eat a calf, I gulped down two oxen and all the other things; and because I was still hungry and had nothing left to eat, I ate her. And so there was no more Hunger in the world, and I am her lieutenant and my body suffers from two hungers: mine and hers.[14]

The hallucinatory image of hunger defeated by a monstrous voracity (that is, by hunger itself) seems a surreal allegory of the most desperate self-devourment. 'True stories' of monstrous excesses that give birth to a proliferation of dreams, sometimes tragically sinister, sometimes grotesquely comical, flow together into the reservoir of fantasies of the poor classes.

Official science was for its own part wholly intent on devising ingenious 'secrets' which would annihilate the 'bestial taste' of the cyclamen's bulbous roots – desperate remedy of the 'most rustic' and 'extremely needy' – or on rendering even the bitterest and most insidious herbs reassuringly edible:

> Without performing a miracle [promised Montalbani] we are able to render darnel non-poisonous, if, before mixing it with the wheat, it is fermented in water by itself, and cooked very well, so that it becomes pleasing, and without any harm whatsoever it can go into wheat bread. The decoction has such a great power to modify and reduce all things to praiseworthy indifference, that at times it is all that is necessary to enable us to obtain the desired intention. The

Mexicans would eat immediate death with their yucca bread that they call *cazaui* if the decoction did not remove every malign quality from the juice of the root itself. The peasants can also rest assured that they will not be harmed at all by the things they know how to cook sufficiently.[15]

The prescriptions of Ovidio Montalbani – alias Giovanni Antonio Bumaldi, broad-minded student of *rei herbariae* and arcadian astrologer, whose *Bibliotheca botanica* was reprinted at the Hague in 1740 – were directed in the first place to rural people, forever accustomed to being wary of advice originating from the city, used to eating what they could scrape together, and healing themselves as they were able, resorting with greater confidence to charlatans, quacks and witches than to doctors. Besides, doctors were too difficult to track down or too far away to be of any benefit. In this same period, at several dozen leagues' distance from Bologna, a chronicler of Lugo, the Franciscan priest G. Bonoli, observed (1649) that 'the poor, and especially those of the countryside . . . are reduced . . . to feeding themselves not only on the leaves and roots of herbs, but on the very faeces of doves mixed with a certain flour, and since these were no foods conducive to the sustenance of men, many died with herbs in their mouths.'[16]

16

The 'Fickle and Verminous Colony'

'Far from the city, far from health', went a proverb recorded by Giulio Cesare Croce in the *Selva di esperienza*. And in fact, outside the walls lay an unprotected space, where epidemics struck harder than in the cities, where famines raged more furiously than within the urban walls, and where bandits, 'regular' soldiers and groups of deserters or stragglers, often united into bands of vagabonds, robbed, raped, burned and black-mailed, spreading dread and fear. At the first suspicion of plague the city gates were opened in order to drive back into the countryside 'rogues, vagabonds, gypsies, beggars, lepers, the diseased, and similar sorts of people who perform no trade and want to procure their bread only by the easy method of begging for it'.[1] Throngs of paupers, irregulars, beggars and sick people had to take to the fields. Basically the need was to 'lighten the city of inhabitants', keeping strangers and beggars away, with the exception of the 'poor natives of the land already become city-dwellers'.

Dirty, almost always barefoot, legs ulcerated, varicose and scarred, badly protected by meagre and monotonous diets, living in humid and badly ventilated 'hovels', in continuous, promiscuous contact with pigs and goats, obstinate in their beliefs (even the most harmful), with dung-heaps beneath their windows, their clothes coarse, inadequate and rarely washed, parasites spread everywhere – on their skin, in their hair and in their beds – their crockery scarce or non-existent, often attacked by boils, herpes, eczema, scabies, pustules, food poisoning from the flesh of diseased animals, malignant fevers, pneumonia, epidemic flus, malarial fevers, *sinoche* fevers (with this term the ancient medical vocabulary denoted lingering and high sthenic fevers, provoked by various agents), petechial fevers, scrofula, physcony, and lethal diarrhoeas (not to mention the great epidemics, the diseases of vitamin deficiency like scurvy and pellagra, the convulsive fits, so frequent in the past, epilepsy, suicidal manias and endemic cretinism), the peasants – overwhelmed by misfortunes – saw other wretched paupers approach their huts, carriers of new miseries and old illnesses, which proceeded to add to their inexhaustible reservoir of trouble and anguish.

But the great hidden enemies of health, on which health or illness depended, were, by common conviction (and not only of popular and rural medicine), worms. Men of the pre-industrial age lived – metaphorically and concretely – in a verminous universe unimaginable today. The obsession with worms, profoundly rooted in the mental infrastructures, gave strong grounds for a fear of cultural contagion in which official medicine also participated. The 'fickle and verminous colony', bad-tempered and unpredictable arbiter of everyone's health, tyrannized old and young, men and women, of any age and condition. Everyone carried them inside, for mysterious reasons that remained obscure. Nearly impossible to eliminate, entrenched in their 'sanctuaries', clinging to the narrow cavities of the intestines, masters of the entire territory bounded by throat and sphincter, they could neither be molested nor irritated, under pain of causing the decline of health into the abyss of illness. If they got angry or sick, the worms inevitably contaminated the blood of their host. They were therefore soothed and treated with appropriate remedies, and gently restored – penalty, the carrier's death – to their primitive equilibrium. Taking care of them, one also cared for the ill themselves, bound as they were by a double thread to the worms, according to the firm belief of Moreali:

> As long as the worms lie placidly in the intestines without being irritated, or reside there in moderate numbers, they cause no harm, at least not noticeable; in fact, they are peaceful and innocent guests. But if occasionally, because of food overabounding in proportion to them, they over-reproduce, or if they are irritated by something unwelcome and harmful to them, they will try to change location, moving away from their home nest, or will climb upwards or across in order to look for a new refuge and shelter. Bumping against the intestinal walls with fury, they sometimes eat into them, or at least violently distend them, which causes pain, as also from just their wriggling and harshly stiffening up are born the most pernicious symptoms and sometimes death.[2]

A country doctor employed in Sassuolo for thirteen years, then called to Reggio Emilia in 1734 during an epidemic of obscure fevers, Giambattista Moreali had formulated a 'theoretico-practical system' to demonstrate how the secret of health was hidden in the 'verminous population' (Antonio Vallisnieri). They were 'able to do innumerable evils to men and . . . deprive them of life', 'so that one can conclude as certain that, depending on the season, we will have inside ourselves a greater abundance of worms which, on being angered, will be capable of causing great harm'. Changes in health were brought about by the evacuation and discharge of worms within the human body, rapidly absorbed by the blood with which they entered into contact:

If the discharge of worms is of good quality, natural, not altered or spoiled, then it will not have the strength to harm man in the least; but if it is of bad quality, spoiled and malignant, it will introduce such disturbances into our blood that it will produce pernicious effects . . . From all this it can be concluded that if the worms are healthy, placid and calm, they do not cause the least harm; and as proof we have seen that 'worms can often be lodged in the human body for a very long time, without noticeable harm or trouble.' And this innocent stay of theirs, it seems, can only result from a condition of theirs of the most perfect soundness. However, if, to our great misfortune, more than that of the worms themselves, they become sickly or fall gravely ill and pass on – as they are wont to – impure and rotten, certainly that portion which is introduced into the blood with the chyle, already altered and rendered impure, will be most capable of fouling the blood mass, so that there could result innumerable diseases announced by these most serious perpetrators. Now, if the said verminous excrements are by nature acrid and very mordant, then vomit, cardialgia, hiccups, stomach pains, headaches, dizziness, convulsions and epilepsy will immediately be re-awakened. On the other hand, if the said verminous excrements are of a viscid and slimy quality, then there will be induced into the blood, and consequently into the entire humoural mass, a material completely suited to rendering the blood denser and more viscid than normal, coming across the slimmest capillary vessels and obstructing them. All the diseases that owe their origin to blockages and staunching can occur from this obstruction, as is the case with angina, pleurisy, rheumatism, loss of consciousness, delirium, sadness, depression, voice loss, paralysis, apoplexy, fevers – chiefly coagulative – and other innumerable, most serious and dangerous illnesses.[3]

These 'internal inhabitants', the absolute masters of human equilibrium, had penetrated so profoundly into the popular conscience and medical debates (for which they constituted an obscure enigma), as to inspire popular cosmologies. The worm-angels formed within the primordial cheese, to which Menocchio often referred during the

153

interrogations of the Inquisition, reproposed the image of a great verminous putrefaction, in the light of an animistic and materialistic religion.[4] Whether they were angels, demons or goblins, these beings which sprung out of liquid matter by spontaneous generation were the noble forebears of a degenerated progeny, converted to the religon of evil: the occult and malign puppeteers of possessions and hauntings, as well as the torturers of children, according to the best traditions of witchcraft.

'In the beginning there was the worm,' preached the bible of the fields, and even the most illustrious clinical doctor of the eighteenth century, Herman Boerhaave (Carlo Goldoni's 'Dutch doctor'), recognized that '[there is] truly no symptom so strange that it does not arise occasionally from worms.' When the patient 'received benefit', in very rare cases, it seems that the experimental doctors were able to obtain extraordinary expulsions similar to the one related by Gioseppe 'Scientia', devoted disciple and assistant to his great 'teacher', Giovan Battista Zapata, which took place with a 'very beautiful Roman woman', who following the vermifuge treatment became 'more beautiful and fatter than ever'.

> You must know that this morning I think more than one hundred worms as long as a palm each went out from below, related the *popolana*. Which, on hearing, seemed almost impossible to me, and – smiling – my teacher had the jar brought, and taking a stick and stirring it in the said jar, it seemed just as if I were stirring it in a pot of short macaroni.[5]

In the books of 'secrets' it is not rare to come across unmasked moments of folk life, caught in their most meaningful and realistic appearance. Extinct characters re-emerge from the dark twilight, almost erased (even from memory) by the inexorable passage of time, particularly hard on the classes without a history. Beyond this line of dark shadows, one catches glimpses of wrinkled faces chiselled by the years: wise old women slinking into their houses, like the Spanish woman appearing in Leonardo Fioravanti's *Capricci medicinali*,[6] who – able expert on herbs – resolved with shocking simplicity a clinical case found mysterious by the doctors. Having entered the room of the rich patient, we know not how, 'the crippled old Spanish woman, with a stick of cane in her hand to help herself along and with her garland', and after having briefly muttered to the sick man, 'gave [him] about a dram of a certain herbal powder dissolved in broth . . . in the presence of all us other doctors [Fioravanti relates]; and the thing took place almost like a comedy.' The sick man, notwithstanding the laughter of the sceptical 'rational' doctors, did, however, manage to recover.

Following the example of the restless and brilliant Paracelsus,

Leonardo Fioravanti 'went walking through the world' in order to learn ever newer 'secrets' and acquire 'the gifts of truth'. Similar in these wanderings to the *sanpaolari* who 'go walking the world', bestowing the blessings of St Paul, he kept company not only with the 'most learned doctors', but above all with 'simple empiricists' and all sorts of people, whether 'peasants, shepherds, soldiers, priests, humble women'.

In the rather crowded gallery of people from every class and profession, and in the innumerable encounters that make up the *Tesoro della vita umana*[7] – an extraordinary, much romanticized biography teeming with *mirabilia* and wonders – one might single out from among many faces that of an old Neapolitan surgeon (surgery was a mechanical art held to be much inferior to noble medicine), who 'operated by slicing, and removed cataracts and similar things'. By extracting the swollen and infected spleen of a Greek woman he was able to save her life.

We know very little about lithotomists, phlebotomists, surgeons, barbers and cutters, very capable in 'removing stones and cataracts, healing fleshy growths and curing urinary pains [the removal of gall-stones], injecting, castrating . . .'.[8] A blank space in the formulation of a structural diagram of popular culture: the importance, social role and cultural properties of this untrained para-medical labour, noteworthy in the alleviation of the sufferings of the flesh, empiricists who have never written a word, eludes us. About the only thing remaining concerning these men are their names, buried in the labyrinthine archives of charitable institutions and hospitals.

Medical culture also discovered what the wild *Calibani* had always known:

> Moreover, almost all diseases are thought to come from worms. Epilepsy, dizziness, drowsiness, delirium, convulsions, headaches, loss of consciousness, palpitations, depression, terror, cough, vomiting, nausea, diarrhoea, hiccups, pains, stomach colic, restlessness, outbreaks, wasting away, chronic and acute fevers, and innumerable diseases in other forms.[9]

The evil primacy as provokers of the most varied diseases was attributed to worms, even by official medicine. However, official medicine remained uncertain as to whether to attribute the worms' revolt to supernatural or purely physical causes. At one moment, it was close to the explanations given by popular culture, of which it probably misunderstood the sense; at another, haughtily critical of popular 'superstitions'.

> Certainly, quite often very severe diseases can be attributed – not just to spells – but solely to the qualities of worms . . . Although not right away, the appearance of unusual symptoms in abundance

from some supernatural cause, in semblance and in reality is due to worms, primarily in the case of multiple convulsions. In fact, this is especially remarkable, since the worms themselves are among the symptoms of spells . . .[10]

The relationship between acute convulsive crises and the outbreak of worms was occasionally emphasized (in this case by Friedrich Hoffmann) in order to disprove what was vulgarly attributed to witch-craft, spells and demonic possessions:

Next, once more so as to not neglect it, if the covering of the intestinal nerves is torn and corroded more severely – amazing and unusual thing – that the more ignorant populace is wont to attri-bute to spells, those worms produce the symptoms: they are clearly among the exemplars of worms, those convulsions of the limbs to numbness all the way up to the joints, incredible circular move-ments twist in a surprising way, immediately afterwards the people are struck with aphonia, and then a strange and harmful coherence and mental confusion is indicated, with a grating of the teeth, and they are excited into a frenzy, asserting that they see demons: nevertheless, it often produces the symptoms of this rage, of course, if the worms desist from gnawing.[11]

The clinical description does not differ much from a case of demonic possession, even if we next discover that the agents of such disorder are worms. But the pathological scenario tends to become complicated by the interventions and analogies deriving from suggestions that originate from a different sphere, the depths of the world of demons. It was said that the devil preferred to enter inside man and take possession of him in a disguised manner, under the form of repulsive and disgusting insects (*animalcula*): 'the most sordid animals . . ., sordid . . . and hateful insects for mankind'.

Demons 'can lie hidden in men in the guise of spiders or flies . . .; so, in the guise of whatever animal, even a smaller fly or spider', wrote Petrus Thyraeus.[12] Spiders, flies, black ants: Beelzebub was considered the 'partner of flies' (*comestor muscarum*), 'prince of flies' (*princeps muscarum*), monarch of the wizard-flies, 'pug-faced witch' (*vetule rencagnatae*) and 'fly-eater'.[13]

Outside of this bewitched atmosphere, flies, mosquitos, horse-flies and the other 'tedious little animals' were also believed to have been 'created unintentionally by nature', and defined by some as 'nature's mistakes' (*naturae peccata*).[14]

Perhaps worms were also unconsciously assimilated into these possible incarnations of the devil. Solomon, wizard and enchanter who had control over the spirits, had succeeded in subjugating the worm Shamir, the prodigious helper without whom the Temple could not have been built. Demons or angels, worms issued 'from the most perfect substance of the world':[15] secret agents of the fermenting mass. Not by accident they appeared among the unmistakable 'signs' of these bewitched and possessed, sure signals of the devil's disguised presence and the masked activity of the evil genius of a thousand stratagems and the great *trasformista*. 'In some, a certain thing like a mortar is disturbed at the stomach opening, and yet they are worms, ants or frogs. Much vomiting of the stomach results from this. In some, [there is] the greatest torment in the internal organs'.[16]

The voice of the Christian sorcerer – the unrelenting exorcist – was raised to a fearful pitch to strike them with the most dreadful anathemas and reduce them, along with the wicked gang of other infernal beasts, to an innocuous and sterile powder.

> I exorcise you pestiferous worms, mice, birds, as well as locusts and other animals. Through God the omnipotent Father and Jesus Christ his son and the Holy Spirit from both proceeding, that you immediately depart from these fields, vineyards and waters, and no longer dwell in them, but pass into those regions where you can harm no one; and by reason of the omnipotent God and the entire heavenly host and holy church of God, damning you wherever your curses may be found, that you may be wanting from day to day and waste away, because it is thought worthy to prove that none of your remains are found opportunely, unless necessary to human health and use, whereby it is good fortune to judge the living and the dead and the times by fire.[17]

The scourge of these worms was therefore feared by everyone as an incarnation of viscid and evil forces, sign and portent of famines, plagues and malignant fevers, constant and uninterrupted. People of the ancient world lived in fear of insects: flies, fleas, bedbugs, lice and locusts, the 'worms that eat the wheat still green' and cause the 'ruin of whole estates'.[18]

A great cloud of flies (*muscarum copia*) foretold the Lausanne plague of 1613. The 'locusts from Mirandola, before the epidemic of Carpi, covered the sky by their great abundance'.[19] The seasons of high humidity and the *scirocco* wind, the 'rainy weather and south winds with the calm seasons' favoured and inevitably preceded epidemics and the spread of insects. 'Famines, wars, and great clouds of insects, visible and outside us, are almost an infallible portent of epidemics of disease and pestilence'.[20] The regular climatic pattern and the persistence of identical weather led to oppressive and uniform diseases, as Benedetto Selvatico noted with regard to the epidemic of 1648: whereas 'changeable illnesses correspond to the changeableness of the weather.' But when *inconstantia* was followed by *constantia*, or when 'uniform turbulence' was 'overtaking, consistent and almost uniform diseases appear, so that fevers are raging at this time not as much in Bergamo as in Bologna, Venice, Cividale del Friuli, the Paduan plain, Vicenza and places almost everywhere'.[21]

Among the many terrors of the *ancien régime*, among the other 'terrible and fierce signs' (Torquato Tasso) of the final catastrophe, that of the multiplication of insects – common among all classes – was perhaps not the lesser terror, by comparison with the fear of the multiplication of the poor and the anguish concerning the proliferation of the wretched masses which struck the propertied classes with horror, fearful of a tide of human insects that would rise until finally submerging them.

The 'greater fecundity and propagation of insects' and of worms especially – as in a well-known film, apparently science fiction, portraying a widespread attack of insects – was darkly feared as a possible universal catastrophe for all humanity, devastated by the diseases contracted from their poisonous contact, devoured from within the body and on the skin's surface by a verminous and repulsive apocalypse.

> . . . and it will be during just this time that a more than ordinary multiplication of all insects of this great World will be seen, and in such circumstances there will be a Universal epidemic. While in particular, infections and verminous diseases will spread constantly and continuously, inasmuch as disease will then be particular to and solely for those who have worms; and if someone eats and lives badly, he will induce a certain corruption in the stomach and primary organs which will disturb and cause considerable damage to the worms which are there placidly and calmly. And this could be equivalent to that which is universally caused by wars, famines and rains in tainting the air and causing influenza in general.[22]

A 'tiny race' (*gens pusilla*) the worms, but 'conquered with great difficulty':[23] a real brainteaser for the Galenic pharmacopoeia. The *specificum anthelminicum* (a vermifuge) 'ideal in drawing out roundworms', is found in all the antidote and prescription books, but it seems that the results were disappointing. It was commonly believed that the worms were gifted with 'cunning and sagacity',[24] and moved within the bodily maze with an astonishing knowledge of the terrain. Driven by hunger, when the host body was itself empty and starving, they ascended from the depths of the intestines towards the throat.

It seemed almost a miracle to many that worms or vermin - largely because they are long and round - climb up and come to the throat and leave by the mouth and nose, being accustomed to doing this when the man has gone hungry for a long time. For this reason they bite into the stomach and long to eat, and having nothing with which to nourish or sustain themselves, they climb up and search for food even at the meatus of the throat. Because of a certain sagacity or natural inclination, they sense that food arrives in the stomach by that route, and since the nose is also a meatus that connects to the throat, they arrive there as well, coming out by means of a sneeze, or else they are removed by one's fingers. I have seen this happen many times in healthy men . . . I have also seen it happen among the sick.[25]

Whether healthy or diseased, man was a verminous being, his internal canals traversed by sly colonies of worms, 'vigorous, lively and reptilian', which the specific anthelminthics tried to render 'languid', drive back down and, if possible, kill or expel ('ad inferiora defluere coguntur et necantur').[26] But, lively and almost indestructible, it was they themselves who abandoned the human body as death approached. A quite certain sign and portent of the *exitus* and unequivocal signal of the final marasmus was the flight from dying flesh of these slimy and very sticky inhabitants of the dark, warm and damp recesses of the body:

When they leave spontaneously and without being forced by any natural power, it is a very fatal sign in a patient, because we see this happen to those who are near death. For, due to a certain natural sagacity, they know that the body is about to die and can no longer give them their usual nourishment, and so they leave it.[27]

The animals were able to pick up and interpret much in advance those obscure signals of ruin and death that remained unintelligible to men. 'This has also been noticed in the houses that are falling into ruin, from whence rats and dormice flee, often leaving three months before they tumble down.[28]

Shocking signs of death, the *animaletti* succeeded in foreseeing the near future which often escaped the glance of men and their scanty and unsteady instruments of knowledge for interpreting the real and the possible.

Lice as well as flees, sensing that the human body is about to die and that the blood has left all the limbs, flee as a result, or else they go to those parts where the blood's natural heat and force last longest. And these gravediggers, or those who bury the body, have observed that they end up around the stomach mouth or under the chin next to the windpipe, since those parts, being closer to the heart, retain heat longer, where it lasts even to the last breath. This being shown to me by several people who were close to a patient, right away I saw that it was an infallible sign that the sick man would die and that his death could not be very long in coming.[29]

Signals of another type – not mournful – were transmitted in nordic lands by the domestic crickets that Olaus Magnus and his sixteenth-century popularizer considered 'divining worms':

During the winter [the crickets] remain close to the fire places and chirp continually, which is very annoying, especially for strangers, since those of the town are used to it. And these are worms that prophesy, since in jumping towards the lights placed above the boards, the more frequently they near them the more snows and storms will follow.[30]

Solar fragments, inhabitants of the dark, with mysterious behaviour that put the domestic microcosm in communication with the infinity of the heavens, these 'worms' predicted stellar disturbances and celestial storms, in the way that earthworms shut up inside a human body foresaw organic decay and physiological catastrophe.

The struggle against the 'inner' worms constituted a social problem, profoundly felt by entire communities, large and small, as a fact of major importance, a sort of popular war against cunning and elusive enemies that also required adequate financial support. In Naples during the second half of the seventeenth century, people resorted to the 'oil' made by the Benedictine fathers, who were subsidized in part by public money to prepare a complicated and tortuous antidote, which had to be spread on the 'usual places, as well as the naval, wrists and hollow of the throat'.

This oil is dispensed [wrote the Neapolitan baron and pharma-cologist Giuseppe Donzelli] by the Reverend Fathers of St Benedict in the monastery of San Severino, and its effectiveness is such that most of this city assembles here, which in times gone by paid the said monastery an income of eighty *scudi* a year, in contributions to the costs necessary in its preparation.[31]

It was a complicated and costly prescription, a therapeutic preparation probably lacking in efficacy, a maniacally concocted super-medicine, the stratified complexity of which – of an idea born from the shadow of an idea, according to the principles of accumulation and opposition – supplies an allegorical key to the impenetrability of the enigma of worms.

160

Take the sweetbread of peach stones, bitter almonds, shallots, half a pound of earthworms, five bundles of gentian, white dittany, ash, couch-grass, masterwort and peony roots, blackberry leaves, zedoary, saffron, sweet calamus, carnations, aloe, ferula, colocynth, ginger, nutmeg, cinnamon, pepper, incense, carpus balm, about two ounces of red coral, seven and a half ounces select theriac. Mint, absinthe, wormwood, superior centaury, peach leaves, leek, dill, hawkweed, oregano, plantain, rue, harehound, celery, bay, thyme, sage and wall germander; rosemary, savory, marjoram, betony, about one bundle of pomegranate and orange rind; celery, purslane, plantain, leek, wormseed, quince, fennel, cauliflower, parsley and lupin seeds; rye (German, that is), kidney beans, about six ounces of laurel berries; three ounces burnt deer's horn, six ounces bull's bile, one pound very strong vinegar; mastic oil, paraffin oil, about six ounces of bay-leaf and ears of wheat; thirty-seven and a half pounds of old oil. It is allowed to putrefy and is prepared according to the art.[32]

No oil came near the grandiose blending of this antidote for worms, a sign of the pharmacological primacy given it in the struggle against their proliferation. In the 'pharmaceutical theatre' where the dramatic prologue to the chemical battle against evil was staged, the most labyrinthine and stratified prescriptions perhaps responded to a hypothesis of total medication, a simulated model of concealed, conflicting forces, and duels between secret elements and powers. Attractions and repulsions regulated the arcane game of affinities, relations and opposites: human worms could even be treated with the powder of earthworms, the scorpion's venom with the very oil of scorpions or with wine in which their powder had been dissolved. Following a magical logic, fox oil was administered to those ill with gout; the oil of frogs was used for those suffering from arthritic pains or against insomnia; ant oil to 'stimulate sensual appetites, spreading it on the places *inter anum et testes*, and all over the pouches of the testicles'; cicada oil 'to excite to coitus', although the fact that 'many bad symptoms have been seen to follow . . . including even death, has caused the refrain to cease in medicine regarding such a useful medication'. Finally, there was 'Venus balm' (cicadas, ants, pyrethrum, euphorbia, etc.): 'With this, one anoints the limb and nerve between the calf muscles and the big toe of the left foot, and in washing it every struggle ends; a word is enough to the wise,' warmly advised the Franciscan Domenico Auda, 'Chief Druggist at the Archiospedale di S. Spirito in Rome'.[33]

The suspicion that the toxicological delirium assailed not only those who prepared themselves for the 'flight' of the sabbath with ointments and hallucinatory potions, but that it involved – especially in the case of the sensual and aphrodisiacal 'antidotes' – vast sections of a society already abundantly intoxicated by a thousand poisons, tainted blood and a conspiracy of alkaloids, becomes ever more firm and plausible.

Nor is it possible to draw a line of demarcation between medicine and charlatanism in a world where magical illusion predominated and the Great Vagabond of Basle, the ingenious quack author of the *Labyrintus medicorum errantium* (1538) – the 'divine' Paracelsus (according to Leonardo Fioravanti) – everywhere found faithful disciples who drew from the enigmatic cup of this visionary alchemist: 'A living worm, tied on to the whitlow, vulgarly called *punticcio*, leaving it there until it dies, Paracelsus says will cure one from the said disease.'[34]

The worm that cures with the slimy touch of its gelatinous flesh – the thaumaturgical earthworm that finds its beneficent transfiguration in death – signals the culmination to the magical power of the worm fetish.

17

Putrid Worms and Vile Snails

The vagabonds and bands of drifters who wandered far and wide almost with impunity were feared as voracious insects that devastated the countryside:

> an independent people who recognized neither law, religion, authority nor police; impiety, sensuality, debauchery, was all that reigned among them; the majority of murders, thefts and violence, by day and night, were the work of their hands; and those people whom the Estate of the poor made the object of the faithful's compassion, were, by reason of their rude manners, their swearing and their insolent talk, the most unworthy of the public's assistance.[1]

The *magasins charitables* were created in 1651 for this 'libertine and idle nation', as it was called across the Alps. But in 1764 a *Mémoire sur les vagabonds et sur les mendiants* (anonymous, but attributed to the pen of Guillaume-François Letrosne) continued to portray it as a 'too comfortable estate', living 'within society without being members of it'.[2] Scourge of the countryside ('les vagabonds et les mendiants sont pour la campagne le fléau le plus terrible'), they were singled out for public disdain in order to urge stricter laws.

> They are voracious insects that infect [the countryside] and devastate it, and who daily devour the sustenance of the farmers. They are, speaking without rhetoric, enemy troops let loose in a certain territory, who do as they wish there, as in a conquered land, and who raise veritable war levies under the guise of alms . . . Often they are not content to ask, but seize what they can, and everything is meet for them: linen, clothes, lambs, poultry of all kinds. When they have amassed their supplies, they buy wine in the taverns and go off to celebrate in the woods.[3]

163

In Italy there was no less hatred for these 'thieving and knavish companies', this 'mob' more voracious than worms:

. . . avid caterpillars in human form.

A 'rabble' who

> are always chewing, and never let up or stop,
> whether by night or by day, dusk or dawn.
> As the putrid worm and vile snail
> are used to devouring beets and lettuce,
> they consume, gnaw and eat us,
> becoming ever more ferocious and cruel.[5]

'Opaque cloud', 'great throng' and 'huge cloud', similar to the scourge of locusts which every year denuded the countryside of all life, the paupers and vagrants were feared and hated to the point of invoking a plague – a diabolical medicine – that would annihilate them:

The plague will be the true theriac.[6]

If the doctors feared the uncontrolled and abnormal multiplication of insects, others – and Bonifacio among them – lived obsessed by the propagation of the knavish beggars:

> So many are they, of an ashen colour,
> faces wasted away, who have no refuge,
> who seem born from decay, and not from Venus,
> nor is there any measure which can count them.
> There is no one who sprouts and germinates more than they,
> who grow fat even in their own filth,
> as if they were beetles or vermin.
> And, even though terrible hunger exterminates them,
> these heads of the Hydra, in rebirth they
> pass through all boundaries and limits.[7]

The fear that they might begin to count themselves, achieve self-awareness – of their numbers and power – became a 'class nightmare' (Giorgio Fulco): a political problem that could develop into proposals for their annihilation or, in a less drastic version, for their containment and neutralization.

The multitude, even of infirm things, always renders itself suspect. Thus, in Livy, Cato said: 'Of no species is there not the utmost danger, if it is allowed as a multitude.' For this reason the Pygmies often kill the enemy crane while still in the egg, before they can advance by multiplying. Centipedes are weak, yet they chased the people of Trier from their land; mice are weak, and the small island of Jaro had to be deserted; frogs are weak, and they almost depopulated Egypt; finally, rabbits and moles are weak, yet the former in Thessaly and the latter in Spain undermined the cities. Many times the ancients waged hateful war against the slaves; and a short while ago Emperor Ferdinand waged a most atrocious war against the peasants. Now what would happen to us if we had to battle with the beggars? 'It would be obvious how much danger threatened if our servants began to count us,' says Seneca, and rightly so, since Athenaeus affirms that there was a certain citizen in Rome who kept ten or twenty thousand [slaves . . . a danger which swayed us]. If our beggars count their numbers here – there being many of them these days – as they did in the age of our ancestors, those prodigious locusts will black out the sun in an extraordinary cloud.[8]

Other learned men, less violent and more experienced, like the clever Montalbani, indicated in the 'free treasure of nature' and the 'most natural larders' the places where the 'thousand helpful remedies for hunger' could be found, suggesting a search for the herbs and roots of survival in the most remote and least cultivated places. Perhaps it was a question of an ignoble trick to keep the starving, dreadful and, in any case, always noisome beggars away from the urban space. It is not possible to state with any certainty if we are faced with some kind of sneaky artifice to relieve the urban economy of the useless and unproductive weight of the *malcibati* ('badly fed'); but we must remember that in the event of famine the countryside was the first to undergo the almost total draining of its resources in favour of the city, and the peasants – having become 'lurid pilgrims', in livid, corpse-like procession (writes Manzoni of *Fermo e Lucia*) – streamed towards the large centres, leaving their worn out bodies at the sides of the roads leading to the urban agglomerations.

Pauperes agrestes ('rural paupers') are what Giuseppe Ripamonti called them in the *Historia patria*, to whom were also added the wealthier peasants (*maiores divitesque rustici*), almost as if they had been punished 'by the very soil which they had exhausted by too much tilling'.[10] In the city streets, the 'bodies' of resident beggars, and even more of the recently urbanized wretched poor and the beggars of circumstance, 'their food consumed by poverty, they fell down here and there, or else wandered about at crossroads and churches; they went about with the appearance of corpses, and then they became corpses'. As a chronicler of Fossano quoted by Nicolini relates:

165

Many poor people were forced to die from hunger, and I, on the thirtieth of May [1630], leaving [Fossano] for the farmstead, came across a man without any hope of life since he had lost the ability to speak and all feeling; who fell heavily to the ground because of weakness, that is, with his face to the ground, and not being able to move from there, he made a hole in the ground with his nose and face, and one of the people with me turned him over, and a few hours later he passed away with his hands full of grass.[11]

This terrifying image of a nearly dead man who, shaking himself like a cadaverous marionette, digging himself a tiny hole with his mouth and nose, scratching at the earth with his teeth, makes the advice of those like Montalbani, who pointed out possible remedies for the attacks of hunger in gathering the wild fruits of the non-cultivated earth, appear idle and academic.

In fact, the vagabonds, isolated or in bands, had always been accustomed to wandering about the countryside, in part because the cities closed their gates in their faces, pushing them out towards the desert of the fields, where they 'nibble continually in the countryside',[12] to quote once again from Letrosne's *Mémoire*. In the malevolent eyes of city-dwellers and burghers, they resembled locusts and rodents, as previously in the verses of Baldassare Bonifacio and Angelo Maria Labia. And for Manzoni too, they appeared similar to beasts, with their 'disheartened and yet grim look' (a sinister quality of which there is not trace in the poor urban 'professionals' and which the *Mémoire* reserves for rural beggars).

Here and there against the walls, under the eaves, piles of straw and stubble, beaten, stale, stinking, mixed with foul rubbish, which at night had served as kennel for the beggars chased by hunger away from the city, where they had no shelter to cover their heads. Many were seen to gnaw with repulsive effort at herbs, roots and bark which they had gathered in the meadows and woods, like provisions for the city where they hoped yet to find more humane fare.[13]

The exhortation directed at the Senate of Bologna by the enrobed Montalbani to persuade them to follow the route of the woods and wild glades therefore takes on a sinister aspect (the route towards certain death). The invitation has all the air of a perverse deceit, an infernal trap devised in order to lead them to a silent grave, a remote destruction to rid the cities, landowners, notables and senators of the sad rabble – forever swayed by riot – of their shouts and laments, their diseased bodies, the stench of their worn out and disgusting rags: worms, devourers of 'beets or lettuce', 'bran' and 'trunks and acorns' (Bonifacio).

Learn from the ant, oh feckless beggar, 'go to the ant, oh lazy one!' the Sage [Solomon] reminds him, and by doing so escapes privation and will not die of hunger . . . perhaps the means to live are lacking for those who appeal, by way of divine help, which no one lacks, to the merciful heart and inexhaustible breasts of the great Ancient Mother, the earth? Come on, use your arts, employ your ingenuity and hands to find new substitutes and surrogates for the bread of Ceres, when it is precisely Ceres who has been negligent in her duty . . .

The beggars can go begging from the earth itself all that is necessary for their lives, and they won't be disappointed in their hopes, returning relaxed and at a decent hour, richly rewarded for their suffering and humility. Nature made *corrude*, or wild asparagus, says Pliny, within everyone's reach . . . The same nature produced hops, commonest where vines do not thrive . . . Not everyone has been granted the ownership of farms and gardens, but no one is forbidden access to the woods, where with lawful theft one can live off uncultivated herbs, picked by anyone. Certainly, in our parts one will not find the *hipice* root of the Scythians, which by merely being held in the mouth keeps hunger away for twelve days; nor the indigo root which, according to Chthesia, when put in wine, condenses it in such a way that it becomes manageable, like wax; but one will easily find roots and herbs that will render most foods not only lasting but virtuous. Cybele is more liberal and merciful in the woods than in the orchards and gardens; in cultivated lands she often shows herself to be mean and even cruel, which we know all too well in this year 1648. It is not enough to have served and fattened her very well, for her to be deaf to the appeals of the wearied farmers. The leafy sides of the ditches, the thick river-banks and the colourful stretches of meadows retain their foodstuffs. I do not think the mallows so celebrated by Horace and Martial can be refused.[14]

Even if we accept the inevitable fancy for classical references and the inevitable *exempla* of healthy, tasty and nutritious herbs drawing from a vast and variegated botanical literature, classical and modern (even references to Platina's *De honesta voluptate* are not absent), it is difficult to rid ourselves of the nagging sense of a studied provocation, played out with cynical hyprocrisy on the skins of soon-to-be corpses: or at least of a mocking and fanciful attempt to direct the starving masses towards non-existent wild reservoirs and natural dream-like larders. 'The begging myriads' were diverted towards the artificial paradises of the woods and

167

the green deserts of the heaths in search of medicinal herbs like plantain, sow-thistle, wild lettuce, scarlet pimpernel, sorb-thistle, dandelion, purslane, water-lilies, with the possible addition of *pandopi*, or 'foods of complete composition',[15] herbs which, with the appropriate 'varied fryings and boilings, give the taste of meat and fish'.[16] Such were the wonderful tricks of Baroque cooks and their prestigious hallucinatory inventions which the starving rabble, however, would never have had either the time or the means to prepare. Nor was it thinkable, in the company of Athenaeus, to suggest hunting for one of the two hundred species of couch grass, 'the most rustic and wild, to be used with burning bush to make a humble, yes, but not bad-tasting bread'.[17]

This bookish science, of the eccentric, versatile Bolognese writer, was insanely removed from every possible reference to the tragic necessities of the lower classes. The maniacal proposal of an official doctor put forth when the cries of the starving pierced the air of the streets. A ridiculous, scientific reincarnation of the Doctor Gratiano who had become the preferred target (even if within the infinite capacity for laughing and making fun of one's own difficulties) of the popular satire of a city hostile to the vacuous, presumptuous and high-sounding science of the corporation of doctors. A satire that could take on the bitter aspect of a most extreme and ferocious protest, as in the case of Costantino Sacardino, paid jester of the Magistracy of Elders and alchemistic distiller (one of Fioravanti's *gattisini*, used to repeating in the master's wake that the 'dovecote has opened its eyes'), who, thirty years before Montalbani's words, had for a period of three years fouled the sacred images of the most pious city of Bologna, with its Cardinal legate, a city placed under the tutelage of St Petronius and the sweet, maternal protection of Our Lady of St Luke. Like his countryman Ulisse Aldrovandi (although without his untiring scientific activity), Ovidio Montalbani interpreted the book of creation without 'seeing or demonstrating', but by contemplating a 'nature that was, from top to bottom, written', recording it according to the catalogue already drafted by others, in a never-ending verbal commentary on a natural reality formed of vegetable things, objects and essences, like the herbs and roots of the Kingdom of Ceres. On Montalbani, too, weighed the 'indistinction between that which is seen and that which is read, between the observed and the reported' (Michel Foucault), typical of the attractive pre-scientific epistemology which put together 'natural histories' (Baldassare Pisanelli), mixing the real with the fantastic, what was seen with what was read.

None the less, while keeping in mind the mental spider-web which imprisoned Montalbani's thought within a labyrinthine gaol of endless commentaries, and the enormous disparity between para-scientific hallucination and the surrounding reality, it is difficult to rid ourselves of the suspicion that lurking behind this altered form of knowledge, this scientific paranoia of words and quotations (and the deep layering of words made up that *Fabrica del mondo* which was built upon the illusion of the Word and the artifice of form without meaning), there lay a considered political strategy aimed at the lower classes and the tight-packed and threatening groups of a floating and alienated population. The university culture of Bologna (certainly not alone in Italy[18]) had formulated an ideology of class directed at sanctioning the biological inferiority of the humble poor in order to crush them politically. It was an ideology that postulated two distinct diets, depending on membership of a group in power or of a class of the destitute. During these same years Torquato Tasso, making use of Aristotle's *Politics* (I. 2. 7), confirmed that the 'difference between servants and masters is established by nature' (*Il padre di famiglia*).

As far back as the second last decade of the sixteenth century the Bolognese doctor Baldassare Pisanelli had hypothesized a twin nutritive and dietetic regimen based on social differences (the clash between high and low culture is here portrayed *sub specie coquinaria*): foods suited for country folk and those for gentlemen, forbidden to the former. If this dietary code were neglected or broken, the dietary transgression would be translated into illness for the presumptuous devourer of foods not destined for him by nature (or for 'his nature'). A kind of sad dietetic fate whose ordinances could not be overstepped without bodily pain and affliction. By constructing dietary taboos, Bolognese medicine (or at least a part of it) placed itself at the service of an ideology of power and social abuse:

> No other harm is written concerning the peasant, other than that it causes asthma in country folk; that these people should abstain from it, and leave it for noble and delicate persons . . . Warblers cause peasants to become consumptive. These are not to be given to them, but shall be served to company of quality.[19]

The leek, on the other hand, 'the worst food, and the most detestable and imperfect . . . is the food for country people'.[20]

In some measure even Giulio Cesare Croce was influenced by this flow of medical ideology founded on pseudo-scientific prejudices that with relative ease concealed their political origin, one harshly opposed to the popular classes, and Croce caused Bertoldo to die at the moment he could no longer feed himself on turnips and beans.[21]

These barriers were also further strengthened and confirmed by the Friulian Giuseppe Rosaccio (1530–*c*.1620), who enjoyed great prestige in Bologna during the first half of the seventeenth century and whose works were continually reprinted. In his *Microcosmo* he delivered the following judgement:

> The meat of the cow, steer and pig, the bread of red wheat, beans, cheese, red wine and other heavy foods cause strong semen and bad temperament: the son who is conceived will have great strength, but will be wild and of animal wits. From this there results that among men of the countryside it would be a miracle if one turned out to be of acute intelligence and prone to study, especially where such coarse foods are eaten. The opposite occurs among city-dwellers, whose sons, we see, have more intelligence and ability.[22]

In the same period when Montalbani was active, the Marquis Vincenzo Tanara, author of the *Economia del cittadino in villa*,[23] repeated the dietetic discrimination. On the one hand, dark bread for the 'lowly people': for the poor, the workers and the 'malnourished', 'the darkest bread made only of pollard', and 'maize flour . . . eaten by itself or mixed with other grain, made into bread or *polenta*, with which the peasants chase hunger away'. On the one hand, 'mouths of grain', and on the other, 'mouths of fodder'.

In this polyphonic discourse arranged for multiple but unidirectional voices there also blends that of Giulio Cesare Croce, ambiguous and hesitating, faltering and uncertain. The Bolognese story-teller – who had access to the glamorous palaces of the senators, author too of sacred and devotional poems, favoured by the influential and omnipresent Church powers, linked by family tradition to the world of the artisan, but unable to ignore the presence of the great reservoir formed by people of the countryside – did not miss the opportunity to ally himself with this political platform in which scientific inconsistency was interwoven with a cynical and deliberate satirical suggestion:

> All those who perform their works for others should behave in the manner of experts, who must first know the constitutions of the patients and then apply the remedy equal to their nature; since if they want to introduce some noble medicine through the mouth of a peasant, without any doubt they will be persuaded when seeing him, because by his nature he is accustomed to coarse and rustic foods, according to his boorish nature.[24]

It was during this same period, more or less, that Cardinal Gabriele Paleotti pointed out, in a curial document of thirty-three points, all the nefarious *abusi e vizi de' contadini* ('abuses and vices of the peasants), giving peremptory and official sanction to centuries of satires, jokes, mockeries, insults, curses and defamations at the peasants' expense.

In this atmosphere of obstinate suspicion towards the countryside felt as a wild space, the 'universal punishment' inflicted on the 'starving and consumed' city-dwellers by 'extreme and horrible famine' is principally commiseration for the misfortunes of the 'calamitous city' and its indifference towards the fate of the countryside: provisioning reservoir and dietary reserve from which the city – by love or by force – drained away foodstuffs and grains of every kind. But for a more than seven-year famine like the one officially initiated in 1590 ('the year Ninety, such a dire one'[25]), even the people of the city – 'helpless / rather, unhappy, sad and wretched' – had to feed themselves, like the tramps of the fields, upon 'herbs most bitter and harsh to the taste' and 'sad and unhappy' foods.

18

A City of Mummies

The *Banchetto de' Malcibati* reflects the definitive collapse of the proud Renaissance myth of the happy city. Immersed in a desolate atmosphere which the black humour of the story-tellers did not succeed in alleviating, it brought to centre stage gloomy and melancholic ghost-like characters such as Master Appetite, Lady Hunger, Master Trouble, Master Poor-harvest, Master Infertile and Lady Famine, fished out of the by now abandoned storehouse of medieval characterizations, literary symptoms of a returning neo-feudalism. Tragic presences which allegorical play could not help put out of mind, as it was unable to distance the mocking spectre of poverty from the ancient figure of the *joculator* ('jester'): 'The man who is keen for a laugh will quickly get a wife, whose name will be Derision'.[1] *Paupertas* and *Derisio* are the sharp and bitter figures of the jester's family evoked by St Bernard, whom we later find faithfully mirrored in the Bolognese buffoon Zaffarino,[2] self-styled son of 'Master Trouble d'Ognibene', making out his will in favour of 'Lady Poverty daughter of Tribulation', the witnesses being 'Crazy, Scabby, Filthy, along with Littlebeef'. Ancestors of the penniless members of those companies of the patched up, bankrupt, ruined, ground down and needy: characters worn out by an unpleasant theatre of hardship and poverty.

With the sad, livid signs of a more sombre and dramatic reality, the Croce-like *Banchetto* – a tragic farce much closer to medieval *jeu* than Renaissance comedy, of which it seems to have forgotten every memory – celebrates the 'triumph of hunger', 'trouble', 'sadness' and 'melancholy'. A mirror reflecting reality ('since all invention is born from life'[3]), this allegorico-grotesque *pièce*, wavering between surreal and hyper-real in a climate of collective drama verging into sacred performance, presents one of the most peculiar examples of folk-inspired theatre, where God's passion and Calvary made flesh are reflected in the gruelling agony of an entire city, prolonged for an absurdly long time. The weak and faint shadows of the 'afflicted', 'malcontents', 'poorly dressed' and 'poorly shod', the grotesque puppets reduced to 'pure waste' (Bonifacio), voided by hunger and tormented by disease, are sucked irresistibly back into abject poverty by the relentless inflation. This struck not only the medium-low artisan and small proprietor classes ('How many couldn't obtain the rents / for their houses, and how many became poor, / wretched, disconsolate and helpless?'), but also those who

> with rich and pompous clothes
> were wont to act like lords, who are now listed
> among the numbers of shamefaced poor.[4]

The *mumie* of Giovan Battista Segni, the 'emaciated mummies' and 'skeletons' of Baldassare Bonifacio and the infants 'much leaner than mummies' of Giulio Cesare Croce, echo as it were the curses of the fleshless starving who, as they lay dying, imprecated the organs which had made their whore-mothers pregnant, denying life at its very source.

> Neither mummies nor skeletons were ever seen
>   leaner than those who lived wretchedly,
>   and for this reason they cursed those male organs
>   that had made their mothers pregnant,
> And them as well, because they hadn't turned
>   the cribs into coffins, as soon as they were born;
>   and many, while they were called whores,
>   fell dead, not being able to speak.
> To watch their falls was a spectacle
>   too morbid indeed and too horrible,
>   there being nothing to prevent these bitter cases.
> And this so dreadful and terrible scarcity,
>   whether omen or miracle,
>   will be ever unbelievable to future ages.[5]

Having become a horror museum, not of a nocturnal or ghostly horror, but – something much worse – of a daytime one, the city-cemetery-hospital put monstrous deformities on display in the doorways and streets.

173

And if you saw how many wretched and miserable paupers
are warming themselves in the sun's rays,
and suffer serious harm from hunger;
    How many blind men, how many widows and infants
much leaner than mummies,
lie on the ground, poor and mean.
    The cries, the screams that are heard
through all the streets, the banging on doors,
and the various and strange diseases.
    The cheeks afflicted, colourless and pale,
that represent, to those who see them,
none other than the image of death.[6]

One person's death reflected in the face of another, a fellow human
being, a neighbour; the persistent mirroring of our slow and daily death
portrayed in the flesh of the 'surrounding starving and destroyed people', all reduced to the condition of 'scroungers, beggars, paupers and
searchers',[7] creates the sinister atmosphere of a city changing face,
agonizing among the cries, screams and the banging on doors. The
image of a desperate collective shipwreck that every year sucks more and
more victims into the abyss, against whom 'various and strange diseases'
have also raged – the inevitable corollary of hunger – and where men
have become 'the object, from one to another, no longer of mercy but of
horror, all of them filthy, each more terrified to find himself among so
many companions of desperation', as Manzoni would later say.

The Mendicants' Institute, an 'infinitely vast Hospital for Poor
Mendicants',[8] progressively expands its sad hospices inside and outside
the walls. The assistance given to paupers and beggars becomes the most
burning question for those in charge of civic order. And Santa Maria
della Pietà, the enormous church of the mendicants, equips itself with
grain silos for the temporary relief of beggars.

Giovan Battista Segni's plaintive lament, his bitter complaint, his
mortal mistrust of the society of his day and the apocalyptic wish for a
'universal plague' that would wipe out and extinguish all the living, offer
the most dramatic evidence of incurable crises of conscience and institutions, and a social and economic breakdown of the utmost depth and
hopelessness.

Alas, if we want to run through all of the conditions of men, we shall
find them all worthy of this scourge [hunger], since all have turned
their backs on God and have given themselves up to this vain world
. . .
    The Princes want to be level with God; judges have banished

174

justice from their courts; doctors no longer counsel what is right; lawyers are full of tricks; notaries false and untruthful; merchants thieves; artisans perjurers; soldiers assassins; fathers rude; sons sinks of iniquity; masters cruel; servants full of deceptions; the rich miserly; the poor without faith; husbands unfaithful; wives without just love; laymen blasphemers; churchmen dissolute; and, finally, search and search again in all our Italy and you will not find anything but abominations. Civic and Christian faith has been lost. Civic, because promises and pacts among men are not observed. Christian, because there is no fear of God, no reverence for the saints, no devotion to sacred things. The cult of God, both interior and exterior, has been reduced almost to nothing. Religion has been made into a fable by the people. Justice is administered only against the poor; and the powerful, who deserve a thousand fires and chopping blocks, escape unpunished. Treachury abounds, hatred doesn't go away, the good are oppressed, rogues are exalted. In other words, our pride – everyone's – is such that we no longer recognize God; we dress sumptuously in luxury, avarice holds the sceptre for everyone. So it is no wonder that Christ holds the sharp scythe in his avenging right hand, because he neither can nor wants to tolerate such confusion any longer. Oh Italy, Christ still bears the scythe in hand, he hasn't put it down yet, your hunger hasn't finished for now. Who is so blind that he cannot see, so stupid that he does not realize that the coming year will perforce be one of famine and perhaps much worse than this year, since most lands have not been sown. The poor farmers have eaten their seeds, many have abandoned their fields, some have died because of these troubles; robbers have in many places turned the farmland upside down, stealing and eating the animals, chasing away the farmers or at least preventing them from working.

And if we do not proceed against them as we must, their numbers will increase every day, even though there are already armies of them, and these predators will besiege states as well as the few crops that manage to grow. How will the princes manage then? How will good citizens live? How will all Italy protect itself from those who want to occupy her? I can only believe that either God must send people very far away to possess these delights which we know not how to enjoy or defend, or with a universal plague must remove from the world all these lawless men and together with all us other ungrateful people, causing men to be born anew for these beautiful and delightful lands, who will be true Italians and perfect Christians, worthy of all good things.[9]

For the Bolognese priest who looks heavenward for the famine's causes – while Croce limits himself to witnessing it on earth and describing it – the angered Omnipotent, instead of manna, has sent a kind of evil celestial poison which from season to season has carried away all food-stuffs, swiftly making the fields barren with a 'foul and cursed dew', diametrically opposed to manna in its evilness, and rapidly drying up every growing thing.

> This past year the astrologers predicted a good harvest because of the favour of the heavens . . . There wasn't excessive heat . . . labourers were not wanting. For many years, thanks to God, we knew neither wars nor sieges. Rather, due to the overabundance of calm, our men have become so lazy that they would sooner let robbers and highwaymen eat their hearts from their bodies than unsheathe sword to defend their things. Locusts have not appeared, nor have fundamental disagreements predominated over us. Therefore, it remains to firmly believe that it came because of divine judgement.[10]

The cities and farmlands become progressively parched beneath the blaze of an evil fire that burned day after day like fire inside a furnace: an immense oven baking and drying out the flesh of the living.

> The skin of their flesh became dry and wrinkled because of hunger, pale because of pain, yellow because of toil, worn out by lack of food and like Penance because of the suffering. The oven . . . when it has been thoroughly warmed by the fire, converts all that is put before it into ash, or it sucks and draws it into the stones of which it is made. So the faces, skin and flesh of these men is similar to ash . . . These wretched folk, because of their continuous labours, bitter hunger and lack of food, have shrivelled and blackened faces, wasted away and laden with soot and exhaustion.[11]

Faces were blackened by consumption and turned dark like the outside of a cooking pot (the *laveggio*), 'where meats are cooked . . . which on the outside, in frequent contact with the fire's flames, becomes black, ugly and covered with soot.'[12]

Such were the sinister metamorphoses performed by hunger on the flesh and skin of reluctant penitents, behind which stands out the shadow of cannibalistic self-destruction, symbolized in Ovid's myth of the transgressor of the vegetable taboo: 'He who violated and cut down the tree of Ceres was hit with such hunger that first it consumed all his

176

faculties and then, finally, he ate his own flesh'.[13] The origin, in either case, is still a transgression of divine law: for the canon Segni the vegetable apocalypse – the revolt of nature upset by divine will – had already begun.

19

The Triumph of Poverty

On 27 February in the year of Our Lord 1581, a strange, colourful procession, exiting from the Hospital of the Trinity, made its way – with Pope Gregory XIII joyfully presiding – through the streets of Rome under the bewildered and incredulous gaze of residents, foreigners and pilgrims. Winding slowly by torchlight among the psalm-chanting choirs and processional music, the unusual procession, 'a truly pitiful and amazing spectacle, perhaps never again seen', was about to climb the Campidoglio, accompanied by 'an infinite number of people, assembled not only because of the wonder of the event, but also owing to the indulgence which had been offered by our Lord to all those who accompanied it'.

A red standard led the way, on which was painted the most holy Trinity, accompanied by two large lanterns; nearby walked many prelates and lords dressed in red sackcloth, bearing red canes in hand, according to the custom of that Confraternity [the Confraternity of the most holy Trinity of convalescents and pilgrims]. Then came the most holy Crucifix carried by people also dressed in red sackcloth and going barefoot, accompanied by a great number of burning white wax tapers, and by a very large number of brothers of the Company dressed in the same red sackcloth and various choirs singing hymns and psalms in good music and plainsong. When this order was finished, it was followed by that of the poor mendicants, with the necessary trappings and emblems, and individuals were seen to go in couples, the blind were led, and those who were crippled were led in carts by other mendicants; there followed fourteen carriages full of those who were so crippled and infirm that they could not be borne in any other way.

A truely pitiful and amazing spectacle, perhaps never again seen like this. Lastly came the primicerius, guardians and other officials of the said confraternity, with an infinite number of people . . . There were eight hundred and fifty poor mendicants, including men and women, young and old, who climbed and came down from the Campidoglio with greater triumph than the ancient Romans ever managed; and lastly they went to the San Sisto gate, where they were received with great piety and charity.[1]

The extraordinary procession of the Roman Court of Miracles in fact represented but a small part of the elusive and unassimilable world of the mendicant, which refused integration and internment, as the rapid decline of this hospital, which Sixtus V tried in vain to develop, makes clear:

Throughout Rome [in the years following the death of Sixtus V] one sees nothing but poor mendicants, and in such numbers that one can neither stand nor go about the streets without being continuously surrounded by them, to the great dissatisfaction of the people and of these poor mendicants. Yet in the said hospital there are very few people, and according to the information I have, the number doesn't reach one hundred and fifty people, including the paupers, officers and the ordinary's servants, and most of the time much less.[2]

The *traversata* of 1581 was also the dress rehearsal for a 'spectacle' that every day splintered into a thousand performances put on at every street corner by ingenious poverty: a grandiose parade where illness and unhappiness had shown their great theatrical potential and the strange capacity of attraction practised on eyes starving for portrayals of horror. Poverty became mass theatre, a shuddering allurement to the senses and a perverse spell of the pitiful and repulsive. The astonishment of the spectators was doubled by seeing, all in a line, regimented and tamed (at least apparently and temporarily), a small number of the extras in this colossal daily spectacle, including the 'depraved will' and 'blindness of intellect' of the vagrants, to whom were attributed 'tremendous and scandalous crimes, in such a way that the practice of begging in Rome could be called a school for theft, lewdness, blasphemy, licentiousness and every kind of abomination.'[3]

But if the 'theatre of Roman beneficence'[4] was the biggest in the world and 'Roman piety and the fruitful breasts of the Church'[5] seemed inexhaustible, every city in the seventeenth century (the 'little ice age',[6] teeming with social catastrophes beneath a lurid, inclement and evil sky, whose fearful writers compounded the suffering of the skeleton-like poor with its blackish, dried up skin) had to defend itself from an 'immense multitude of commoners',[7] whose number had 'become so horrible that one could no longer live in the streets, churches or houses because, besides the importunity, there was also violence and confusion.'[8]

> [The beggars] were no longer seen one by one, but they actually went about in swarms, old wretches falling from hunger; boys without father and mother, who because of age and the lack of training and upbringing were incapable of earning their bread other than by roguery; women of every kind, but especially suspected widows, whose husbands had gone off out of desperation with musket over their shoulders, leaving them burdened with the children . . .; and lastly, an incredible quantity of sick people who – persuaded or shown that by waiting to be assisted in their hovels and on the straw of their kennels they would die of hunger before their fever or sores killed them – dragged themselves like so many skeletons, expiring in the public streets, in order to see whether horror and nausea would serve as a better exhortation than charity and faith.
>
> And this still would have been little. Worse was the fact that among this frightening multitude of real poor there was an even greater one, causing much more fear, of fakes, idlers and vagrants, all of whose deeds, since they have made a career out of roguery, consist of robbery, dishonesty, blasphemy, impiety and every sort of abomination.[9]

'Idleness', 'licentiousness' and 'scandalous importunities' governed the lives of vagabonds 'capable of committing any misdeed.'[10] 'Full of tricks and artifices', 'they live without religion and without faith . . .; they are always in the churches but they never pray there . . .; they despise the sacraments and hardly ever experience that of marriage, mixing indifferently with one another . . .'

These were the 'fake' and 'idle' poor, the 'libertine' poor (as the abbot Carlo Bartolomeo Piazza defined them with surprising perfidy),[11] 'lovers of idle liberty . . . with false and deceitful pretexts exempt from the check of the laws of Princes and Christian discipline: odious to the public, toublesome to private persons, mistrusted in commerce, a bother in churches and a contagion in civil conversations'.[12] For these *mali pauperes*, 'the bodily mutilations, twisted limbs, fistulated sores, patched-up rags, nerve spasms, apparent bruises, rolling of the eyes, artificial tremors, studied paralyses . . . serve as a rich and studied patrimony.'[13]

They were quite different from the authentic poor – *fideles et boni* – dressed in the 'livery of Jesus Christ', and the 'poor of Christ's school',[14] 'ragged, wan, lean, pale, emaciated, wasted away',[15] whose

> blindness, maimed limbs, bleeding sores, uncomfortable hovels, dry and insufficient bread, torn coats, putrid bandages, vile rags . . . sticks and crutches are the glorious trophies of their Christian patience . . . doctors for the rich, surgeons to the avaricious . . . cauteries of health . . . stairs of paradise . . . trustees of divine mercies . . . banks of celestial usuries . . . gate-keepers of Heaven . . . philosophers of the Gospel . . . salubrious leeches.[16]

The finger of the great Roman prosecutor, ideologue of the vigorous policy of social improvement desired by Innocent XII, points (beyond the begging masses, among whom the 'poor man of Christ' becomes ever rarer, while the alarming figures of the vagabond and criminal under the rags are perceived as ever more numerous) to all those who are tossed indiscriminately into the infernal cauldron of the 'depraved poor':[17] men of ambiguous professions, often at the borderline of the law, nomads and pedlars, but also *cantimbanchi* ('bench singers'), charlatans, conjurers and jugglers.

Suspicion and distrust, along with these characters, hit popular culture hard, and it was rebuked and attributed with demoniacal origins by the same words (sign of a cultural policy of the Church unaltered for centuries) with which the relentless Tertullian condemned the 'badly born race', the 'false poor' (distinguished from the 'valid mendicants') of his time, 'miserable martyrs of Satan'.[18] As for vagabondage itself, in the eighteenth century it was still considered an offence (and not solely *in criminalibus*): but this was only for the poor man, in no way for the rich. So too with idleness which, while considered a crime for the wretched pauper, was certainly not so for the lord. 'Petty thieves are hanged, major ones let off' (*Parvi fures suspenduntur, magni dimittuntur*). The criminology of class, it seems, was not an invention of advanced capitalism.

The itinerant and cursed trades, the 'wandering' men, were banished (while the never-forgotten ghost of the 'devil's family' reappears) to suspect and inauspicious marginality, to wicked 'depraved poverty', branching out – like a contorted and ghastly tree of evil – into instable families, resistant to social improvement and forced integration (or seclusion). The ancient Church condemnation of *comici* and actors re-emerges vehemently in perfect accord with the 'rationalizing' of the fight against vagrancy and against a negative society in ideological opposition to elite cultural models. There was a growth, it was said, of indifference to religion or unbelief, embodied in ragged 'libertines', spreaders of every physical and moral contagion, vile and overbearing carriers of 'atheism', diabolical cheats ready for any moral 'plague-spreading' and spiritual poisoning:

> sly vagabonds, wandering beggars, ill-mannered rogues, noisome mountebanks, artful swindlers, cheating charlatans, superstitious inventors of sainthood, fraudulent cheats, sellers of tales, dealers in falsehoods, slothful hypocrites and cunning quacks . . . whose fortunes are aided primarily by trickery, deceitfulness, cunning and atheism: insolent in wretchedness, bold in their rags, fraudulent in their distress, rash in nakedness, pompous in misfortune, eloquent in abjection and fearlessly ingenious in their practised frauds.[19]

At the threshold of the *Settecento* the ancient notion of poverty persists almost unchanged, so much so as still to constitute a 'profound cultural conditioning, which prevents contemporaries from considering the material data of indigence in problematical terms, and intentionally draw up an analysis of the processes of impoverishment'.[20]

The true Christian poor, the only ones worthy of the *cristiana economia* and apostolic charity, had to fall within a stereotypical model (the only one favoured by the Church) of humble pauper, servile, acquiescent, 'wasted away on the inside by hunger, on the outside by shame',[21] old, weak, relentlessly persecuted by misfortune: mutilated human forms, wrecks of every war, laden with starving children: 'battered by the outrages of fortune, lying on the bare earth with faint voices, on dung-heaps, with a distressed appearance, with the hollowed-out cavities of lost eyes; with maimed hands barely able to beg . . . with the trunks of their bodies exposed to brutalities, to iron, fire and attacks.'[2]

In many Italian cities (between the last half of the seventeenth century and the first half of the eighteenth) the public almshouse opened wide its doors to the docile, meek and integrated poor: a general hospital erected for the purpose of 'eradicating begging forever, and of spiritually and temporally assisting all the paupers of a city, with *economy, order* and *method*'.[23] 'Institutes of piety and public order, relief and punishment, charity and prevention, their apparent paradox suggests in fact to the historian the in-depth analysis of a contradiction: that of a concern for the poor which attempts to fulfil itself by means of the very social structures which have produced the poverty'.[24]

Refuges, shelters, hospitals (*ptochotrophia*) and homes for the aged were opened with magnificent ceremonies and solemn pomp, with a sequence of spectacular events, including solemn masses, processions, music and banquets. Before being swallowed up by the hospice–prison, the delights of the senses and the sanctity of the spirit were charitably donated to the poor for the first and last time. Served at table by noblewomen and knights, the young girls were washed and cleansed of their 'filthiness' and reclothed, before they were locked up for good and before they became accustomed to the food of the almshouse (unfailingly 'frugal and suited to their condition',[25] so that the 'poor closed inside . . . are not spoiled by excess').[26] The poor 'males [are accompanied] by a boy dressed as an Angel, and each female by a young maiden'; and after the singing of a solemn *Te Deum* the last act commenced, 'the most beautiful of this function, that is, the public supper . . . in the main square, with a good number of soldiers sent by His Excellency for this purpose'.[27]

> Two large and long tables were set up, one for the men and the other for the women, in the style of a theatre. The tablecloths or covers were among the finest available. At the head of the two great tables there were two large sideboards full of cutlery, washbasins, saucers and other very beautiful vessels of silver. The tables were set with royal plates for three courses, and every table and twenty-four dishes for each course. All the Ladies, with Her Excellency Madame Deshays, requested to serve the girls and the poor women, as all the most important knights the men.
>
> While the paupers received this charity, concerts of musical instruments were heard, of trumpets, oboes and others, which restored more and more the faith of these poor people that are nourished by Jesus Christ.[28]

Poverty utilized as a theatrical mechanism has its choreographic apotheosis, its spectacular sublimation, in this piazza of Vercelli (1719). Then, 'having finished the supper and given due thanks to the Lord, they sang several spiritual lauds which they had learned in the preceding days; after which they were once again conducted in procession to their hospice where, having entered the chapel and been made to recite their prayers, each sex was conducted to its apartment to put themselves to bed'.[29]

After the songs, the pieces of music, the prayers, the sparkling of the silverware and the magnificence of the courses, the long night of silence and want began. With the vagabonds shut in, the foundlings 'hospitalized', the silverware put away, the tablecloths all washed, the lights put out and the purifying exorcism recited, the great parade dispersed. The performance was over, 'begging banished', the defeated monsters,

. . . in a long line of vanquished
Behind the cart they marched, necks tied with chains,
The countless plagues of Erebus: in every way pressed
Under the yoke of poverty: for this sordid look, and
Lazily dragging their feet, and like their ancestor
Descendants of idleness, to whom ensued many offspring:
Quarrel, brawl, trickery, heartfelt frenzy,
And impestuous gluttony of the stomach, gaming and fraud,
And now, dejected face shaking for fear of their daring . . .
And the fraud that hates daytime, with its disguise torn off,
On its face the wickedness is nakedly revealed: the perjuries
Of the tongue and the robberies, are here at last evident
On the naked mouth. Behind the cart, in the middle, the most
Ugly faces, with heads wrapped in dark veils, a perverse
Ignorance of things follows, most hideous companion to the sight,
Despiser of the living, faithless despiser of the laws,
Impiety . . .[30]

With the 'libertines' segregated, the 'countless plagues of Erebus' enchained, and the beggars' mouths spitting out abuse and blasphemy reduced to the monotonous silence of short devout prayers mumbled in mechanical repetition, the society of the just and good – through the voices of scholars *humaniorum litterarum* – celebrated, with the inauguration of the General Hospital (*in solenni renascenti Ptochotrophii instauratione*),[31] the happy return to order, the 'new feast', the triumph over poverty: *paupertatis triumphus*.

Notes

Introduction

1 M. Savonarola, *Trattato di molte regole, per conservare la sanità, dichiarando qual cose siano utili da mangiare, e quali triste e medesimamente di quelle che si bevono per Italia. Aggiontovi alcuni dubij molto notabili* (Venice: Eredi di Gioanne Padovano, 1554), fol. 5r-v.

2 M. Savonarola and B. Boldo, *Libro della natura et virtù delle cose che nutriscono et delle cose non naturali. Con alcune osservationi per conservar la sanità, et alcuni quesiti bellissimi da notare . . . riformato, accresciuto, et emendato, et quasi fatto un altro per Bartolomeo Boldó* (Venice: D. & G. B. Guerra, 1576), p. 34. The book is an ample and thorough re-working of M. Savonarola's *Trattato*.

3 *Secreti diversi et miracolosi. Racolti dal Falopia, et approbati da altri medici di gran fama. Nuovamente ristampati . . .* (Venice: Alessandro Gardano, 1578), p. 346.

4 Levino Lennio, medico zirizeo, *Della complessione del corpo humano libri due. Sommamente necessarij à tutti coloro, che studiano alla sanità* (Venice: Domenico Nicolino, 1564), fol. 121v.

5 T. Campanella, *Del senso delle cose e della magia. Testo inedito italiano con le varianti dei codici e delle due edizioni latine*, ed. A. Bruers (Bari: Laterza, 1925), p. 193.

6 C. Lévi-Strauss, *La pensée sauvage*, Paris, 1962; English translation *The Savage Mind* (London: Weidenfeld & Nicolson, 1966), p. 46.

7 Io. Michaelis Savonarolae, *Practica maior. In qua morbos omnes, quibus singulae humani corporis partes afficiuntur, ea diligentia, et arte pertractat . . .* (Venice: Iuntas, 1559), fol. 25r.

8 Sabadino degli Arienti, *Le porretane* (Bari: Laterza, 1914), p. 242. Available in English in *The Italian Novelists*, vol. II, London, 1825.

9 Campanella, *Del senso delle cose*, p. 192.

10 Marin Sanuto (1466–1536), a Venetian chronicler and member of the Great Council, acquired fame for his *Diari*. (Trans. note)

11 *Brevi*: small pouches with devotional objects sewn in or covered with magical formulas, worn from the neck as a sign of piety or as a talisman. (Trans. note)

12 Luca Landucci, *Diario fiorentino, dal 1450 al 1516*, continued by an anonymous writer till 1542, published on the codices of the Comunale di Siena and Marucelliana libraries with annotations by Iodoco del Badia (Florence:

185

Sansoni, 1883), pp. 299–300.

13 Marie de France was a French poetess of the second half of the twelfth century, best known for the *Lais*, a series of poems inspired by Breton legends. (Trans. note)

14 Paulus Aegineta medicus, *Opera*, Ioanne Guinterio Andernaco medico peritissimo interprete. (Lyons: G. Rovillium, 1566), p. 253.

15 Girolamo Manfredi, *Libro intitulato Il Perché, tradotto di latino in italiano, de l'eccell. medico et astrologo, M. Hieronimo di Manfredi* . . . (Venice: Ventura di Salvador, 1588), p. 15.

16 J. Raulin *Istruzioni sulla maniera di raccogliere i parti scritte dal celebre Sig. Raulin per ordine del Ministero di Francia, ed ora tradotte nella nostra volgar favella* . . . (Venice: Caroboli & Pompeati, 1771), p. 113. The original French version is *Instructions succinctes sur les accouchemens*, Paris, 1770.

17 S. A. Tissot, *Avis au peuple sur sa santé, ou Traité des maladies les plus fréquentes, par Mr. Tissot* . . . (1760; new edn. Liege: Bassompierre & Van Den Burghen, 1763), p. 269. English translation by J. Kirkpatrick, *Advice to the People in General with Regard to their Health* (London, 1765).

18 P. Boccone, *Museo di fisica e di esperienze variato, e decorato di osservazioni naturali, note medicinali, e ragionamenti secondo i principii de' moderni* (Venice: G. B. Zuccato, 1697), p. 149.

19 T. Campanella, *La Città del Sole*, translated and annotated by D. J. Donno (Berkeley: University of California Press, 1981), pp. 89–93.

20 *La commare o raccoglitrice* (Venice: Gio. Francesco Valvasense, 1686), p. 289.

Chapter 1 The 'Disease of Wretchedness'

1 Quoted in J. Delumeau, *La Peur en Occident (XIVe–XVIIIe siècles). Une cité assiégée* (Paris: Fayard, 1978), p. 164.

2 G. B. Segni, *Trattato sopra la carestia e fame, sue cause, accidenti, provisioni e reggimenti, varie moltiplicationi, e sorte di pane. Discorsi filosofici* (Bologna: Gio. Rossi, 1602), p. 53.

3 Ibid., p. 55.

4 J. P. Migne (ed.), *Patrologia Greca* (Paris, 1845), vol. 31, III, columns 322–3.

5 Delumeau, *La Peur en Occident*, p. 163.

6 Procopius, *The Gothic War*, in book VI of *History of the Wars*, pp. 41–5. Translated by H. B. Dewing, Loeb Classical Library, London and New York, 1924.

7 Henrici Rantzovii [Heinrich Rantzau], *De conservanda valetudine* . . . (Antwerp: Christophori Plantini, 1580), p. 115.

8 Ibid., p. 114.

9 Gio. Maria Bonardo, *Della Miseria et Eccellenza della vita humana. Ragionamenti due* (Venice: Agostino Zoppini, 1586), fol. 4a.

10 Ibid., fol. 9b.

11 Ibid.

12 Ibid.

13 Rantzovii, *De conservanda valetudine*, p. 17.

14 See the recipe for it in the *Tesoro delle gioie. Trattato curioso nel quale si dichiara brevemente la virtù, qualità e proprietà delle gioie* (Padua: P. P. Tozzi, 1626), pp. 195-7.

15 Gio. Antonio Vignati, Bolognese, *Antidotario contro la peste* (Bologna: Clemente Ferroni, 1630), p. 27.

16 *I maravigliosi secreti di medicina, et chirurgia . . . raccolti dalla prattica dell'eccellente medico e cirugico Gio. Battista Zapata* per Gioseppe Scientia (Venice: Santo Lanza, 1629), p. 1. For the attacks against the 'rational' doctors cf. the works of the Veronese, Zefiriele Tomaso Bovio: *Flagello de' medici rationali* (Venice: Nicolini, 1583), *Fulmine contro de' medici putatitii rationali* (Verona: Dalle Donne & De' Rossi, 1592), and *Melampigo overo confusione de medici sofisti* (Verona: G. Discepoli, 1585).

17 *I maravigliosi secreti di medicina*, p. 3.

18 Ibid., p. 1.

19 Domenico Auda, *Breve compendio di maravigliosi segreti* . . ., (Rome: Angelo Bernabò, 1660), p. 178.

20 Marsilio Ficino, *Della vita sana*, in *Della religione christiana*: 'a most useful and erudite work, and translated by the author himself into the Tuscan tongue. Together with two books by the same on maintaining the health and prolonging the life of lettered people' (Florence: Giunti, 1568), p. 109.

21 Giulio Getto, of Treviso, *Diacameron id est Dator Vitae. Il principale delli singolari segreti di medicina affermato dagli antichi filosofi . . . Opera nova* (Treviso: Grispoldi, 1623), p. 9.

22 Ibid., p. 9.

23 Ibid., pp. 9-10.

24 Strozzi Cicogna, *Palagio de gl'incanti, et delle gran meraviglie de gli spiriti, et di tutta la natura . . .* (Vicenza: Roberto Meglietti, 1605), p. 390. Cf. G. Bonomo, 'I folletti nel folklore italiano', in *Studi demologici* (Palermo: Flaccovio, 1970), pp. 95-140.

25 Strozzi, Cicogna, *Palagio de gl'incanti*, p. 390.

26 Ibid., p. 388.

27 Ibid., p. 390.

28 T. Campanella, *La Città del Sole e scelta d'alcune poesie filoso fiche* ed. A. Seroni (Milan: Feltrinelli, 1962), p. 276.

29 Strozzi Cicogna, *Palagio de gl'incanti*, p. 396.

30 *Vaticinio et avertimenti per conservare la sanità, et prolongar la vita humana*: 'collected by Lampridio Anguillara, from an ancient Arab writer, known as Elbymitar' (Ferrara: Vittorio Baldini, 1589), pp. 18-19. 'One must stay cheerful, since cheerfulness excites the natural colour and tempers the spirits, and renders them purer, strengthens the natural virtue, rejuvenates the body, not in years but in strength, prolongs life, sharpens the intellect and renders men more suited to affairs'. (Auda, *Breve compendio*, pp. 277-8).

31 Arcibaldi Pictarnii, *Elementa medicinae phisico-mathematica* (Venice: Antonium Bartoli, 1733), p. xvii. The six 'non-natural' things represent an obligatory element of Galenic medicine.

32 Cf. W. H. McNeill, *Plagues and Peoples* (Garden City, NY: Anchor Press, 1976).

33 T. Fasano, *Della febbre epidemica sofferta a Napoli l'anno 1764* (Naples: Giuseppe Raimondi, 1765); quoted in F. Nicolini, '1764: Napoli nell'anno della fame', *Rivista Storica Italiana*, LXXXV, 2 (1973), p. 406.

Chapter 2 Elusive Bread

1 B. Bonifacio, *Il Paltoniere*, ed. G. Fulco, in *Strumenti Critici*, 36–7 (1978), p. 186.
2 Ibid., p. 187.
3 Ibid., p. 185.
4 Keith Thomas, *Religion and the Decline of Magic* (London: Penguin Books, 1971), p. 108; quoted by Thomas in 'Problemi sociali, conflitti individuali e stregoneria', in M. Romanello (ed.), *La stregoneria in Europa* (Bologna: Il Mulino, 1975), p. 215.
5 Ruzante, *Teatro*, trans. and annotated Ludovico Zorzi (Turin: Einaudi, 1967), p. 697; the complete works are also available in French in *Un Dramaturge populaire de la Renaissance italienne. Ruzzante, 1502–1542*, trans. A. Mortier, 2 vols. (Paris, 1925).
Angelo Beolco was an actor and writer of satirical comedies in the Paduan dialect during the first half of the sixteenth century, acquiring the name 'Ruzante' from the part of a peasant he played. Despite their popular nature, his works were intended for the aristocratic circle of Alvise Cornaro, whose lands he helped administer. (Trans. note)
6 Ibid., p. 693.
7 Ibid.
8 Ibid., p. 695.
9 Ibid.
10 Ibid., p. 709.
11 Ibid., p. 1439.
12 Ibid.
13 Ibid.
14 M. Dobb, *Studies in the Development of Capitalism* (New York: International Publishers, 1947), p. 222.

Chapter 3 Sacred and Profane Cannibalism

1 Delumeau, *La peur en Occident* (ch. 1, n. 1), p. 164.
2 Ibid., p. 164.
3 G. S. Menochio, *Stuore* . . . (Venice: Stefano Monti, 1724), II, p. 380. Menochio (1575–1655) was a Jesuit theologian and exegete. (Trans. note)
4 Ibid., pp. 380–1.
5 *Le Nove Muse di Erodoto Alicarnasso*: 'translated and illustrated by Andrea Mustoxidi Corcirese' (Milan: Gio. B. Sonzogno, 1820), vol. I, p. 126. According to the sixteenth-century gloss, one should believe that putrefaction and the worms' banquet was the much feared 'disgrace'. In fact, Tommaso Garzoni writes that 'the Messagetae eat their dead relatives, since they think a burial in a man's stomach more decent than in that of worms' (*La*

piazza universale di tutte le professioni del mondo (Venice: G. B. Somasco, 1587), p. 446). 'The Issedones [added Garzoni], at the death of their fathers and mothers, were accustomed to singing and tearing apart their bodies with their teeth, and ate them mixed with the meat of sheep' (ibid.).

6 The Padam too in the East Indies followed a not dissimilar rite: 'Every time that one of them, man or woman, happens to get ill, if he is male, his closest family and friends kill him, saying that with his illness he would cause their flesh to spoil; and if a poor wretch denies that he is ill, they kill him anyway without mercy and eat him. If it is a woman, the women closest to her do the same. And he who reaches old age, doesn't for this reason escape being likewise killed and then eaten by his relatives; and yet because many are killed on becoming ill, very few of them reach old age' (*Della Selva rinovata*, by Pietro Messia, fourth part added by Mambrino Roseo da Fabriano, (Venice: G. Imberti, 1638), p. 4. Available in English as Pedro Mexia, *The Foreste; or, Collection of Histories*, London, 1571).

7 F. Pomey, *Libitina seu de funeribus* (Lyons: A. Molin, 1659), pp. 170-1. During the seventeenth century thanatology aroused increasing interest. The theme of the *Barocco e la morte* has also recently attracted the attention of some scholars. Here we shall limit ourselves to mentioning the work of Francesco Perucci, *Pompe funebri di tutte le nazioni del mondo. Raccolte dalle storie sagre e profane* (Verona: Rossi, 1646); Ulisse Aldrovandi, *De ritu sepeliendi apud diversas nationes* (Bologna: University Library, MS. 30), vol. I (cf. *Catalogo dei manoscritti di Ulisse Aldrovandi*, L. Frati ed. (Bologna, 1907).

8 Vladimir Propp, *Edipo alla luce del folclore* (Turin: Einaudi, 1975), p. 59.

9 Vladimir Propp, *Feste agrarie russe. Una ricerca storico-etnografica* (Bari: Dedalo, 1978), p. 53.

10 Dioscoride Pedacio, *Libri cinque della historia et materia medicinale tradotti in lingua volgare italiana*: 'by M. Pietro Andrea Matthiolo, Sienese doctor . . .' (Venice: Nicolò de Bascarini, 1544), p. 204. Cf. Galeottus Martius narniensis, *De doctrina promiscua*, ch. X: 'De cicuta herba ubi mors Socratis, de hyoscyamo, et de herba sardonia et risu sardonico'.

11 G. C. Croce, *Invito generale . . . per veder segare la vecchia*. Croce (1550-1609), writer of poetry in the Bolognese dialect, is most famous for *Bertoldo*, which portrays with vivacity and comedy many aspects of contemporary peasant life. Cf. Piero Camporesi, *La maschera di Bertoldo* (Turin: Einaudi (1976). (Trans. note)

12 M. Ficino, *Della vita sana* (Florence: Giunti, 1568), pp. 87-8.

13 G. M. Savonarola, *Practica maior* (Venice: Giunti, 1559), fol. 175a.

14 Vignati, *Antidotario contro la peste* (ch. 1, n. 15), p. 7.

15 F. Sirena, *L'arte dello spetiale . . .* (Pavia: Gio. Ghidini, 1679), p. 86.

16 *Antidotarium generale a Io. Iacobo Vueckero Basiliense nunc primum laboriosae congestum, methodicae digestum* (Basel: Eusebium Episcopium and Nicolai Frat., 1580), p. 301.

17 Camillo Brunori, *Il medico poeta ovvero la medicina esposta in versi e prose italiane* (Fabriano: Gregorio Mariotti, 1726), II, p. 374.

18 Ibid., p. 374.

19 Ibid., p. 375.

20 Johann Schroeder, *Pharmacopoeia medico-chymica, sive thesaurus pharmacologicus* . . . (Frankfurt: Joan. Görlini, 1677; first edn., 1646), p. 327.

21 Ibid., p. 324.

22 The Italian translation is from Vittorio Putti, *Berengario da Carpi. Saggio biografico e bibliografico seguito dalla traduzione del 'De Fractura calvae sive cranei'* (Bologna: Cappelli, 1937), p. 317.

23 'Now expanded with important secrets by Francesco Pignocatti, and with an index of all the diseases in order to find medications to cure them. Seventh printing' (Venice: Curti, 1680). With another title, *Secretario degli animali cioè secreti medicinali, che dalle parti d'ogni uno d'essi si cava* (Milan: Filippo Ghisolfi, 1649).

24 Schroeder *Pharmacopoeia medico-chymica*, p. 325.

25 Ibid., p. 325.

26 Cf. the term *mumie* in the *Allgemeines Lexicon der Künste und Wissenschaften* (Leipzig, 1721).

27 L. Leys, *De iustitia et iure caeterisque virtutibus cardinalibus* . . . (Milan: Petri Martyris Locarni and Io. B. Bidellum, 1616), p. 566.

28 Ibid., p. 566.

29 Paulus Aegineta, *Opera* (Intro., n. 14), p. 101.

30 'Nuova Aggiunta al nuovo Sistema del Moreali'. published as an appendix to Giam-Battista Moreali, *Delle febbri maligne, e contagiose. Nuovo sistema teorico-pratico* . . . (Venice: Giuseppe Corona, 1746), p. 282.

31 Gio. Felice Astolfi, *Della officina istorica* . . . (Venice: Sessa, 1622), p. 411.

32 Ibid., pp. 411–12.

33 Ibid., p. 415.

34 Montaigne, *Essais*, book I, ch. 30.

35 Marvin Harris, *Cannibals and Kings: The Origins of Cultures* (New York: 1977), p. 109.

36 Girolamo Cardano, *De rerum varietate libri XVII* (Avignon: Matthaeum Vincentium, 1558), p. 851.

37 Astolfi, *Della officina istorica*, p. 415.

38 C. Lévi-Strauss, *Tristes tropiques* (Paris: Plon, 1955). English translation by J. Russell (New York: Criterion Books, 1961), pp. 385–6.

39 G. Botero, *Relatione universale dell'isole fino al presente scoverte* (Rome: G. Ferrari, 1595), p. 114.

40 Guillaume Raynal, *Storia filosofica e politica degli stabilimenti, e del commercio degli Europei nelle due Indie* . . . : 'translated from the French by Remigio Pupares, noble patrician of Reggio', vol. VI (n.p., 1776). Published in France in 1770 under the title *Histoire philosophique et politique des établissements et du commerce des Européens dans les deux Indes*. Available in an English translation by J. Justamond, *A Philosophical and Political History of the Settlements and Trade of the Europeans in the East and West Indies* (Dublin, 1776).

41 Ibid., vol. IX (1777), p. 28.

42 Ibid., p. 32.

43 M. Eliade, 'Les représentations de la mort chez les primitifs', in *La Mort et l'Au-Delà*, in the *Cahiers de la Pierre qui vive* (Paris: Desclée De Brouwer, 1954), p. 169.

44 G. Botero, *Delle relationi universali*, part IV, (Rome: G. Ferrari, 1596), pp. 9–10. Available in English translation by R. Johnson, *Relations of the most Famous Kingdoms and Commonweales through the World* (1616).
The rite – with a few variations – was performed among the Aztecs, where the massacres were more numerous and severe. Francesco Saverio Clavigero wrote that 'if the victim was a prisoner of war, they immediately sacrificed him and cut off his head to keep it in the bone pile, and they threw the body down the stairs to the lesser atrium where it was picked up by the official or soldier who had put him in prison, and it was taken to his house to be cooked and prepared and make a dinner for his friends out of it' (*Storia antica del Messico* . . . (Cesena: G. Biasini, 1780), II, pp. 46–7).

45 P. Messia, *Della Selva rinovata* (above, n. 6) p. 31.

46 Ibid., p. 8.

47 Ibid., p. 30.

48 Raynal, *Storia filosofica e politica degli stabilimenti*, VI, pp. 40–1.

49 Ibid., IX, p. 30 and *passim*.

Chapter 4 *'They Set Out into the World of the Vagabond'*

1 *Lamento de uno poveretto huomo sopra la carestia* (n.p., n.d.), verse 1ff.

2 Ibid.

3 *Provisione elemosinaria per li poveri di qualunque sorte della città di Bologna* (Bologna: A. Giacarelli, 1548); quoted in P. Camporesi (ed.), *Il libro dei vagabondi* (2nd edn; Turin: Einaudi, 1980), p. 410.

4 Quoted in E. Grendi, *'Pauperismo e albergo dei poveri nella Genova del Seicento' Rivista Storica Italiana*, LXXXVIII, 4 (1975), p. 629.

5 Franceso Vettori, *Viaggio in Alemagna* (1507), in E. Niccolini (ed.), *Scritti storici e politici* (Bari: Laterza, 1972), p. 32. Vettori (1474–1539), friend and defender of Machiavelli, was active in Medicean politics until he fell out of favour with Cosimo I. (Trans. note)

6 Teseo Pini, *Speculum cerretanorum*, in Camporesi, *Il libro dei vagabondi*, pp. 38–9.

7 Reprinted in Camporesi, *Il libro dei vagabondi*, pp. 336–42.

8 G. B. Andreini, *Lo schiavetto* (Milan: Pandolfo Malatesta, 1612), p. 16. Andreini (1579–1654), from a family of actors, wrote comedies, poems and religious dramas, and was principal actor of the 'Comici Fedeli'. (Trans. note)

9 Cf. D. Fabre and J. Lacroix, *La tradition orale du conte occitan* (Paris: Presses Universitaires de France, 1974), I, pp. 23ff.

10 G. L. Basini, *L'uomo e il pane. Risorse, consumi e carenze alimentari della popolazione modenese nel Cinque e Seicento* (Milan: Giuffrè, 1970), p. 14.

11 L. Ferrante, ' "Tumulto di più persone per causa del calo del pane . . ." Saccheggi e repressione a Bologna (1671, 1677)', *Rivista Storica Italiana*, XC, 4 (1978), p. 798.

12 Basini, *L'uomo e il pane*, p. 76.

13 Ibid., p. 83.

14 E. Piscitelli, 'Le classi sociali a Bologna nel secolo XVIII', *Nuova Rivista*

Storica, XXXVIII, 1 (1954), p. 105.

15 Ibid., p. 102.
16 Ibid., p. 109.
17 Ibid., pp. 109-10.
18 Basini, *L'uomo e il pane*, pp. 64-5.
19 Ibid., p. 65.
20 G. Duby, *The Early Growth of the European Economy. Warriors and Peasants from the Seventh to the Twelfth Century*, trans. H. B. Clarke (London: Weidenfeld & Nicolson, 1974), p. 29.

Chapter 5 'They Rotted in Their Own Dung'

1 C. Ginzburg, C. Poni, 'Il nome e il come: scambio ineguale e mercato storiografico', *Quaderni Storici* (1979), pp. 181-90, n. 40. The quotation of S. L. Kaplan is taken from *Bread, Politics and Political Economy in the Reign of Louis XV* (The Hague: Martinus Nijhoff, 1976), pp. xx-xxi.
2 Abbot Giuseppe Parini (1729-99), a Milanese writer of Horatian odes, is remembered primarily for *Il giorno* (*The Day*, Eng. trans. 1927), a satirical poem on the selfishness and superficiality of the Milanese aristocracy. (Trans. note)
3 G. C. L. Canali, *La carità del prossimo celebrata, spiegata e promossa in più ragionamenti*. . . (Bologna: Gaspare de Franceschi, 1763), II, p. 23.
4 *Lamento nuovo sopra la andata di Tofalo zafo Sbirro de poveri mendichi cosa bella e ridicolosa*: 'newly brought to light by Giacomo Cieco of Verona' (Bologna: Vittorio Benacci, 1593).
5 C. Lévi-Strauss, *Tristes Tropiques* (ch. 3, n. 38), p. 293. Cf. Jack Goody and Ian Watt, 'The Consequences of Literacy', in *Literacy in Traditional Societies* (Cambridge: Cambridge University Press, 1968).
6 Canali, *La carità del prossimo*, II, p. 39.
7 Ibid., p. 39.
8 Ibid., pp. 32, 31.
9 Ibid., p. 38.
10 Giambattista Melloni, *Vita del Servo di Dio Giulio Cesare Luigi Canali* . . . (Bologna: Longhi, 1777), pp. 238-9.
11 Canali, *La carità del prossimo*, II, pp. 55-6.
12 Ibid., p. 57.
13 *Lettera portata nuovamente da Gianicco ambasciatore del Freddo a i poveretti avisandogli, che l'Inverno è per viaggio per venir a visitargli, e che stiamo parati, che il Mese di Novembre vol far l'entrata* (Bologna: Bartolomeo Cochi, 1610).
14 Melloni, *Vita del Servo di Dio*, p. 140.
15 Ibid., p. 138.
16 A. Saitta (ed.), *De subventione pauperum* (Florence: La Nuova Italia, 1973), p. 19.
17 Canali, *La carità del prossimo*, II, p. 57.
18 Ibid., p. 57.
19 Ibid., p. 71.

20 Ibid., p. 70.
21 Ibid., p. 91.
22 Ibid., pp. 91-2.
23 Ibid., p. 95.
24 Ibid., p. 92.
25 Melloni, *Vita del Servo di Dio*, p. 237.
26 Ibid., p. 139.
27 Ibid., p. 235.
28 'Stampata in Fiorenza, in Torino, in Bergamo, in Verona e in Mantova per l'Osanna Stampator Ducale', n.d.
29 Pastarino, *Preparamento del Pastarino, per medicarsi in questi sospettosi tempi di peste* (Bologna: Gio. Rossi, 1577), p. 6.
30 Ibid., p. 12.
31 Ibid., p. 11.
32 Ibid., p. 15.
33 Ibid., p. 16.
34 Ibid., pp. 16-17.
35 Pastarino, *Instruttione sopra la universal peste* . . . (Bologna: Gio. Rossi, 1584).
36 Pastarino, *Preparamento*, p. 14.
37 G. C. Canali, *Raccolta delle sagre canzoni altre volte date in luce* da Giulio Cesare Canali Dottor Teologo Collegiato, Lettor pubblico, e Curato di Sant'Isaia (Bologna: Lelio dalla Volpe, 1747), pp. 105-8. Canzonetta 'Sopra la carestia'.
38 Ibid., pp. 127 and 129. Canzone 'Della morte'.
39 'Lamento della povertà per l'estremo freddo del presente anno 1587', in M. Dursi (ed.), *Affanni e canzoni del padre di Bertoldo* (Bologna: Alfa, 1967), pp. 115-17.
40 *Lettera portata nuovamente da Gianicco ambasciatore del Freddo*, fol. 3r.
41 Ibid., fol. 3v.
42 'Lamento della povertà', p. 116.
43 Ibid., p. 116.
44 *Lamento de' poveretti i quali stanno a casa a pigione, e la convengono pagare* (Bologna: Cochi, 1617), fol. 1r-1v.

Chapter 6 The World Turned Upside Down

1 G. C. Croce, *Il solennissimo trionfo dell'Abbondanza, per la sua fertilissima entrata nella Città di Bologna, il dí primo d'Agosto 1597. Con l'amaro pianto, che fà la Carestia, nella dolorosa sua partita*, in Dialogo. (Bologna: Gio. Battista Bellagamba, 1597), fol. 6r.
2 E. De Martino, *La fine del mondo. Contributo all'analisi delle apocalissi culturali* ed. C. Gallini, (Turin: Einaudi, 1977), p. 222.
3 *Libre de Fortuna e Prudència*, quoted in G. Cocchiara, *Il mondo alla rovescia*, preface by P. Camporesi (Turin: Boringhieri, 1981), pp. 143-4.
4 R. Garapon, *La fantasie verbale et le comique dans le théâtre français du moyen âge à la fin du XVIIe siècle* (Paris: Colin, 1957), p. 87.

5 E. De Martino, *Furore Simbolo Valore*, Introduction by L. M. Lombardi Satriani (Milan: Feltrinelli, 1980), p. 174.
6 Giovanni di Mo. Pedrino depintore, *Cronica del suo tempo*, ed. G. Borghezio and M. Vattasso, with historical notes by A. Pasini (Rome: Biblioteca Apostolica Vaticana, 1934), II, p. 447.
7 G. B. Spaccini, *Cronaca modenese (1588–1636)*, ed. G. Bertoni, T. Sandonnini and P. E. Vicini (Modena: Ferraguti, 1911), I, p. 38.
8 The term refers to those people suspected of spreading the plague in Milan during the seventeenth century by smearing a poisonous substance on the walls. (Trans. note)
9 Spaccini, *Cronaca modenese*, I, pp. 3–4.
10 Ibid., II (1919), p. 177.

Chapter 7 *'Famine of Living' and 'Times of Suspicion'*

1 Delumeau, *La peur en Occident* (ch. 1, n. 1), p. 162.
2 P. Vizani, *I due ultimi libri delle historie della sua patria*, (Bologna: Eredi di Gio. Rossi, 1608), p. 138.
3 Segni, *Trattato sopra la carestia e fame* (ch. 1, n. 1), p. 52.
4 Cf. Emile Benveniste, *Il vocabolario delle istituzioni indo-europee*, II, *Potere, diritto, religione* (Turin: Einaudi, 1976), pp. 419ff. Trans. of *Le vocabulaire des institutions indo-européennes. Pouvoir, droit, religion* (Paris: Les Editions de Minuit, 1969).
5 G. B. Segni, *Discorso sopra la carestia, e fame* (Ferrara: B. Mamarello 1591), p. 46.
6 P. Vizani, *Diece libri delle historie della sua patria* (Bologna: Eredi di Gio. Rossi, 1602), p. 455.
7 *Ce fastu?*, 1–6 (1965–7), p. 62.
8 J.-P. Peter, 'Malati e malattie alla fine del XVIII secolo', in F. Braudel (ed.) *Problemi di metodo storico* (Bari: Laterza, 1973), p. 504.
9 L. Fioravanti, *Del Tesoro della vita humana* (Venice: Eredi di Melchior Sessa), c. 82r. Fioravanti (1518–88) was a Bolognese doctor and alchemist, and creator of a spirit solution once used in the treatment of rheumatic pains. (Trans. note)
10 Quoted in Basini, *L'uomo e il pane* (ch. 4, n. 10), p. 83.
11 L. A. Muratori, *Li tre governi, politico, medico ed ecclesiastico, utilissimi, anzi necessari in tempo di peste*, 3rd edn. (Milan: Vigoni & Cairolo, 1721), p. 119.
12 Ibid., p. 21.
13 Landucci, *Diario fiorentino* (Intro., n. 12), p. 174.
14 Muratori, *Li tre governi*, p. 23.
15 Ibid., p. 22.
16 Ibid., p. 25.
17 Ibid., p. 96.
18 Ibid., p. 97.
19 Ibid., p. 128.

Chapter 8 Night-time

1 Anonymous, *Vita della Beata Beatrice seconda d'Este fondatrice dell'insigne monastero di S. Antonio in Ferrara della regola di S. Benedetto* (Ferrara: G. Rinaldi, 1777), p. 125. The book is a reprint, with several modifications and additions, of the *Vita* written by Girolamo Baruffaldi, noted archpriest of Cento, published at Venice in 1723.

2 Ibid., p. 124.

3 Ibid., pp. 119-21.

4 Mongitore (1663-1743) collected anecdotes on his native Sicily, and was canon of the Cathedral of Palermo and member of the Arcadian Academy. (Trans. note)

5 Strozzi, Cicogna, *Palagio de gl'incanti* (ch. 1, n. 24), p. 275.

6 Ibid., p. 404. Cf. S. Battaglia, 'Il mito del licantropo nel "Bisclavret" di Maria di Francia', in *La coscienza letteraria del Medioevo* (Naples: Liguori, 1965), pp. 361-89.

7 Muratori, *Li tre governi* (ch. 7, n. 11), p. 90.

8 Martino d'Arles, *Tractatus de superstitionibus, contra maleficia seu sortilegia quae hodie vigent in orbe terrarum* (Rome: Vincentium Luchinum, 1559), fol. 9r.

9 *The Eclogues of Baptista Mantuanus*, Introduction and notes by W. P. Mustard (Baltimore: Johns Hopkins University Press, 1911), p. 105. Along with bat's blood, hallucinogenic herbs, 'plantae soporiferae' or sleeping drugs (elaeoselinum, aconite, poplar leaves, somniferous solanum . . .), and soot, the fundamental ingredient in the witches' ointment was *puerarum pinguedo*, the fat of infants. Cf. G. Aquilecchia, 'G. B. Della Porta e l'Inquisizione', in *Schede di Italianistica* (Turin: Einaudi, 1976), p. 227.

10 Prospero Domenico Maroni, 'De superstitiosi in generale', in *Decisiones prudentiales casuum et quaesitorum conscientiae* . . . (Forlì: Fastorum Eruditorum, 1702), pp. 317, 322.

11 Francisci Pamphili 'praestantissimi poetae sanctoseverinatis', in *Picenum* . . . (Macerata: Sebastianus Martellinus, 1575), p. 47.

12 J. P. Migne, *Patrologia Graeca* (Paris, 1845), CXXII, col. 827.

13 *Roma ristaurata, et Italia illustrata*: 'di Biondo da Forlì tradotte in buona lingua volgare per Lucio Fauno' (Venice: M. Tramezzino, 1548), fol. 126r.-v. Biondo (1392-1463) was an Italian humanist and pontifical secretary. (Trans. note)
On the theme of the ingestion of sacrificed infants cf. Norman Cohn, 'The Myth of Satan and his Human Servants', in M. Douglas (ed.), *Witchcraft, Confessions and Accusations* (London: Tavistock, 1970).

14 G. Merula, *Nuova selva di varia lettione* (Venice: Valvassori, 1559), p. 35.

15 J. Le Goff, quoted in J.-L. Goglin, *Les misérables dans l'Occident médiéval* (Paris: Editions du Seuil, 1976), p. 204.

16 P. Ripa, *Tractatus de nocturno tempore* (Pavia: P. Bartoli and O. Bordoni, 1601), p. 314.

17 Girolamo Menghi, *Compendio dell'arte essorcistica* . . . (Bologna: Giovanni Rossi, 1582).

18 Strozzi Cicogna, *Palagio de gl'incanti*, p. 275.
19 Vizani, *Diece libri delle historie della sua patria* (ch. 7, n. 6), pp. 452–5. For the 'symptoms of collective anguish', cf. B. Farolfi, *Strutture agrarie e crisi cittadina nel primo Cinquecento bolognese* (Bologna: Patron, 1977), pp. 41ff. For 'signs' and prophetic omens, cf. O. Niccoli, 'Profezie in piazza. Note sul profetismo popolare nell'Italia del primo Cinquecento', *Quaderni Storici*, 14 (1979),: *Religioni delle classi popolari*, ed. C. Ginzburg, pp. 300–39.
20 Quoted in Moreali, *Delle febbri maligne e contagiose* (ch. 3, n. 30), p. 117.
21 Vizani, *I due ultimi libri delle historie della sua patria*, (ch. 7, n. 2), pp. 81–2.
22 Cf. E. Le Roy Ladurie, 'Difficulté d'être et douceur de vivre', in P. Wolff (ed.), *Histoire du Languedoc* (Toulouse: Privat, 1967), pp. 265–311.

Chapter 9 Ritual Battles and Popular Frenzies

1 G. Rosaccio, *Fabrica universale dell'huomo sotto titolo di Microcosmo dichiarata . . .* (Venice: G. Imberti, 1627), pp. 45–6.
2 Canali, *La carità del prossimo* (ch. 5, n. 3), II, p. 32.
3 Ibid., p. 42.
4 *Il solennissimo trionfo dell'Abbondanza, per la sua fertilissima entrata nella Città di Bologna; il dí primo d'Agosto 1597. Con l'amaro pianto, che fà la Carestia, nella dolorosa sua partita, in Dialogo* (Bologna: Gio. Battista Bellagamba, 1597), fols. 5r.–6v.
5 Published in Rome and republished in Bologna: Vittorio Benacci, 1597.
6 Bologna: Vittorio Benacci, 1603.
7 Remained in MS, but has re-surfaced now thanks to the research of L. Ferrante and published in "Tumulto di più persone per causa del calo del pane . . .", Saccheggi e repressione a Bologna (1671, 1677)', *Rivista Storica Italiana*, XC, 4 (1978), pp. 801–2, in note.
8 Segni, *Trattato sopra la carestia e fame*, pp. 54–5. *Zarabottana* was a medieval game of chance. (Trans. note)

Chapter 10 Medicina Pauperum

1 Vizani, *I due ultimi libri delle historie della sua patria* (ch. 7, n. 2), pp. 138–9.
2 Basini, *L'uomo e il pane* (ch. 4, n. 10), p. 14.
3 Landucci, *Diario fiorentino* (Intro, n. 12), p. 46.
4 G. Fantaguzzi, *Caos. Cronache cesenati del sec. XV pubblicate ora per la prima volta di su i manoscritti con notizie e note*, ed. Dino Bazzocchi (Cesena: Bettini, 1915), p. 17.
5 Ibid.
6 O. Montalbani, *Il pane sovventivo spontanascente succedaneo intero del pane ordinario, overo aumentante l'istesso pane di biade, breve discorso teorico e prattico . . .*, 'to the Most Illustrious Senators of Bologna' (Bologna: Ferroni, 1648). With the dedication altered, the *discorso* was republished the following year by the same publisher with the title *Urania, e Cerere pacificate insieme. Discorso astrologico per l'anno 1649 . . .*

7 O. Montalbani, *Formolario economico cibario, e medicinale di materie più facili di minor costo altrettanto buone, e valevoli, quanto le più pretiose* (Bologna: G. Monti, 1654).

8 N. Serpetro, *Il mercato delle meraviglie* (Venice: Tomasini, 1653), p. 10.

9 G. Della Porta, *Magia naturalis* (Naples: Horatium Salvianum, 1589), pp. 93–5. [Available in a reprint of the 1658 English edition as Derek Price (ed.), *Natural Magick*, (New York: Basic Books, 1958).]

10 Montalbani, *Il pane sovventivo spontenascente*, p. 14.

11 Montalbani, *Formolario economico cibario, e medicinale*, p. 10. 'Gratianesque' refers to Commedia dell'Arte character of Doctor Gratiano. (Trans. note)

12 Ibid., p. 8 and *passim*.

13 Ibid., pp. 10–11.

14 Fioravanti, *Dello specchio di scientia universale* (Venice: M. Sessa, 1583), p. 41a.

15 Ibid., p. 41b.

Chapter 11 *'Tightness of Purse'*

1 Croce, *Della famosissima Compagnia della Lesina. Dialogo, Capitoli e Ragionamenti*, (Venice: Soineda, 1610), fol. 21a.

2 Ibid, fols. 21b–22a.

3 Ibid., fol. 23a.

4 Ibid., fol. 22a–b.

5 G. C. Croce, *Le Nozze di M. Trivello Foranti, e di Madonna Lesina de gli Appuntati* (Bologna: Cochi, 1620), p. 3.

6 Ibid, p. 5.

7 Croce, *Della famosissima Compagnia della Lesina*, fol. 73a–b.

8 Croce, *Le Nozze di M. Trivello Foranti*, p. 5.

9 Ibid., p. 7.

10 Ibid., p. 8.

11 Ibid., p. 48.

12 The names are difficult to render into English, but they are, roughly, as follows: Miser Loot, Thick-skinned O'the Thick-skinned, Boor Peasant, Pincher Flannels, Hooked O'the Hooked, Clutch Big-miser, Howsoever, Little-skinflint of Carpi, Stretch-those Grape-stalks, Truffaldino (referring to a swindling character in the Commedia dell'Arte) of Graffignano, Jest O'the Jests, Eversnatching, Clutchall, Loan-nothing, Skinflint, Sharp, Worker ant, Put-in-pocket, Tight-cone, Fleecer, Big-skinflint, Open-eye, Weeding, and Shut-tight. (Trans. note)

13 Croce, *Della famosissima Compagnia della Lesina*, fol. 16a.

14 *Galeria de' Lesinanti*, Bologna, University Library, MS 3878, chapter LI, part VI., fols. 101r–102v.

15 The full title is worth translating: 'The true rule for keeping thin with very little expense, written by Master Miser of Stingy, Official for the Most Noble Company of Stinginess, to Master Needle Unbridged, his godfather. A work most useful to all those who suffer tightness of purse'. (Trans. note)

16 Croce, *Della famosissima Compagnia della Lesina*, fol. 56b.

17 Ibid., fol. 103a.

18 G. C. Croce, *La vera regola per mantenersi magro* (Bologna: Gliheredi di Bartolomeo Cochi, 1622), fol. 4v.

19 Croce, *Della famosissima Compagnia della Lesina*, fol. 25a.

20 Ibid., fol. 89a.

21 Quoted in Venturi, '1764: Napoli nell'anno della fame' (ch. 1, n. 33), p. 406.

Chapter 12 *Collective Vertigo*

1 G. C. Croce, *Contrasto del pane di formento e quello di fava per la precedenza. Con un sonetto in Dialogo fra un Maestro, e un Garzone, sopra il pane alloiato* (Bologna: B. Cochi, 1617), fols. 1v.-2r.

2 Ibid., fol. 3r.-v.

3 M. Savonarola and B. Boldo, *Libro della natura et virtù delle cose che nutriscono* . . . (Intro., n. 2), p. 21.

4 Pietro Andrea Mattioli, *Discorsi ne' sei libri di Pedacio Dioscoride Anazarbeo della materia medicinale* . . . (Venice: N. Pezzana, 1744), p. 340.

5 Ibid., p. 276.

6 Croce, *Contrasto del pane di formento*, fol. 2v.

7 Anon., *Instruzioni mediche per le gente di campagna* (Bassano: Remondini, 1785), part I, p. 25.

8 *Erbolario volgare* (Venice: F. Bindoni, 1536), chapter 'De lo papavero'.

9 Mattioli, *Discorsi ne' sei libri*, p. 597.

10 Ibid., p. 600.

11 Ibid., p. 603. Cf. S. Marszalkowicz, 'L'elemento tossicologico nella stregoneria medievale', in *Lavori di storia della medicina compilati nell'anno aceademico 1936-37* (Rome: Bedonia, 1938), pp. 80–93.

12 Osvaldo Crollio, *Tractatus de signaturis internis rerum* (Venice: Combi, 1643).

13 Cardano, *De rerum varietate* (ch. 3, n. 36), pp. 734-5.

14 K. Kerényi, Preface to the Italian edition of *The Trickster in Relation to Greek Mythology, Il briccone divino*. (Milan: Bompiani, 1979), p. 19).

15 Croce, *Contrasto del pane di formento*, fol. 2v.

16 Ibid., fol. 4r.

17 Aldous Huxley, *The Doors of Perception: Heaven and Hell*. (London: Chatto & Windus, 1960), p. 19.

18 G. C. Croce, *Sogni fantastichi della notte* (Bologna: Cochi, 1629), p. 4v. and *passim*.

19 Giovanni Maria Bonardo, *La minera del mondo* (Venezia: A Turini, 1611), fol. 42a. The first edition goes back to 1589.

20 Ibid., fol. 43a.

21 Lazaro Grandi, *Alfabetto di segreti medicinali* (Bologna: Longhi, 1693), p. 128.

22 P. Zacchia, *De' mali hipochondriaci* (Rome: V. Mascardi, 1644), p. 44.

23 Ibid., p. 45.

Chapter 13 Hyperbolic Dreams

1 J.-P. Peter, 'Malati e malattie alla fine del XVIII secolo' (ch. 7, n. 8), p. 506.

2 Ibid.

3 Savastano (trans. Giampietro Bergantini,), *I quattro libri delle cose botaniche del Padre Franceso Eulalio Savastano della Compagnia de Gesù. Colla traduzione in verso sciolto italiano* (Venice: P. Bassaglia, 1749), p. 399.

4 Translated literally into English, the names are as follows: falling sickness, blessed sickness, fits, sacred disease, Herculean disease, comitial disease, principal sickness, great sickness and lunatics' sickness. (Trans. note)

5 Moreali, *Delle febbri maligne, e contagiose* (ch. 3, n. 30), p. 12.

6 Ibid., pp. 12-13.

7 Zacchia, *De' mali hipochondriaci* (ch. 12, n. 22), p. 398.

8 Ibid., p. 397.

9 Ibid., p. 396.

10 Ibid.

11 Ibid., pp. 398-9.

12 Savastano, *I quattro libri delle cose botaniche*, p. 401.

13 Thomas, 'Problemi sociali, conflitti individuali e stregoneria' (ch. 2, n. 4), p. 204.

14 L. Fioravanti, *De capricci medicinali* (Venice: L. Avanzo, 1568), fol. 118r.

15 Cited in C. Corrain and P. Zampini, 'Documenti etnografici e folklorici nei Sinodi Diocesani dell'Emilia-Romagna', reprinted from *Palestra del Clero*, 15-17 (Aug.-Sept. 1964), p. 9, n. 56.

16 *Episcopale bononiensis civitatis et dioecesis* (Bologna: Benacci, 1580), fol. 1v.

17 G. Duby *The Early Growth of the European Economy* (ch. 4, n. 20), p. 67.

18 Maroni, *De superstitiosi in generale* (ch. 8, n. 10), p. 323.

19 Ibid., p. 317.

20 Verses by Giovan Battista Refrigeri, in L. Frati (ed.), *Rimatori bolognesi del Quattrocento* (Bologna: Romagnoli-Dell'Acqua, 1908), p. 94.

Chapter 14 Artificial Paradises

1 Montalbani, *Il pane sovventivo spontenascente* (ch. 10, n. 6), p. 23.

2 Segni, *Discorso sopra la carestia, e fame* (ch. 7, n. 5), p. 44.

3 Giovanni Lorenzo Anania, *L'universale fabrica del mondo overo cosmografia* (Venice: I. Vidali, 1576), p. 156 and *passim*. Giulio Cesare Croce is also author of a poetic *Cosmografia* in verse.

4 Battista Codronchi, *De morbis veneficis . . . opus non modo medicis ac exorcistis apprime utile ac necessarium, sed omnibus litterarum professoribus iucundissimum* (Venice: Franciscum de Franciscis senensem, 1595), fol. 95b. In Pietro Spano's *Libro dimandato il Tesoro de' Poveri*, diabolical possessions were also considered, for the most part, the responsibility of doctors. Cf. ch. XXXV, 'Contra lo male et demoni cioè fatura' (Venice: Giovanni Alvisi de Varesi, 1500).

5 G. M. Bonardo, *La minera del mondo* (1st edn. 1589; Antonio Turini, Venice, 1611), III, fol. 40a and *passim*.

6 G. Menghi, *Compendio dell'arte essorcista* . . . (Bologna: G. Rossi, 1582), pp. 570 and 573.

7 Ibid., pp. 571-2.

8 Codronchi, *De morbis veneficis ac veneficijs*, fol. 191a.

9 Ibid., fol. 192a.

10 Quoted from J. Céard, 'Folie et démologie au XVIe siècle', in *Folie et déraison à la Renaissance* (Brussels: Ed. de l'Université de Bruxelles, 1976), p. 141. Cf. A. Delatte, *Herbarius. Recherches sur le cérémonial usité chez les anciens pour la cueillette des simples et des plantes magiques* (Bibl. de la Faculté de Philosophie et Lettres de l'Université de Liège, 1938), fas. LXXXI, p. 158.

11 Levino Lennio, *De gli occulti miracoli e varii ammaestramenti delle cose della natura, con probabili ragioni e artifiziosa congiettura confermati* (Venice: Lodovico Avanzi, 1560), fol. 81a.

12 Ibid., fol. 79a.

13 Ibid., fol. 72a.

14 Pietro Castelli, *Memoriale per lo speziale romano* (Venice: Gio. Francesco Valvasense, 1678), p. 311 and *passim*. The *mitridato* mentioned was an antidote for poisons. (Trans. note)

15 Ibid., p. 311.

16 Cf. G. Amalfi, 'A proposito di danze macabre', in Giambattista Basile, *Archivio di letteratura popolare*, I (1883), no. 8, pp. 59-60.

17 Cf. *Lettera sulle insalate. Lectio nona de fungis*, Introduction by E. Cecchini, contributions by G. Arbizzoni, D. Bischi, G. Nonni and S. Scaramella Petri (Urbino: Accademia Raffaello, 1977), pp. 68 and 118. By the same doctor and naturalist see *Lettere a Ulisse Aldrovandi*, ed. G. Nonni (Urbino: Quattro Venti, 1982).

Chapter 15 Poppyseed Bread

1 Montalbani, *Il pane sovventivo spontenascente* (ch. 10, n. 6), p. 3.

2 Cf. A. Guenzi, 'Un mercato regolato: pane e fornai a Bologna nell'età moderna', *Quaderni Storici*, 37 (1978), 370-97; and, by the same author, 'Il "calmiero del formento": controllo del prezzo del pane e difesa della rendita terriera a Bologna nei secoli XVII e XVIII', *Annali della Fondazione Luigi Einaudi*, XI, (1977), pp. 143-201.

3 Montalbani *Il pane sovventivo*, p. 4.

4 Ibid., p. 7.

5 Ibid., pp. 7-8.

6 Ibid., pp. 7-8.

7 Ibid., p. 7.

8 Ibid., p. 11.

9 G. Della Porta, *Magia naturalis* (ch. 10, n. 9), pp. 94-5.

10 Savonarola and Boldo, *Libro della natura et virtute delle cose che nutriscono* (Intro., n. 2), p. 33.

11 Mattioli, *Discorsi ne' sei libri di Pedacio Dioscoride Anazarbeo* (ch. 12, n. 4), pp. 594-5.

12 Savonarola and Boldo, *Libro della natura* p. 31.

13 Ibid., p. 31.

14 G. Della Porta, *Gli duoi fratelli rivali*, act I, scene IV, in *Le Commedie*, ed. V. Spampanato, Bari: Laterza, 1910, vol. II, p. 216.

15 Montalbani *Il pane sovventivo*, p. 13.

16 G. Bonoli, *Storia di Lugo ed annessi* (Faenza: Archi, 1732), p. 206.

Chapter 16 The 'Fickle and Verminous Colony'

1 Muratori, *Li tre governi, politico, medico ed ecclesiastico* (ch. 7, n. 11), p. 21.

2 Moreali, *Delle febbri maligne, e contagiose* (ch. 3, n. 30), p. 27.

3 Ibid., pp. 53-4.

4 Refers to the miller of Carlo Ginzburg's study *The Cheese and the Worms: The Cosmos of a Sixteenth-Century Miller*. trans. John and Anne Tedeschi (Harmondsworth: Penguin, 1982). (Trans. note)

5 *I maravigliosi secreti di medicina e chirurgia* (ch. 1, n. 16), p. 57.

6 Fioravanti, *De Capricci medicinali* (ch. 13, n. 14), fol. 117r.

7 *Tesoro della vita umana* (Venice: Marco Sessa's heirs, 1570), fols. 25v.-26v. and *passim*.

8 Cf. L. Samoggia, 'Empirici litotomi e oculisti negli Ospedali della Vita e della Morte in Bologna nel 1600 e 1700' in Samoggia et al., *Sette secoli di vita ospitaliera in Bologna* (Bologna: Cappelli, 1960), pp. 183-201.

9 Quoted in Moreali, *Della febbri*, p. 47.

10 Ibid., pp. 47-8.

11 Ibid., p. 49.

12 Petrus Thyraeus, *Daemoniaci, hoc est de obsessis a spiritibus daemoniorum hominibus* . . . (Coloniae Agrippinae: Cholini, 1598), pp. 8-9.

13 Cf. Lucia Lazzerini, 'Arlecchino, le mosche, le streghe e le origini del teatro popolare', *Studi Mediolatini e Volgari*, XXV (1977), p. 110.

14 A. Tassoni, *De' pensieri diversi, libri dieci* (Venice: D. Miloco, 1676), p. 283. Cf. the 'horrid monsters . . . vice and fault / Of the matter' (Torquato Tasso, *Il Mondo creato*, VI, 1319-22).

15 Ginzburg, *The Cheese and the Worms*, p. 57.

16 Hieronymus Mengus, *Eversio daemonum e corporibus oppressis* . . . (Bononiae: Io. Rossium, 1588), p. 9.

17 Ibid., p. 539.

18 Moreali, *Delle febbri*, p. 40.

19 Ibid., pp. 42-3.

20 Ibid., p. 42.

21 Ibid., p. 119.

22 Ibid., p. 44.

23 Giuseppe Donzelli, *Teatro farmaceutico, dogmatico, e spagirico*, (Venice: A. Poletti, 1728), p. 505 and *passim*.

24 Lennio, *De gli occulti miracoli* . . . (ch. 14, n. 11), fol. 87a.

25 Ibid., fol. 87a.-b.

26 Donzelli, *Teatro farmaceutico*, p. 505.

27 Lennio, *De gli occulti miracoli*, fol. 87b.
28 Ibid., fol. 87b.
29 Ibid., fols. 87b.-88a.
30 Olao Magno Gotho Vescovo di Upsala, *Historia delle genti et della natura delle cose settentrionali* (Venice: Giunti, 1565), p. 158a. Available in English as Olaus Magnus, *A Compendious History of the Goths, Swedes, Vandals, and other Northern Nations* (London: Streater, 1658).
31 Donzelli, *Treatro farmaceutico*, p. 459.
32 Ibid., p. 459.
33 Auda, *Breve compendio di maravigliosi segreti* . . . (ch. 1, n. 19) pp. 222-3.
34 Donzelli, *Teatro farmaceutico*, p. 457.

Chapter 17 *Putrid Worms and Vile Snails*

1 *L'Hôpital général* (1676), quoted in Michel Foucault, *Folie et déraison. Histoire de le folie à l'âge classique* (Paris: Plon, 1961), p. 645. Available in English as *Madness and Civilization: a history of insanity in the Age of Reason* (London: Tavistock, 1967). Translator Richard Howard.
2 G.-F. Letrosne, *Mémoire sur les vagabonds et sur les mendiants* (Paris: P. G. Simon, Imprimeur du Parlement, 1764), p. 8.
3 Ibid., p. 4 and p. 6.
4 Bonifacio, *Il paltoniere* (ch. 2, n. 1), p. 182.
5 Ibid., pp. 183-4.
6 Ibid., p. 184.
7 Ibid., p. 180.
8 Ibid., pp. 171-2.
9 Montalbani, *Il pane sovventivo spontenascente* (ch. 10, n. 6), p. 3.
10 Quoted in F. Nicolini, 'La carestia e le epidemie del 1629', in *Aspetti della vita italo-spagnola nel Cinque e Seicento* (Naples: Guida, 1934), p. 206. Ripamonti, 1573-1643, was a Milanese chronicler. (Trans. note)
11 Ibid., p. 209.
12 Letrosne, *Mémoire sur les vagabonds*, p. 11.
13 A. Manzoni, *Fermo e Lucia*, vol. IV, ch. 1.
14 Montalbani, *Il pane sovventivo spontenascente*, pp. 5 and 19-20.
15 Ibid., p. 21.
16 Ibid., p. 21.
17 Ibid., p. 21.
18 For the same aristocratic and class polemic in Alessandro Piccolomini and Paolo Paruta cf. G. Benzoni, *Gli affanni della cultura. Intellettuali e potere nell'Italia della Controriforma e barocca* (Milan: Feltrinelli, 1978), pp. 36ff.
19 B. Pisanelli, *Trattato della natura de' cibi e del bere . . . con molte belle historie naturali* (Bergamo: Comino Ventura, 1587), pp. 80, 84.
20 Ibid., p. 47.
21 A reference to the peasant turned king's adviser who is the protagonist of Croce's *Bertoldo*. Available in a 1903 translation as *Bertholde; or, Wonderful Sallies of Wit . . . Freely translated with considerable improvements*. (Trans. note)

22 *Il Microcosmo . . . nel quale si tratta brevemente dell'anima vegetabile, sensibile, e rationale dell'huomo . . .* (Bologna: Eredi d'Antonio Pisarri, 1688), p. 40.
23 V. Tanara, *Economia del cittadino in villa* (Venice: G. Battista Tramontin, 1687), p. 409 and *passim*.
24 G. C. Croce, *La sollecita et studiosa Academia de Golosi. Nella quale s'intendono tutte le loro leccardissime scienze . . .* (Bologna: Vittorio Benacci, 1602), fol. 2r.
25 Giulio Cesare Croce, *Banchetto de' Malcibati. Comedia dell'Academico Frusto. Recitata da gli Affamati nella Città Calamitosa . . .* (Ferrara: Vittorio Baldini, 1601), p. 4 and *passim*.

Chapter 18 *A City of Mummies*

1 St Bernard, 'De Gubernatione rei familiaris', in E. Faral, *Les jongleurs au Moyen Age* (Paris: Champion, 1910), p. 278.
2 The 'Testamentum seu stentamentum', in E. Levi, *Un giullare del Trecento: Zaffarino* (Livorno: Giusti, 1915), pp. 65–76.
3 Croce, *Banchetto de' Malcibati* (ch. 17, n. 25), p. 5.
4 Ibid., p. 27.
5 Bonifacio, *Il paltoniere* (ch. 2, n. 1), p. 189.
6 Croce, *Banchetto de' Malcibati*, p. 39.
7 Ibid., p. 3.
8 Montalbani, *Formolario economico, cibario, e medicinale* (ch. 10, n. 7), p. 4.
9 Segni, *Discorso sopra la carestia, e fame* (ch. 7, n. 5), pp. 22–4.
10 Ibid., pp. 19–20.
11 Ibid., p. 21.
12 Ibid., p. 21.
13 Ibid., p. 21.

Chapter 19 *The Triumph of Poverty*

1 Camillo Fanucci, *Trattato di tutte l'opere pie dell'alma città di Roma* (Rome: L. Faccij and S. Paolini, 1602), pp. 65–6.
2 Ibid., p. 67.
3 *La mendicità proveduta nella città di Roma coll'ospizio publico, fondato dalla pietà, e beneficenza di Nostro Signore Innocenzo XII Pontefice Massimo. Con le risposte all'obiezioni contro simili fondazioni* (Rome: Gio. Giacomo Komarek, 1693), p. 24.
4 Carlo Bartolomeo Piazza, *Euseuologio romano, overo delle opere pie di Roma* (Rome: Domenico Antonio Ercole, 1698), p. ix.
5 Ibid., p. xii.
6 Fernand Braudel, *Capitalismo e civiltà materiale* (Turin: Einaudi, 1977), p. 47. Available in English as *Capitalism and Material Life, 1400–1800*, trans. M. Kochan (London: Weidenfeld & Nicolson, 1973).
7 *Il mendicare abolito nella città di Montalbano da un Pubblico Uffizio di Carità. Con la replica alle principali obiezioni che potrebbon farsi contro questo Regolamento.* (Florence: Gio. Filippo Cecchi, 1693), p. 18.

8 Ibid., p. 19.

9 Ibid., pp. 19-20.

10 *La mendicità proveduta*, p. 8 and *passim*.

11 Piazza, *Euseuologio romano*, p. iii.

12 Ibid., p. iv.

13 Ibid., pp. iii-iv.

14 Ibid., p. v.

15 Ibid., p. xi.

16 Ibid., p. v and *passim*.

17 Ibid., p. iv.

18 Ibid., p. iv.

19 Ibid., p. iv.

20 G. Severino Polica, 'Storia della povertà e storia dei poveri. A proposito di una iniziativa di Michel Mollat', *Studi Medievali*, XVII, 1 (1976), p. 385.

21 Piazza, *Euseuologio romano*, pp. xi-xii.

22 Ibid., p. xii.

23 *La mendicità proveduta*, p. 1. The beginning of this work was copied literally in Andrea Guevarre, *La mendicità sbandita col sovvenimento de' poveri . . .* (Turin: Mairesse, 1717). *La mendicità proveduta nella città di Pisa . . .* (Pisa: C. & F. Bindi, 1714), also faithfully follows *La mendicità proveduta nella città di Roma*.

24 Polica, 'Storia della povertà e storia dei poveri', p. 384.

25 *Istruzioni, e regole degli Ospizi Generali per li Poveri da fondarsi in tutti gli Stati della S. R. Maestà del Re di Sicilia . . . Di ordine della Medesima Maestà* (Turin: G. Mairesse & G. Radix, 1717), p. 132.

26 Ibid., p. 133.

27 *Stabilimento dell'Ospizio generale della carità nella città di Vercelli* (Turin: Radix & Mairesse, 1719), p. 13.

28 Ibid., p. 14.

29 Ibid., p. 14.

30 Ibid., in Appendix, p. 2.

31 Ibid., p. 1.

Index

Accolti, Girolamo, 105
aged, sacrificial killing of the 41–2, 43–4
Albertus Magnus, 24
Aldrovandi, Ulisse, 145, 168, 189
almshouses, *see* hospices and hospitals
amulets, 113–14, 141
Anania, Giovanni Lorenzo, 199
Andreini, Giovan Battista, 60
Anguillara, Lampridio, 187
anointing, 24–5
anthropophagy, *see* cannibalism
apothecaries, *see* druggists
aqua divina, 46
Aquilecchia, G., 195
Arienti, Sabadino degli, 185
Ariosto, Ludovico, 93, 97
Astolfi, Giovanni Felice, 190
astrology, herbs and, 143–4
athrepsia, 82
Auda, Domenico, 161, 187
autophagy, 38, 40
Avicenna, 29
Aztecs, 52

baara root, 142
bakers' shops, looting of, 106
Balordìa, 79
Barigazzi family, 47
Baruffaldi, Girolamo, 195

Basil, Saint, 26–7
Basini, Gian Luigi, 62, 191, 196
Basle, Great Vagabond of, 162
Battaglia, S., 195
Battara, Giovanni, 43
beggars, *see* poor, the; vagabonds, rural
beliefs, interpretation of, by historians, 2–4
Benveniste, Emile, 194
Benzoni, G., 202
Beolco, Angelo, *see* Ruzante
Berengario, 47
Bernard, Saint, 172
Bianchi, Tomasino de', 62, 109
Biondo, Flavio, 55, 97, 195
blood, human, 19
  drinking of, 44–5
Boaistuau, Pierre, 142
Boccone, Paolo, 24
body, the
  history of conceptions of, 12–13
  medicinal use of, 7–8, 46–50
Boerhaave, Herman, 154
Boldo, Bartolemeo, 148, 198, 201
Bologna, 44
  druggists in sixteenth century, 72–3
  famine in sixteenth century, 86–7, 100–1, 104–6, 146–7, 172–7
  looting of bakers' shops in, 106

Mendicants' Institute, 174
poor in eighteenth century, 61, 63–70
poor in sixteenth century, 58–9, 108–9
Bonardo, Giovanni Maria, 141, 186, 198
Bonifacio, Baldassare, 35, 108, 164, 165, 166, 173
Bonoli, G., 150
Bonomo, G., 187
borage, 140
Borgarucci, Prospero, 73
Botero, Giovanni, 53, 54
Bovio, Zefirele Tomaso, 187
Boyle, Robert, 24
Braudel, Fernand, 194, 203
Brazilian Indians, 53–4
bread, 17–18
adulteration by authorities, 84–5
narcotic substances in, 18, 122–3, 126–7, 137–8
poppyseed, 18, 137, 147–8
seasoning of, 148
types of, and social distinctions, 10, 17, 120–1, 170
wheat substitutes in, 62, 110–11, 119, 121–2, 123, 138, 148
brevi, sellers of, 22
Brunori, Camillo, 46, 189
Bumaldi, Giovanni Antonio, see Montalbani, Ovidio
Burke, Peter, 5

Calabria, 83
Campanella, Tommaso, 21, 24, 187
Camporesi, Piero
Bread of Dreams, 8–16
La Carne Impassabile (The Incorruptible Flesh), 7–8
La Casa dell'Eternita, 6–7
Canali, Giulio Cesare, 63–4, 66, 67–70, 196
verse quoted, 74–6
cannibalism, 23, 28–9, 40–1, 44–55, 87

cantastorie (story-tellers), 64–5
Cardano, Girolamo, 51, 53, 125, 129, 198
Caribs, 52
Carnaro, Alvise, 36, 38–9
Casanova, Giacomo, 61
Castelli, Pietro, 200
Castiglione, Sabba, 95
Céard, J., 200
Ce fastu?, 88, 194
charity, see hospices and hospitals; poor relief
children, narcotics administered to, 23–4, 25, 124
Cicogna, Strozzi, 99, 187, 195
Citaredo, Vincenzo, 71
class, social, and diet; see diet, social class and
Clavigero, Francesco Saverio, 191
Clement XIV, Pope, 61
coca, 138, 139
Cocchiara, G., 193
Cockaigne, Land of, 80–1
Codronchi, Battista, 142, 199
Cohn, Norman, 195
comedies, seventeenth-century, 60
Commare o raccoglitrice, La, 186
consumer society, development of, 13–14
Contratto, Hermano, 87
Cordo, Valerio, 73
corpses, human, medicinal uses of, see mummified flesh
Corrain, C., 199
Crespi, Giuseppe Maria, 67
crickets, as omens, 160
crime, 58–9, 98, 102
Croce, Giulio Cesare, 59, 66, 67, 71, 99, 151, 169, 170
Banchetto de' Malcibati, 172–3, 174
Contrasto, 120–1, 126
Della famosissima Compagnia della Lessina, 115–16
Dialogo fra un Maestro e un garzone sopra il pano alloiato, 126–7

Invito per veder . . . segare la vecchia, 44

Le Nozze di M. Trivello Foranti, 115, 116

Sogni fantastichi della notte, 128

Il solemnissimo trionfo dell'Abbondanza, 78, 104–5

La vera regola per mantenerse magro con pochissima spesa, 118

Crollius, Osvaldus, 73, 124

Cromero, Martino, 87

Cupramontana (Massaccio), sacrificial rites in, 96–7

cyclamen, 149

dancing, group fits of, 18, 83–4; *see also* St Vitus's dance

darnel, 121–2, 123, 149

Darnton, Robert, 5

death, attitudes to, 30, 47

Delatte, A., 200

deliria, 132–3
  collective, 18, 83–4

Della Porta, Giambattista, 110, 148, 149

Delumeau, J., 186, 188

De Martino, E., 193, 194

De natura rusticorum, 96

Diacono, Paulo, 87

diet
  social class and, 10, 17, 103–4, 120–1, 169–70
  see also bread

Di Nola, A. M., 18

disease, 68–70, 88–91, 101–2, 112–14, 131–2, 151–2
  popular belief as to causes of, 30
  see also medicine; worms, intestinal

Dobb, Maurice, 39

Donzelli, Giuseppe, 201, 202

Douglas, M., 195

Dove si contiene il lamento della Povertà (anonymous poem), 71

drama, 36–9, 60, 172–3

dreams, 128–30, 132–3
  medicinal control of, 133

druggists, in sixteenth-century Bologna, 72–3

drugs, *see* hallucinogens; herbs; narcotics

Dubé, Paul, 23

Duby, Georges, 136, 192

Duden, Barbara, 12

effluvia, plant, 24

Elbymitar, 187

elecampane, 140

Eliade, M., 190

elixir of life, belief in, 31–2

Emilia, 86, 109, 123, 152

England, 14

epilepsy, 45, 132

epomphalia, 24

Erasmus, 140

Erbolario vulgare, 124

ergot, 127

estates, small, elimination of, 39

Este, Beatrice II d', oracular tombstone of, 92–4

Eustachia, the Blessed, coffin of, 94

exorcism, herbs used in, 141–2

Fabre, D., 191

Fabriano, 97

Faenza, dance of the sick in, 84

Fallopio, Gabriele, 19

famine, 14, 26–9, 32–4, 35–9, 87
  in Bologna (sixteenth century), 86–7, 100–1, 104–6, 146–7, 172–7
  as divine retribution, 72
  in fifteenth century, 109–10
  in France, 27, 38, 40
  in Naples (eighteenth century), 119

Fantaguzzi, Giuliano, 110

Fanucci, Camillo, 203

Faral, E., 203

Farolfi, B., 196

fat, human, medicinal uses of, 48–9

feast-days, 136

Febvre, Lucien, 24

Ferrante, L., 191
Ferrara, 84
Ferrari, Giovan Battista, 145
Ficino, Marsilio, 44, 187
Filandro, Evonomo, 141
Fincelius, J., 95
Fioravanti, Leonardo, 73-4, 89, 114, 135-6, 154-5, 162
flax flour, 149
folklore studies, 4-6
food poisoning, 84-5
Fossano, 164-5
Foucault, Michel, 202
foxglove, 125
France
    famine in, 27, 38, 40
    rural vagabonds in, 163
Francis, Saint, 21-2
Fraticelli sect, 97
Frati, L., 199
Friuli, 101
Fronde, the, 40
Frugoni, Francesco Fulvio, 60
funeral rites, comedy in, 42-3

Galen, 148
Galeria de Lesinante, 117-18
Garapon, R., 193
Garmann, Christian, 92
Garzoni, Tommaso, 109, 188
Gaul, 62
Genoa, 59
Getto, Giulio, 187
ghiottone (type of herb), 121-2
Gianicco, 67
Ginzburg, Carlo, 3, 192, 196
Giovanni di Maestro Pedrino, 84
Gnostics, 98
Goglin, J. L., 195
Goldoni, Carlo, 154
Goody, Jack, 192
Grandi, Lazaro, 129
Gregory XIII, Pope, 178
Grosius, Henningus, 92
Guenzi, A., 200
Guevarre, Andrea, 204

hallucinations, hunger-induced, 125-6, 127
hallucinogens, 14-15, 18, 20-1, 124-30, 137-8
    political control through, 137-8
    see also narcotics
Hamsun, Knut, 126
Harris, Marvin, 52
Helianus, 44
hemlock, 44, 139
hemp, 18, 123, 140, 149
henbane, 124
herbalism, astrology and, 143-4
herbs
    hallucinogenic, see hallucinogens
    medicinal use of, 139-45
    signaturae and, 143
    used in exorcism, 141-2
    used in salads, 144-5
    used to quell hunger, 139
Herodotus, 41
Hoffmann, Friedrich, 156
hospices and hospitals, 34, 63, 68, 69-70, 108, 174, 179
    ceremonial opening of, 182-4
humours, 29-30
hunger, 32-4
    hallucinations caused by, 125-6, 127
    herbs to quell, 139
    see also famine
Huxley, Aldous, quoted, 127
hysteria, 131-2
    mass, 18, 83-4

Innocent XII, Pope, 181
insects, plagues of, 157-8
insomnia, remedies for, 25
Instruzione mediche per le genti di campagna, 124
Ireland, 53
Istruzioni, e regole degli Ospizi Generali . . ., 204
Italy
    famine in, see famine

poverty in, *see* poor, the; vagabonds, rural

Jakobson, Roman, 43

Kaplan, Steven, 63
Kerényi, K., 198
Khoi people, 41

Labia, Angelo Maria, 166
Lacroix, J., 191
'Lamento della povertà per l'estremo freddo del presente anno 1587', 75-7
Lamento de'poveretti i quali stanno a casa a pigione, 193
Lamento de uno povero huomo sopra la carestia, 191
Landucci, Luca, 22, 109-10, 196
language, as compensation for poverty, 81
Lausanne, plague of 1613 in, 157
Lavater, Loys, 92
Le Goff, Jacques, 23, 195
Le Loyer, Pierre, 92
Lennio, Levino, 19, 201, 202
Leo IV, Pope, 42
Le Roy Ladurie, Emmanuel, 4-5, 196
Letrosne, Guillaume-François, 163, 166
Lettera portata nuovamente de Gianicco ambasciatore del Freddo, 192, 193
Lettera sulle insalate, 200
Levi, E., 203
Lévi-Strauss, Claude, 20, 65
on cannibalism, 52-3
Leys, Leendert, 49, 53, 190
Libre de Fortuna e Prudencia, 193
life-span, 135
linseed, 149
Locatelli, Ludovico, 73
Lombardy, migration of peasants to and from, 109-10
Loredano, Giovanni Francesco, 42
Loux, Francoise, 5
Lugo, 150

Lullo, Raimondo, 141-2
lycanthropy, 23, 95
lysergic acid, 127

Machiavelli, Niccolo, 83
McNeill, W. H., 187
Magalotti, Lorenzo, 145
magasins charitables, 163
Manetti, Saverio, 111
Manfredi, Girolamo, 23
Mansi, Marcello, 70
Mantegazza, Paolo 138, 139
Mantuanus, Baptista, 195
Manzoni, Alessandro, 57, 165, 166
maravigliosi secreti di medicina, I, 187, 201
Marie de France, 23
market relationships, food and, 13-14
Maroni, Prospero Domenico, 195, 199
Marseilles, 44
Marszalkowicz, S., 198
Martino d'Arles, 195
Massaccio region, *see* Cupramontana
mass hypnosis, 18, 83-4
Massonio, Salvatore, 145
Mattioli, Pietro Andrea, 43, 122, 123, 141, 148
medicine, 19-20, 101-2
dreams and, 133-4
eighteenth century, 111-12
human body used in, 7-8, 46-50
for the poor, 112-14
popular, 30-2, 135-6
of rich and poor compared, 103
see also druggists; herbs; worms, intestinal
Melloni, Giambattista, 66, 68
Melusina, 97
Mémoire sur les vagabonds et les mendiants, 163, 165
Mendicare abolito nella città di Montalbano, Il, 203
Mendicita proveduta nella città di Roma coll'ospizio publico, La, 203, 204

Menghi, Girolamo, 99, 141, 195
Mengus, Hieronymus, 201
Menocchio, Giovan Stefano, 41, 188
mental health, 122–3
Mercuri, Scipione, 25
Merula, Gaudenzio, 98, 195
Meruli, 44
Messagetae, 41
Messia (Mexia), Pedro, 189, 191
Messina, 94
Metge, Bernart, 80
Michiele, Pietro, 42
Migne, J. P., 186
migrations, peasant, 58, 60–1, 109–10
Modena, 58, 60, 62, 94
   adulteration of bread in, 84–5
   migrants in sixteenth and seventeenth centuries, 60–1
Mongitore, Antonio, 94
'monkey disease', 82
Montaigne, Michel Eyquem de, 51
Montalbani, Ovidio, 110, 111–12, 137, 139, 146, 147, 165
   advice to rural poor given by, 149–50, 166–9
Monti, Alessandro de', 105
Moreali, Giambattista, 50, 132–3, 152–3, 201
morsus diaboli (type of herb), 141
mummified flesh, medicinal uses of, 46–7, 49
Muratori, Ludovico Antonio, 89, 194, 195

Naples, antidote for worms made in, 160–1
narcotics
   administered to children, 23–4, 25, 124
   in bread, 18, 122–3, 126–7, 137–8
   see also hallucinogens
narks, 64–6
negotiana (type of herb), 139
Nicaragua, 54
Niccolini, E., 191
Niccoli, O., 196

Nicholas of Salerno, 25
Nicolini, F., 165, 202
nightshades, 124–5
Nove Muse di Erodoto Alicarnasso, Le, 188

ogres, 50–1
oils, as antidotes, 160–2
ointments, 24–5
Olaus Magnus, 160
omens, 21, 157–8, 160
opium, 123, 137, 140
   administered to children, 23, 25, 124
orgies, 96–8
Ospedale degli Abbandonati (Foundling Hospital, Bologna), 63, 68, 69–70

Padam people, 189
Padua, famine in, 26
Paleotti, Cardinal Gabriele, 170
Palmieri, Matteo, 87
Pare, Ambroise, 24
Parini, Abbé Giuseppe, 63
Paruta, Paulo, 202
Pastarino, 72–4
Paulus Aeginata, 50, 186
Pavia, 109
peasants
   diet recommended for, 168–9
   diseases suffered by, 151–2
   migrations of, 58, 60–1, 109–10
   see also vagabonds, rural
Pedacio, Dioscoride, 189
Percato, Caterina, 37
Perucci, Francesco, 189
Peruvian Indians, 54
Peter, Jean-Pierre, 131, 194
pharmacology, see herbs; medicine
Piazza, Carlo Bartolemeo, 203, 204
Piccolomini, Alessandro, 202
Pictarnii, Arcibaldi, 187
Pini, Teseo, 191
Piobicco, Constanzo Felici da, 145
Pisanelli, Baldassare, 169

Piscitelli, E., 191
plague, 87–91, 101, 102
  magical remedies against, 91
plays, *see* drama
Pliny the Elder, 140
Polica, G. Severino, 204
Pomey, François, 41
Poni, C., 192
poor relief, 174; *see also* hospices and
  hospitals
poor, the, 18–19, 32–4
  culture of, 79–85
  diet of, *see* bread; diet
  in eighteenth century, 61, 63–70,
    74–7, 119, 182–4
  explusion from cities of, 108, 151
  'fake' and 'genuine', 180–2
  in fifteenth century, 90, 109–10
  internment of, 108
  literary treatment of, 36–9, 57
  medicine for, 112–14
  priests concerned with, 63–4
  revolts of, 35–6, 108
  in Rome, 178–82
  in seventeenth century, 61,
    179–82
  in sixteenth century, 58–60, 71,
    86, 108–9, 172–79
  see also peasants; vagabonds, rural
poppyseed bread, 18, 137, 147–8; *see
  also* opium
population, growth in, 34
Porri, Alessio, 142
prayers, sellers of, 22
Prévost, Jean, 23
Price, Derek, 197
priests, concern with poverty of,
  63–4
printing
  influence on medicine, 114
Procopius of Caesarea, 27, 44
Provisione elemosinaria per li poveri, 191
Provost, Jean, 113
Psellus, Michael, 97
Putti, Vittorio, 190

Quintilian, 41

radice Hipice (type of herb), 139
Raulin, Josephe, 23
Raynal, Abbé Giullaume, on
  cannibalism, 53–4, 55
Refrigeri, Giovan Battista, 199
Regino of Prum, 43
revolts, of the poor, 35–6, 108
Rimini
  cannibalism in Second World
    War, 28
Ripa, Polidoro, 98–9, 195
Romagna, 44, 84, 110, 123
  festa dei becchi, 98
Romanello, M., 188
Romans, 41–2
Rome
  poverty in, 178–80
  procession of Court of Miracles,
    178–9
Rosaccio, Giuseppe, 169–70, 196
rosemary, 141
Roseo, Mambrino, 54, 55
rue, 142–3
Ruzante (Angelo Beolco), *Dialogo
  facetissimo*, 36–9

Sacardino, Costandino, 168
saffron, 141
St John's wort, 141
saints, 21–2
St Vitus's dance, 127; *see also*
  dancing, group fits of
Saitta, A., 192
salads, herbs used in, 144–5
Salvinius, *De gubernatione Dei*, 41–2
Samoggia, L., 201
Sanseverino, Francesco Panfilo da,
  96
Sanuto, Marin, 185
Sardinia, killing of the aged in,
  43–4
'sardonic' herbs, 41, 42, 43
Savastano, Francesco Eulalio, 199
Savonarola, Giovanni Michele, 17,
  45, 185, 198, 201
Schama, Simon, 11
Schroeder, Johann, 49, 73, 190

Scientia, Gioseppe, 187
Scythians, 139, 140
Secreti diversi et miracolosi, 19
Segavecchia rite, 44
Segni, Giovan Battista, 26, 67, 87, 87-8, 107, 110, 138,173, 203
  on famine as divine retribution, 174-6
Selvatico, Benedetto, 158
senna, 111-12
Serpetro, Nicolo, 110
Sigisberto, 87
Sirena, Fra Francesco, 45
Sixtus V, Pope, 179
skulls, human, belief in properties of, 45-6
social structure, 36
Sonuto, Martin, 21
Spaccini, Giovan Battista, 61, 84, 108
Spano, Pietro, 199
spartanata (type of herb), 139
Speculum cerretanorum, 59
Spinelli, Doctor, 101-2
Spinola, Orazio, 104
Stephen VII, Pope, 50
story-tellers, 64-5
supernatural, belief in the, 19-25, 92-101, 155-8, 160
surgeons, 155
Swertius, Franciscus, 42

Tacconi, Gherardo, 106
Taillepied, Noël, 92
Tassoni, A., 201
Tasso, Torquato, 139, 169
Taxil, Jean, 142
Telemacus, 140
Tertullian, 181
Tesoro della vita umana, 155
Thirty Years War, 40
Thomas, Keith, 3, 135
Thompson, E. P., 11
thorn-apple, 125
Tissot, Samuel André, 23

Tofalo, 64-6
Tozzetti, Giovanni Targioni, 110
triaca (theriac), 103
Trotula da Salerno, 48
Turner, Byran, 13

unrest, social, 35-6, 108

vagabonds, rural
  in France, 163
  in Italy, 164-8
Valesio, 149
Venturini, Alessandro, 48
Vercelli, ceremonial opening of hospice at, 183-4
Veronese, Giacomo Cieco, 71
Vettori, Francesco, 59
Vignati Giovanni Antonio, 189
Villanova, Arnoldo da, 141
Vincenti, Giovanni Maria, 92
Virgil, 41
Vives, Luis, 68
Vizani, Pompeo, 86, 100-1, 108, 194
Watt, Ian, 192
werewolves, 23, 95
witchcraft, 21, 124-5, 134
Wolff, P., 196
wolves, 101
worm-angels, 153-4
worms, intestinal, 152-62
  and death symptoms, 159-60
  exorcism of, 157
  Neapolitan antidote for, 160-1
  supernatural explanations for, 155-6
wormwood, 20

Zacchia, Paolo, 129-30, 134, 198, 199
Zaffarino, 203
Zampini, P., 199
Zapata, Giovan Battista, 154